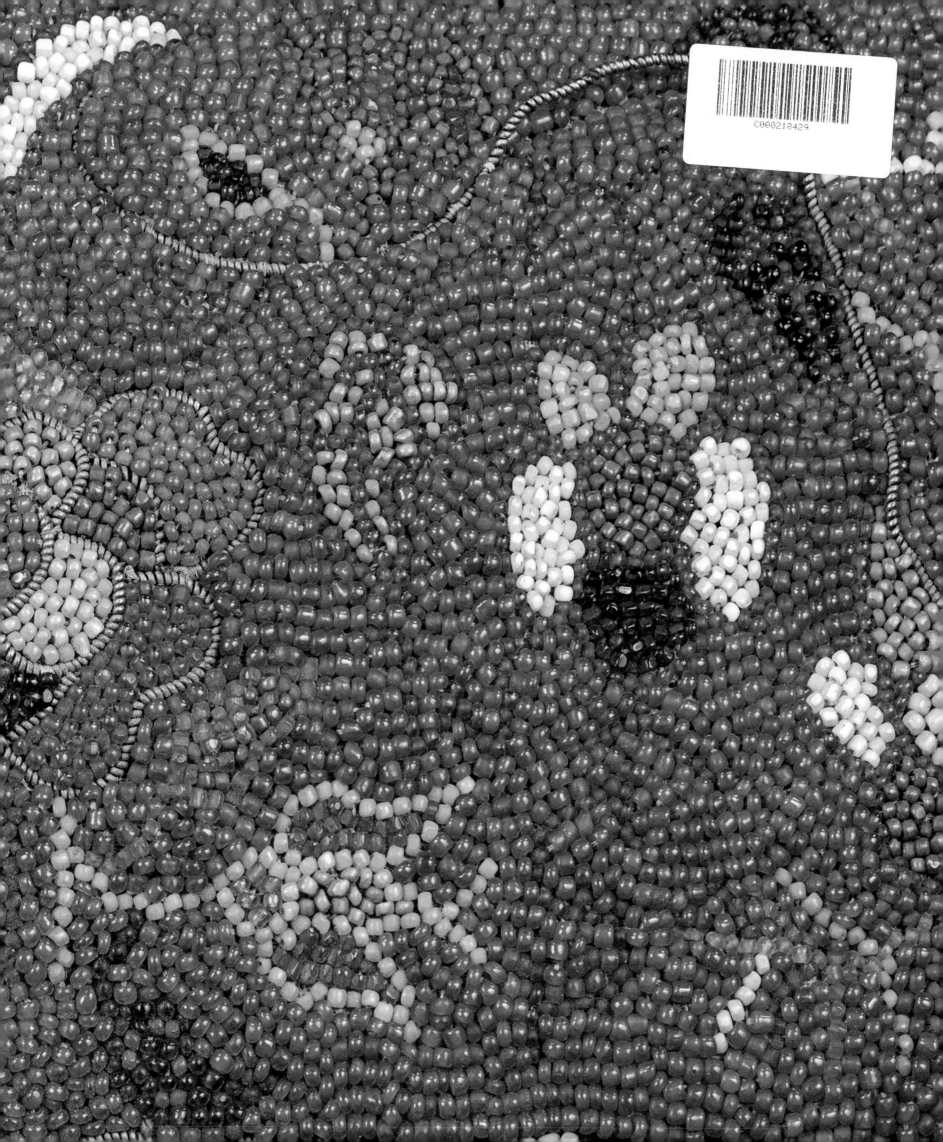

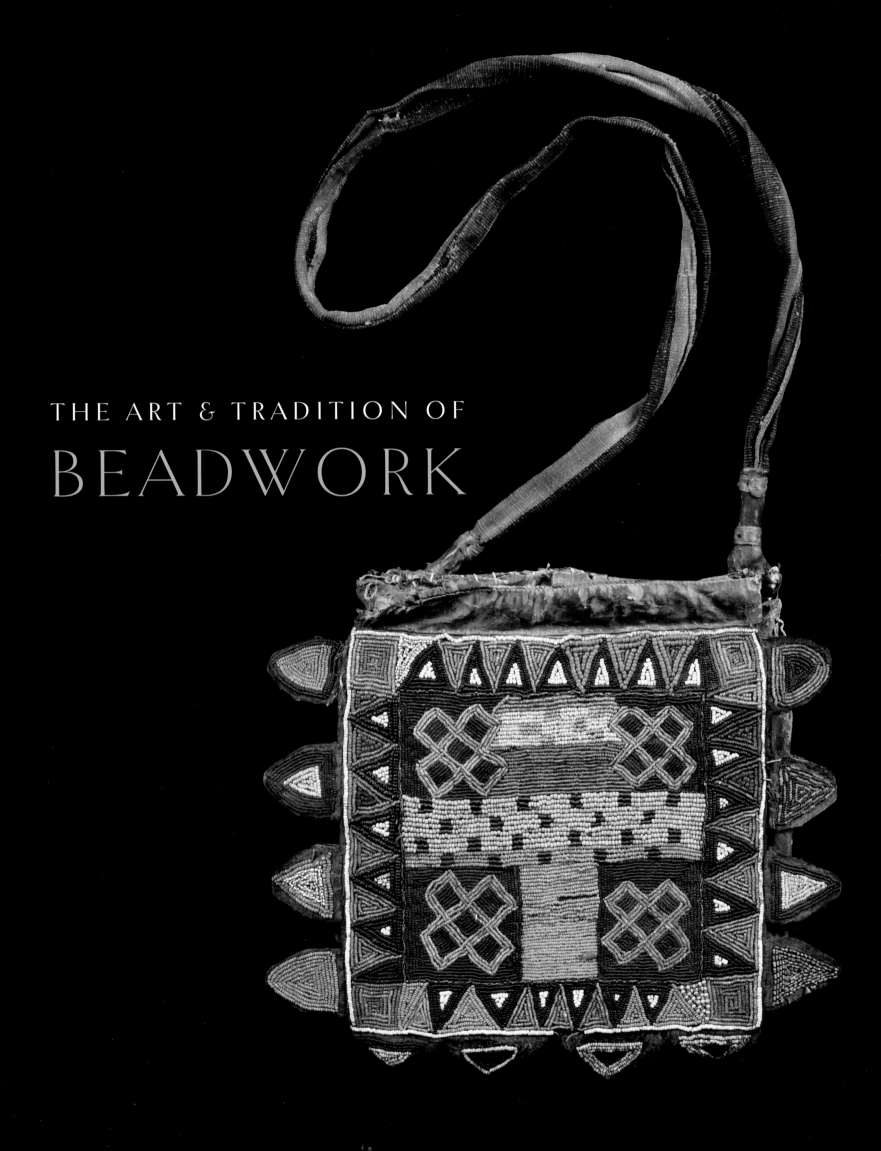

THE ART & TRADITION OF
BEADWORK

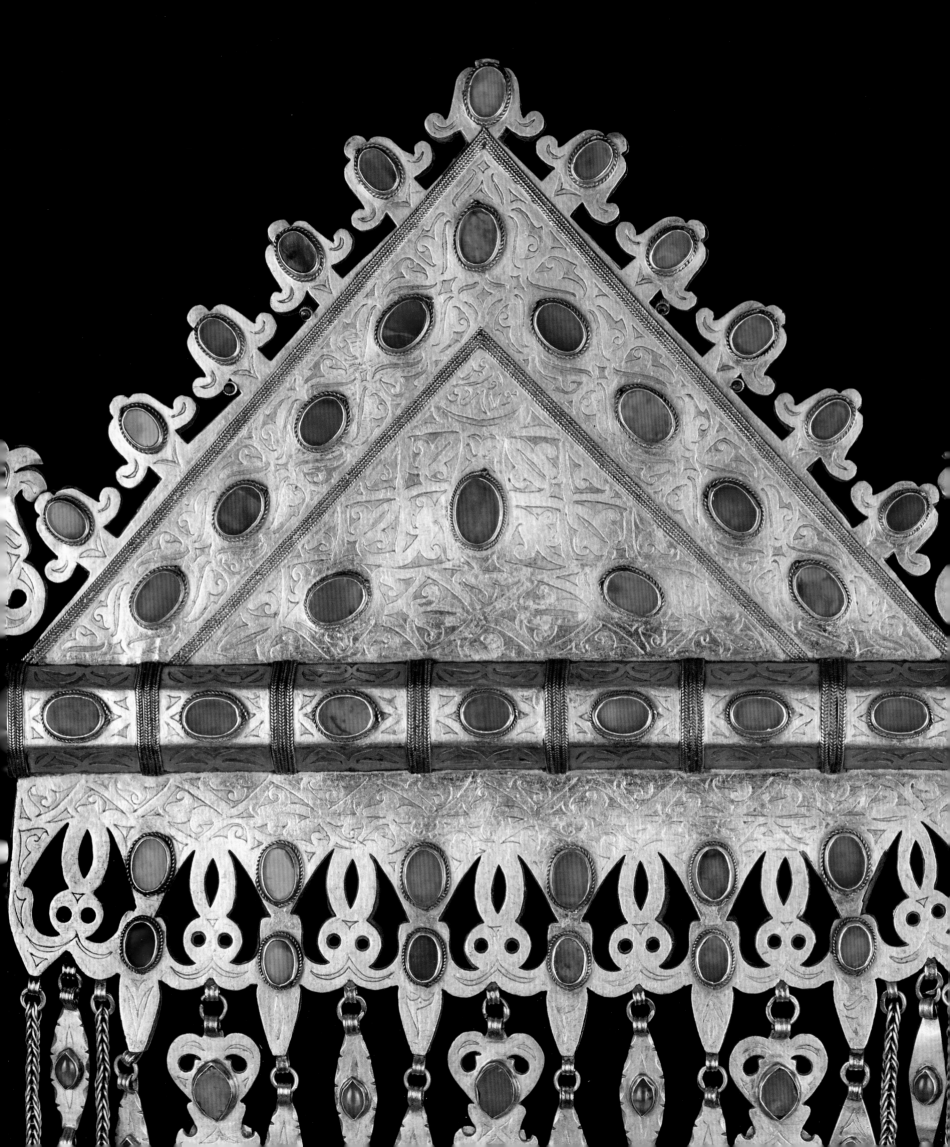

THE ART & TRADITION OF
BEADWORK

MARSHA C. BOL

GIBBS SMITH
TO ENRICH AND INSPIRE HUMANKIND

First Edition
22 21 20 19 18   5 4 3 2 1

Text © 2018 Marsha C. Bol
Photographs © 2018 Blair Clark or as noted throughout

Published by
Gibbs Smith
P.O. Box 667
Layton, Utah 84041

1.800.835.4993 orders
www.gibbs-smith.com

Designed by Rita Sowins / Sowins Design
Printed and bound in China
Gibbs Smith books are printed on either recycled, 100% post-consumer waste, FSC-certified papers or on paper produced from sustainable PEFC-certified forest/controlled wood source. Learn more at www.pefc.org.

Library of Congress Cataloging-in-Publication Data

Names: Bol, Marsha, author.
Title: The art and tradition of beadwork / Marsha C. Bol.
Description: First edition. | Layton, Utah : Gibbs Smith, 2017. | Includes bibliographical references.
Identifiers: LCCN 2017032646 | ISBN 9781423631798 (hardcover)
Subjects: LCSH: Beadwork.
Classification: LCC NK3650 .B65 2017 | DDC 745.58/209—dc23
LC record available at https://lccn.loc.gov/2017032646

TO THOMAS "RED OWL" HAUKAAS,
AND THE MEMORY OF NELLIE STAR BOY MENARD
AND ROSALIE LITTLE THUNDER

CONTENTS

INTRODUCTION

EXTRAORDINARY HOW A SMALL GLASS BEAD FROM THE ISLAND OF Murano (Venice, Italy) or the mountains of Bohemia (Czech Republic) can travel around the world, entering into the cultural life of peoples far distant. Glass beads are the ultimate migrants. Where they start out is seldom where they end up. No matter where they originate, the locale that uses them makes them into something specific to their own worldview. This book is about what happens to these beads when they arrive at their final destination.

"Where are beads from? Only a person from the river mouth would ask this sort of question! The Bornean bead owners' reactions typically range from 'don't know and don't care' to polite bewilderment. One very common answer is: 'We got the beads from our mothers, our grandmothers, our great-grandmothers.'" (Munan 2005: 34).

So completely have glass beads become embedded into various cultures throughout the world, that, for example, when the world thinks of Plains Indians in North America, we associate the people with their beaded buckskin clothing. We think of beadwork as a wholly American Indian art form. Again, when envisioning Samburu or Maasai women of Kenya with their many layers of beaded neckrings, we think of these neckrings as uniquely theirs.

Each cultural tradition has color preferences and its own design aesthetics and sewing techniques, so that we do not mistake Crow Indian beadwork of the American Plains with Ndebele beadwork of South Africa. Beadwork adornment conveys many culturally specific messages to those members of the group. Even so, looking at beadwork around the world reveals many parallel uses among the various beadworking societies, thus allowing the opportunity to compare the myriad of creative ways in which humankind works their beads.

This book is not actually about beads. There are many fine publications on this subject. Rather this book is about *working beads* resulting in *beadwork*, and what a collective of beads in a garment or an object reveals about the intentions of its makers or users. While these intentions aren't always determined only by the beadwork, it is the bead embellishment that, working in tandem with other factors, makes clear the purposes of these objects. As Coomaraswamy (1956: 18) has observed: "The beauty of anything unadorned is not increased by ornament, but made more effective by it . . . It is generally by means of what we now call its decoration that a thing is ritually transformed and made to function spiritually as well as physically."

Much of an object's meaning is necessarily associated with how it is used in its society. In most parts of the world, beads, having value, are often used at peak moments in life. With their luster and sparkle, used as an adornment or surface additive, they help to heighten the effect, the impact, the meaning. Beads were (and still are) called upon to adorn garments and objects, when attention is meant to be drawn to the adornee. These special moments in the adornee's life tend to revolve around life stages and passages (chapters 1–4); power, position, or status in the community (chapters 6 and 7); the high meaning of the occasion (chapter 9); or communication with the spirits, who are attracted to the beads (chapter 8).

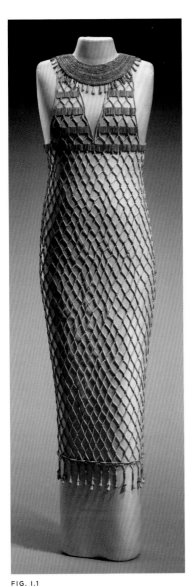

FIG. I.1

FIG. I.1
BEAD-NET DRESS WITH BROAD COLLAR, 2551–2528 B.C.E.

Giza Tomb G7740Z, Old Kingdom, Dynasty IV, Reign of Khufu, Egypt

Faience beads

44½ x 17⅓ in. (113 x 44 cm)

Harvard University—Boston Museum of Fine Arts Expedition, 27.1548.1–2

FIG. I.2
PFC. EVA MIRABAL (EAH HA WA) SERVING IN THE AIR FORCE DURING WORLD WAR II, 1944

Photograph by AAF Air Service Command, courtesy of Jonathan Warm Day Coming

FIG. I.3
YA-LEI CHIANG, 2014

Paiwan peoples, Taiwan

Photograph by Bob Smith, courtesy of International Folk Art Alliance

FIG. I.4
LAKOTA "CREATION NARRATIVE" SHIRT, 2016

Maker: Thomas "Red Owl" Haukaas (b. 1950, Sicaŋgu Lakota/Creole)

Wool cloth, antique glass beads

Nerman Museum of Contemporary Art, Johnson County Community College, Overland Park, Kansas, acquired with funds provided by the Barton P. and Mary D. Cohen Art Acquisition Endowment at the JCCC Foundation

FIG. I.2

FIG. I.3

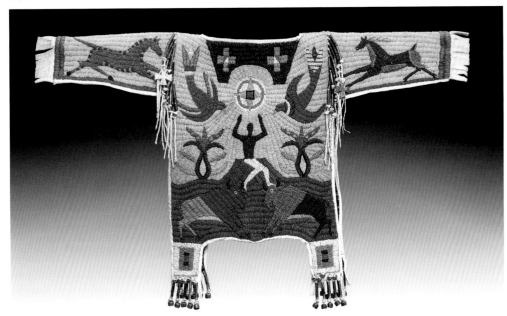

FIG. I.4

A blue and green faience bead-net dress (Fig. I.1) was found in an Egyptian tomb on a female mummy during a 1927 expedition. The threads holding the beads together had disintegrated. Yet the beads and their impressions were still in place, allowing the dress to be reconstructed some 4,500 years later. This finery surely identified a woman of high status during Egypt's Old Kingdom.

Faience beads were made from powdered quartz covered with a transparent blue or green glasslike coating. Not all beads used in the beadwork in this book are made of glass. Beads made from metal, cloth, stone, and other materials worked into objects served equally well to distinguish their wearer.

As Arnold Rubin (1975: 39) has stated emphatically: "In a traditional context, whatever else objects may be and do, they are first of all perceived as making statements about the self-identification of their makers and users." Self- and ethnic-identity loom large in this book. Ndebele beadwork from South Africa provides a clear example of this concept. "These little round imported objects [glass beads] became possibly the single most important way of publicly expressing personal or group identity as well as the deepest personal and social relationships between women and men, mothers and daughters, chiefs and commoners, elders and young men. Beadwork thus had the dual effect of transforming the wearers' identities and defining relations between them." (Procter and Klopper 1994: 58). When uprooted from their territory and scattered far from other members of the Ndebele community, the women reclaimed their group identity via beadwork by reviving their distinctive beaded apparel (See chapter 2).

Eva Mirabal enlisted in the Women's Army Corps (WAC) in 1943, saying that since there were no sons in her Taos Pueblo family, she felt that she should join in the fight. (Gerdes 2016: 27). In this photograph (Fig. I.2) of her image in the mirror, Mirabal sees herself dressed as a WAC, yet her Lakota beaded vest shows she identifies with her Native American heritage. Moreover, even though she is a Puebloan from Taos Pueblo, not a Lakota, her pueblo has long been an important center for trade between tribes from the Plains and the Southwest United States.

While beadwork has a lengthy history, it is truly a living art. The majority of the art works in this book date from the nineteenth to the twenty-first centuries. Beadwork today comes in many forms— it may be a continuation of an unbroken tradition, perhaps with contemporary innovations, or it may be a revival of a lost form. Ya-Lei Chiang, a Paiwan indigenous beadworker from Taiwan, along with her husband, Omass, have worked for over 25 years to revive their traditional glass bead-making used for jewelry and embroidery for rituals, weddings, and gifts (Fig. I.3).

Lakota beadworker, Thomas Haukaas, continues sewing beadwork in the traditional Lakota way, which he learned from his elders (chapter 1). However, he does not slavishly reproduce the beadwork of his forbearers. Haukaas selects pieces of his tradition and recombines them in new ways, allowing him to stay true to his traditions without becoming stale. His pictorial shirt (Fig. I.4) is worked in nineteenth-century beads to tell the story of the Lakota peoples' origin, using a shirt form that was stylish in the late nineteenth century especially for Lakota boys. Even so, the shirt has been treated as a canvas for a twenty-first-century painting.

All of the objects in the book are from the past, the far past to the recent past. They "represent a world receding further into a past that is a present rolling back, much like a stretch of dirt road that slips under a fast-moving vehicle. The dust remains hanging behind or settling on the vegetation around even after the car has hit tarmac—the modern era—and is going to inhabit the atmosphere as long as there is still such an element around the globe. The dirt road is a metaphor for a past that is still with us, especially in Greater Africa." (Mphahlele 1991: 6).

ACKNOWLEDGMENTS

THIS BOOK BEGAN WHEN A TALL, stately, white-haired gentleman walked into my office at the Museum of International Folk Art (MOIFA) in Santa Fe, New Mexico, where I was the director. This gentleman, Gibbs Smith, had come to convince me that a book on beadwork around the world needed to be written, and that the Museum of International Folk Art, with its vast international collections, was the right institution to collaborate with Gibbs's publishing company to do this. So began a multi-year collaboration.

Many people contributed to its contents. Photographer Blair Clark, from the Museum Resources Division of the New Mexico Department of Cultural Affairs, worked with me to photograph nearly 1,000 objects over four years. In the end, we both ended up still smiling, but retired! It took four project assistants to keep the documents and photos in order and accessible. Three completed their doctorates while working on this project. Their assistance was invaluable, and I thank Ruth LaNore, Dr. Elaine Higgins, Dr. Cristin McKnight Sethi, and Dr. Thomas Grant Richardson. MOIFA's librarian, Caroline Dechert, located obscure publications and ordered stacks of interlibrary loans for me without even a whimper.

Other members of the MOIFA staff pointed me in the direction of beaded objects, contributed information and ideas, and helped in numerous ways. My thanks to curators Laura Addison, Nicolasa Chavez, Nora Fisher (retired), Amy Groleau, Carrie Hertz, Felicia Katz-Harris, Barbara Mauldin (retired), Bobbie Sumberg (moved on), and guest curator Suzy Seriff; collections staff Polina Smutko, Ruth LaNore, Bryan Johnson-French, Ernst Luthi, Deborah King, and Carrie Haley; office staff Ellen Castellano, Aurelia Gomez, Laura Lovejoy-May, Angelina Maestas (retired), Chris Vitagliano; conservators Angela Duckwall and Maureen Russell, and the guards, who were always encouraging, especially Ritchie Lujan.

The International Folk Art Foundation supported this project with publications funds and a Bartlett Research Grant. Their support of the museum is beyond measure. Sister museums and arts division (Museum of Indian Arts and Culture / Laboratory of Anthropology, the New Mexico History Museum / Palace of the Governors, and the New Mexico Arts) and their staff members—Cathy Notarnicola, Meredith Davidson, and Michelle Laflamme-Childs—opened their collections' storage for me to hunt for needed objects.

Many museums, artists, scholars, and private collectors generously shared their collections, which filled gaps in the MOIFA collection, and their knowledge, greatly enriching the book's contents. Listed are some, though certainly not all, who contributed to this book: Kelsey Arrington-Ashford, National Museum of African Art; James Barker, Naomi Bebo, Linda Belote, Walther Boelsterly Urrutia, Director of the Museo de Arte Popular, Mexico City; Don Cole, Fowler Museum at UCLA; Herbert M. Cole, Anyieth D'Awol and Pam McKulka, the Roots Project; Marcus Dewey, W. Garth Dowling, Marilyn Eber, Natalie Fitz-Gerald, Judy Frater, Anne and Bill Frej, Ingrid Cincala Gilbert, Sue Grinois, Fine Arts Museums of San Francisco; Lauren Hancock and Christopher Philipp, the Field Museum; Robert Hart, McGregor Museum; Deborah Harding, Carnegie Museum of Natural History; Thomas Haukaas, Emil Her Many Horses, Kit Hinrichs, Earl Kessler, Cory Kratz, Genevieve Lemoine, The Peary-MacMillan Arctic Museum and Arctic Studies Center; Sara and David Lieberman, David McLanahan, Esther Mahlangu, Martha Manier, Linda Marcus, Stephanie Mendez, Iris M-L Model, Heidi Munan, Pam Najdowski, Valarie Nebres, Harry Neufeld, Edric Ong, Jan Ramirez, National September 11 Memorial & Museum; Penny and Armin Rembe, Fr. Andreas Rohring CMM, Mariannhill; Bob and Lora Sandroni, Marlane Scott, Bernard Sellato, Sharon Sharpe, Linda Sherwood, High Noon Western Americana; Bob Smith, Gaylord Torrence and Stacy Sherman, Nelson-Atkins Museum of Art; Jonathan Warm Day Coming, Whitney Williamson, Nerman Museum of Contemporary Art; Rafael Cilaunime Candelario Valadez; Jannelle Weakly, Arizona State Museum; Terry Winchell, Fighting Bear Antiques; Rachel Wixom and Bruce Bernstein, Ralph T. Coe Foundation; Sara Woodbury, Roswell Museum and Art Center; and Alice Zrebiec.

At Gibbs Smith, I sincerely thank Gibbs, Michelle Branson, Leslie Stitt, Rita Sowins, and Renee Bond.

LIFE
BEGINS

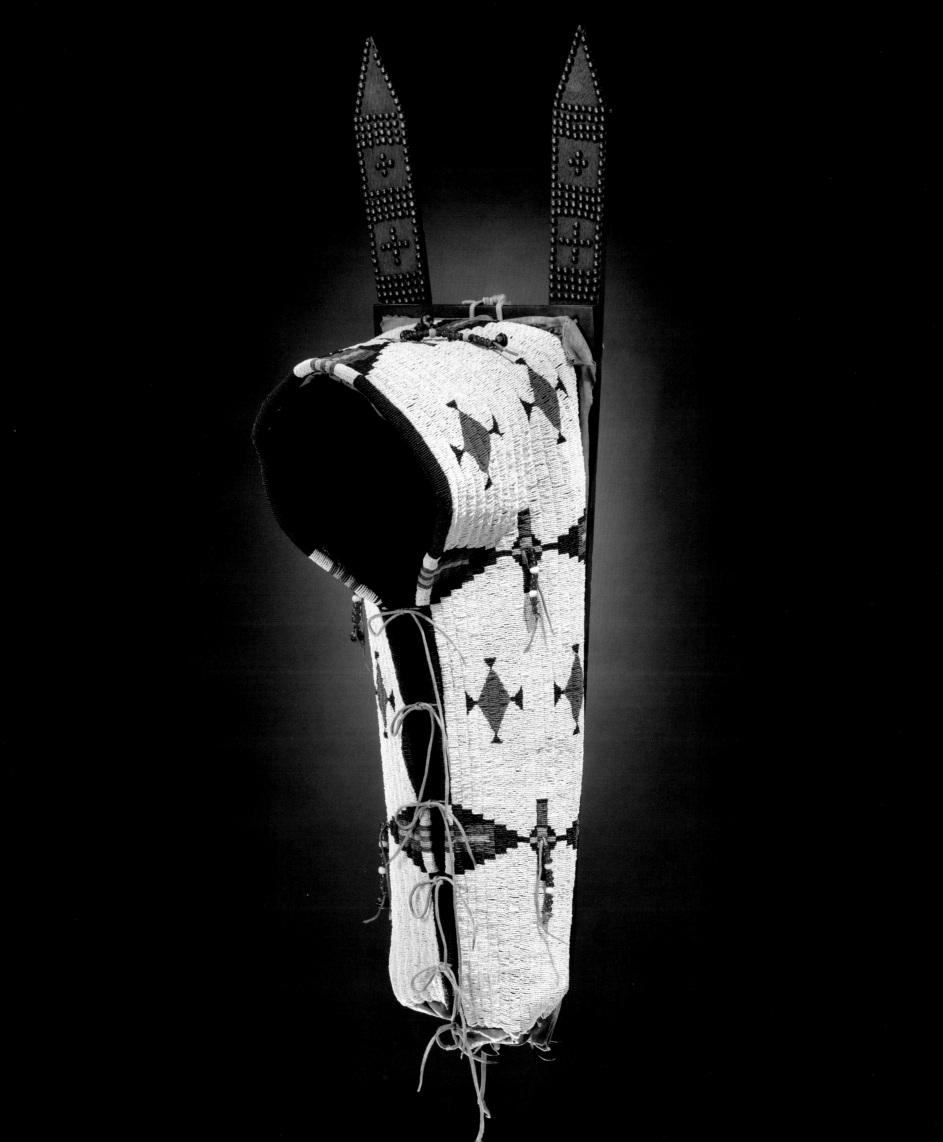

"ALL LIFE GOES AROUND IN A CIRCLE, BEGINNING WITH BIRTH, CHANGING THROUGH THE SEASONS, ALWAYS ENDING WITH DEATH, FROM WHICH WILL SPRING NEW LIFE."
—Adolf and Star Hungry Wolf, Blackfoot, 1992 (Hungry Wolf 1992: 3)

All humanity shares the biological life cycle. Yet the teaching of cultural values and worldview specific to each society begins at the moment of birth.

ADORNING LAKOTA CHILDREN

NOT JUST A CRADLE

Like children everywhere, Plains Indian children are the treasures of the tribe. Traditionally among the Lakota (western Sioux) people of the central Plains of the United States, a baby began life swaddled in a lovingly decorated soft cradle. This cradle provided more than a warm, cozy bodily protection. It wrapped the newborn into his/her network of social relationships that would become a central part of a child's life. The paternal aunt, sister of the baby's father, was responsible for providing the beaded cradle, although other female relatives might do so as well. In making this cradle, the aunt was conferring honor upon the baby and indirectly upon her brother. Brothers and sisters had very special respect relationships throughout their lifetimes, with gift-giving nurturing the bonds of this relationship.

A cradle revealed a child's place in society. The baby's relatives could confer a special status on the infant by giving more than one cradle, ranging in size as the child grew. Making a fully beaded cradle required a major commitment of time and expense on the part of the beadworker (Fig. 1.1, Fig. 1.2, Photo 1.1). One greatly honored baby reportedly received twenty-two cradles. (Hassrick 1964: 271–72).

The portable baby cradle form was well adapted to the seminomadic lifestyle of the Plains people. The cradle could be propped against the tipi wall so that the child could watch the family's interactions, held in the mother's arms, carried on the back of the baby's mother or sister while she was working, or hung from the saddle of the horse whenever the tipi camp was on the move.

Childhood mortality, always a grave concern, prompted beadworkers to apply protective designs to cradles as a prayer for an infant's good health and long life. Often the meaning of those designs were known only to the maker, but in the Lakota case, the cradle design above the head was intended to represent a turtle. (Wissler 1904: 241). Why a turtle? A turtle's ability to operate in more than one world, in water and on land, and to transform itself by withdrawing into its shell, makes it a likely candidate for supernatural association. Its perceived attributes are linked to longevity. (Deloria n.d.: 312).

PHOTO 1.1
ARAPAHO MOTHER AND CHILD, C. 1882

Darlington Agency, Oklahoma, USA

Photo by William S. Soule

Trustrim Connell Collection, Billie Jane Baguley Library and Archives, Heard Museum, Phoenix, Arizona

FIG. 1.1, *Previous Overleaf*
CRADLE, C. 1875

Cheyenne nation, Oklahoma or Wyoming, USA

Native-tanned hide, rawhide, muslin, cotton cloth, wood, brass tacks, brass bells

39 in. (99 cm)

Hirschfield Family Collection, courtesy of Fighting Bear Antiques

Photograph by Garth Dowling

FIG. 1.2
CRADLE, C. 1885–1890

Lakota nation, South Dakota, USA

Native-tanned hide, rawhide, glass beads

22 1/16 x 7 1/16 x 9 13/16 in. (56 x 18 x 25 cm)

Museum of International Folk Art, Gift of the Art Institute of Chicago, A.1951.16.316

Babies were well dressed in their totally beaded cradles. Complete beading of cradles was a trait shared by several Plains tribes on the central and southern Plains including the Lakota, Cheyenne, Arapaho, and Kiowa. It is often difficult to distinguish with complete certainty between the beadwork of Lakota beadworkers and their Cheyenne and Arapaho allies. All three nations used the "lazy stitch" technique where the beadworker strings 6–12 beads on a sinew thread before attaching it to the skin. Repeating this step creates a lane of beads, which works especially well for geometric designs, with a preference for white backgrounds and similar geometric patterns and design compositions.

Anthropologist Clark Wissler (1902) noted in a letter to Franz Boas: "The Arapaho and the Sioux [Lakota] visit a great deal even at the present time and the custom of giving presents has introduced many decorated objects."

Although the general belief is that all Plains Indian cradles have a wooden framework to support the cradle with the weight of the baby, Lakota and Cheyenne women commonly made soft cradles with no framework. These soft cradles allowed mothers and family members to hold the baby cradled in their arms. (Greene 1992: 96). This particular cradle (Fig. 1.2) is unusual because the beadwork fully encircles the child with no opening at the bottom.

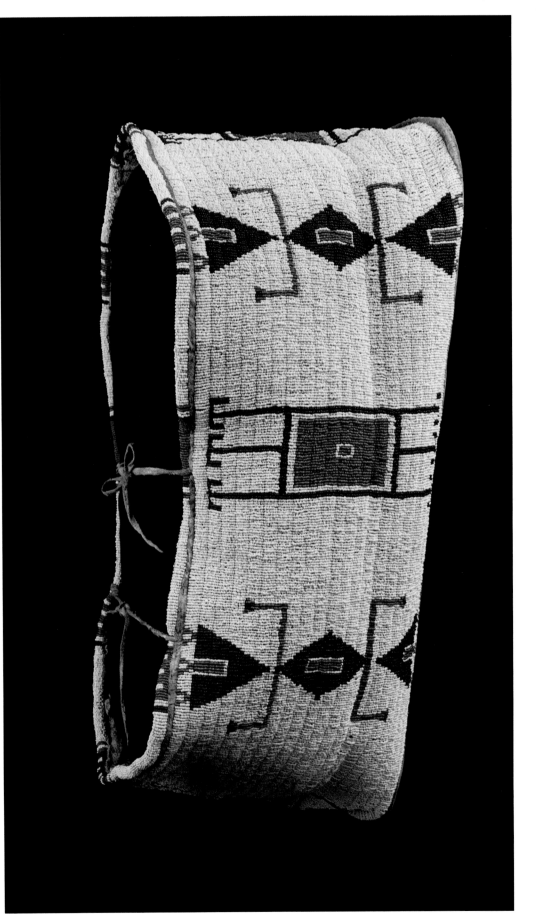

FIG. 1.2

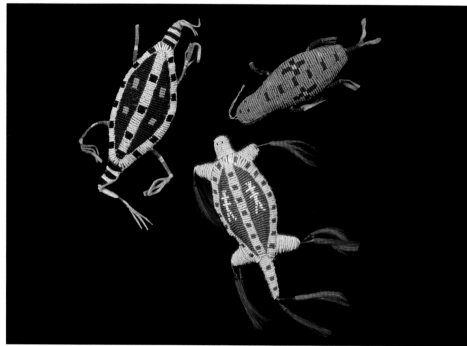

FIG. 1.3

The turtle and the lizard are the
purposefully selected forms for
umbilical amulets. These animals are
generally considered the guardians
of life because of their natural
abilities to protect themselves.
The turtle's hard shell provides
complete protection when the
animal withdraws into it. Some
lizards detach their tails to distract
predators; others change color to
camouflage themselves. Thus, they
are both good candidates to ensure a
child a long, safe life.

Lakota women embroidered prayers for protection and long life into other things
they made for their children. Every baby received a decorated navel amulet containing his or her dried umbilical cord. When the cord dried and fell off, a female
family member stuffed the cord along with sweet grass into a beaded amulet, made
especially for the infant in the shape of a turtle or a lizard. This amulet was tied
to the infant's cradle and later worn by the female child in her hair, around her
neck, or on her belt or her back, so that she would continue to carry the protective
power once out of the cradle (Fig. 1.9). (Powers, M. 1986: 55). Some girls wore
two amulets, their own and their brother's. (Deloria 1937: 45).

Less frequently a navel amulet might be made into the shape of a lizard (Fig.
1.3). Considered a friend of the turtle, the lizard can also transform itself for protection by detaching its tail or camouflaging itself through color blending. (Walker
1983: 359). Alice New Holy, Oglala Lakota, lamented that today a child's cord is
often thrown away. She asked, "How will the child know where he is?" (New Holy
1992). I never quite fully understood what Alice New Holy meant by her statement, until I encountered something similar from the neighboring Arapahos: "If
a navel bag is lost, Arapahos believe that the owner will wander, crazily searching
for it by means such as snooping in or even stealing other people's belongings."
(Anderson 2013: 120).

CHILD-BELOVED

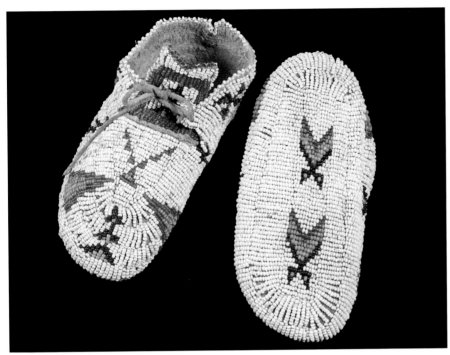

FIG. 1.4

Although it seems surprising that
a pair of children's moccasins
would be beaded on the soles, such
lavish adornment, irrespective of
practicality, signaled the special
status of the child dressed in them.

On occasion a favored child was honored by his/her family with a *Hunka* ceremony, which involved a feast and regaling the guests with many gifts. Henceforth
the child was known as a "child-beloved." Child-beloved status was made visible
by dressing the recipient in fine, beaded clothing, which included such impractical
items as moccasins with fully beaded soles. Dressed in these fully beaded moccasins, clearly not meant to be walked on, the child was carried into the tipi where
the ceremony was to take place (Fig. 1.4).

This lifetime designation committed the favored child to take personal responsibility throughout life for the welfare of others. (Deloria 1983: 42–43).

If a man had a beloved child, that child whether a boy or girl did not go
about at random, to any and every place, but they remained at home; and
when anything was going on, the child was caused to give property away,
while the old women sang his praises, and called out his name. Moreover,
nobody must ever snap the fingers in an insult at such a child, and never
must they laugh or mock at him; and such children were never whipped, but
instead they were brought up gently, and were greatly loved. And on their
account, their relatives expended much in property and horses. They were
never allowed to wear old clothes and their discarded clothes were placed
upon somebody who was poor and in need of them.

A beloved was made to possess only fine goods, and such apparel, etc. as
only Huka [*sic*] initiates possess. . . . (Deloria 1937?: 532)

COVERED IN BEADS

Lakota women, in partnership with Lakota men in the work of supporting the family, had separate spheres of activity. A major responsibility of Lakota women was to make and adorn beautiful clothing for all family members. Handsome clothing was a sign of the esteem which the wearer was accorded by the maker. This in turn created admiration in the eyes of observers and ultimately supplemented the status of both the wearer and the maker. As a result, it significantly added to the prestige of a woman's family if the members were dressed in fine clothing.

In applying beadwork embroidery, she adorned her family as lavishly as possible. With the introduction of Venetian glass seed beads to the Plains Indians by traders around 1840–50, beadwork emerged as the predominant feminine art form, eclipsing porcupine quillwork and the earlier "pony" (large-sized beads in few colors) beadwork. Lakota women became the most prolific producers of beadwork in the Plains. As noted by one outside visitor to the Lakota (Sioux) in 1876, "The more heavily an article of dress is adorned with beads the better it is suited to their tastes. Some of the buckskin coats are stiff with beadwork, and are really beautiful." (Brackett 1876: 469).

Lakota women spent many hours applying beads to tanned hide and trade cloth in order to dress their family in the finest attire. In particular, their children's clothes were the center of their attention. Fine apparel was, and still is, a sign of affection and honor from mothers, sisters, aunts, and grandmothers. A Lakota

FIG. 1.5, *Opposite*
BABY BONNET, C. 1890

Lakota nation, North or South Dakota, USA

Native-tanned hide, glass beads

Bob and Lora Sandroni Collection

Photograph by LA High Noon, Inc.

Lakota mothers thought the Euro-American-style sunbonnet, like the umbrella, was quite sensible on the treeless Plains. They preferred, however, to make it in the Lakota style by constructing their baby bonnets from tanned hide decorated with beads, rather than from calico or other cotton fabrics.

PHOTO 1.2
LAKOTA WOMAN AND HER THREE CHILDREN, 1895-99

Probably Rosebud Reservation, South Dakota, USA

Denver Museum of Nature and Science, Neg. No BR61-309

Photo by J.H. Bratley

In this photo a woman has dressed her three children in annuity-issue goods, but each child also has items of heavily beaded attire including a doll cradle holding a Victorian porcelain doll. The boy wears a fully beaded vest, or waistcoat, and fully beaded trousers, a change in clothing from the more traditional hide shirt and leggings. These beaded pieces may have been cut using cloth examples for patterns, but they were actually fashioned from Native-tanned hide, often cowhide.

Such items of clothing were considered no less Lakota even with the use of Euro-American-introduced clothing, such as the vest and trousers. Lakota people were particularly adept at selective borrowing of foreign materials and synthesizing them into Lakota culture.

"Even though a number and variety of European-made materials were in common use among the tribes of this region . . . we should not forget that Indians controlled the ways in which these materials were employed, so that these articles came to bear an undeniable stamp of Indian ingenuity. Uses made of some European-made objects by these Indians would have surprised their makers, had they seen them." (Ewers, et al. 1984: 75).

PHOTO 1.2

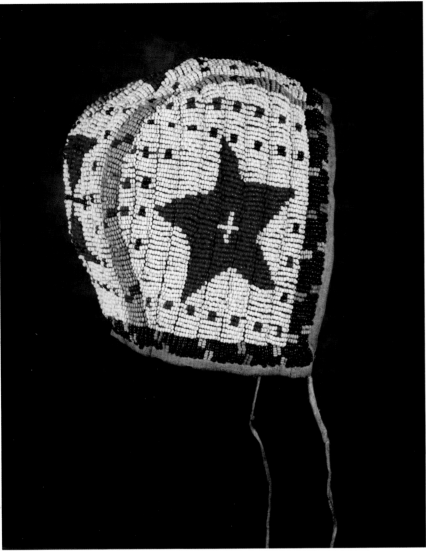

FIG. 1.5

FIG. 1.6
BOY'S VEST AND PANTS, C. 1890

Lakota nation, North or South Dakota, USA

Native-tanned hide, glass

Bob and Lora Sandroni Collection

Photograph by LA High Noon, Inc.

During the reservation era, Plains men and boys were expected to give up wearing breechcloths and leggings and instead wear white men's pants and waistcoats, which were more acceptable to Euro-Americans with whom they came in contact in towns and at boarding schools. Lakota women found a way to successfully mediate between both worlds by making fine fully beaded pants and vests for their sons. These special outfits were acceptable to white society, while at the same time they protected their sons' ethnic identity.

FIG. 1.6

beadworker not only concerned herself with how lavishly she dressed her family but also how she might protect them by ameliorating the potency of the designs:

> Another peculiarity of the Sioux women's technique for beadwork of any kind is that they first mix the beads of all colors and then pick out each bead as it is to be used. This is because glass beads are made by white men who do not know how to control their potencies and by mixing the beads their potencies are equalized so that no bead may have the power to overcome other beads, and the potency of the design will not be disturbed. (Walker 1982: 107).

Lakota clothing traditionally functioned as a personal identifier, a means of distinguishing oneself and one's family from others, and as a collective identifier, demonstrating the ethnic pride of the group in wearing specifically "Lakota" clothing. As the Lakota people entered the reservation era, they were still wearing clothing which served both of these purposes.

In the final decades of the nineteenth century, life changed radically for Lakota society as the last of the life-sustaining buffalo, or American bison, were hunted out in 1882–83, and the people were placed on U.S. government reservations. Contrary to popular belief, Lakota women responded to these dark days not only by continuing to practice their traditional art but by producing their most elaborate beadwork yet. "The common joke is that if anything didn't move, an Oglala [Lakota] woman would bead it." (Powers, M. 1986: 137).

The U.S. government applied intense pressure on the Lakota people to make a change of clothing, particularly in the case of children and men, both of whom had more contact with the Euro-American world. Children were the particular target of assimilation through education in the late nineteenth century. In an all-out effort to assimilate children into white society, the government mandated that Indian children must attend school and wear white men's clothing while doing so.

The Lakota belief that clothing served as protection through its beaded designs and prayers was a pre-reservation value that was carried into the reservation era. By creating especially fine traditional clothing, heavily laden with beadwork, for her children, a Lakota mother found a method for combating the threat of assimilation (Figs. 1.5, 1.6, and 1.7, Photos 1.2 and 1.3).

"When the reservation was first established and up through the 1940s, traditional costuming flourished. . . . [Today] Oglalas constantly fear that the old arts and crafts, like the language, are disappearing. . . . " (Powers, M. 1986: 137). Cherished traditional beaded clothing continues to be passed down through the generations and carefully stored away in chests to be taken out and worn by descendants at local and regional powwows and other special occasions. And many fine beadworkers still make beautiful clothing today for these occasions (Photo 1.4).

FIG. 1.7, *Opposite*
GIRL'S DRESS, C. 1900

Lakota nation, North or South Dakota, USA

Native-tanned hide, glass beads, brass bells, silk ribbon

Bob and Lora Sandroni Collection

Photograph by LA High Noon, Inc.

One Lakota mother carried her beading to its ultimate by totally covering her small daughter's dress in beads. Certainly wearing comfort and practicality were not the thoughts uppermost in her mind. The sheer weight of the glass beads would make it difficult for a small child to stand, let alone wear such a garment for very long. There are a surprising number of such dresses in museum and private collections.

PHOTO 1.3, *Opposite*
YOUNG LAKOTA GIRL IN HER BEADED DRESS AND BONNET, C. 1900

Smithsonian Institution, National Anthropological Archives, Neg. # 54,662

Photographer unknown

This little girl is all dressed up in her fully beaded dress, leggings, moccasins, concho belt, and beaded bonnet. Her dress is remarkably similar to Fig. 1.7.

PHOTO 1.4, *Opposite*
UNITED TRIBES POWWOW, SEPTEMBER 1992

Bismarck, North Dakota, USA

Photograph by Marsha Bol

Beaded clothing continues to be used for special occasions, such as parading and dancing in powwows. Women dress in family heirlooms or in newly made beaded dresses, destined to become family heirlooms.

FIG. 1.7

PHOTO 1.3

PHOTO 1.4

FIG. 1.8
DOLL, C. 1880

Lakota nation, North or South Dakota, USA

Native-tanned hide, glass beads, pigment, human hair, dentalium shells, steel beads, silk ribbon

18 in. (45.7 cm)

Hirschfield Family Collection, courtesy of Fighting Bear Antiques

Photograph by Garth Dowling

This elaborately dressed doll has all the accoutrements of a well-dressed Lakota woman. She wears a finely beaded dress, leggings, and moccasins, along with long dentalium shell earrings and plentiful necklaces. From her belt hangs a woman's tools: an awl case for sewing, a strike-a-light pouch, and a knife case.

Mothers made these dolls for their daughters to play with, but this doll shows no signs of playful wear. Such an elaborate doll as this was likely made for sale to a collector to keep on the shelf.

FIG. 1.9
GIRL'S BELT SET, C. 1884

Southern Cheyenne artist, Oklahoma, USA

Commercial and Native-tanned hide, German silver conchos, glass beads, metal cones, cowrie shells, brass beads, bone, deer tail, pigment, shells, wooden bead, brass gear, metal key

$12^{3}/_{4}$ x $22^{3}/_{8}$ in. (32.4 x 56.8 cm)

Kansas City (Missouri), Union Station / Kansas City Museum, Daniel B. and Ida Dyer Collection, 1940.617

Photograph by Joshua Ferdinand, courtesy of The Nelson-Atkins Museum of Art

---

A Euro-American woman, Mrs. Dyer, collected this extraordinary belt set in 1884 from the mother of a three-year-old Cheyenne girl. While the small belt mimics a grown woman's belt, it has many more accoutrements than usual, likely bestowing high status and protection upon its young owner.

Hanging from the belt are the girl's navel amulet in the shape of a lizard, an awl case for her sewing tool, three bags for her strike-a-light fire starting equipment or her ration ticket, and other protective items, such as a deer's tail and shells.

FIG. 1.10, *Opposite*
MINIATURE TIPI, C. 1890–1910

Plains, USA

Native-tanned hide, glass beads, porcupine quills

$12^{3}/_{4}$ x $11^{1}/_{8}$ in. (32.4 x 28.3 cm)

Museum of Indian Arts and Culture / Laboratory of Anthropology, 7412/12

This small tipi, made in the image of a life-size tipi, may have been made as a toy for a Plains girl, much as Euro-American girls play with dollhouses. It has small tipi poles, so that it can be set up properly.

REHEARSAL FOR ADULT LIFE

Play and toys are often dismissed as the frivolous activities of children in Western society. In most societies, however, play is meaningful practice for the serious business of becoming an adult. The playthings that Lakota parents provided taught their children the social roles they were expected to assume when they grew up. Mothers made miniature versions of women's equipment for their daughters to play with while practicing for their future roles as women (Figs. 1.8 and 1.9, Photo 1.5).

> My chum and I each had doll cradles which were beaded. . . . We also had play-tepees and poles. Whenever the camp broke for a move we were made to take care of our playthings, that is, to bundle them up and to see that they were properly packed on the travois [horse-drawn carrier], and when camp was pitched it was also our duty to unpack them and to place them in our tepees where they ought to be (Fig. 1.10, Photo 1.6).
> —An Arapaho Woman, 1933 (Michelson 1933: 598)

PHOTO 1.5

PHOTO 1.5
KATIE ROUBIDEAUX WITH HER DOLL, 1898

Rosebud Reservation, South Dakota, USA

Nebraska State Historical Society, RG2969-02-165a

Photograph by John A. Anderson

Katie, shown at age eight, lived well into old age on the Rosebud Reservation with her Roubideaux and Blue Thunder descendants. In the photo, she is dressed in traditional Lakota dress and stands on a Lakota beaded saddle blanket.

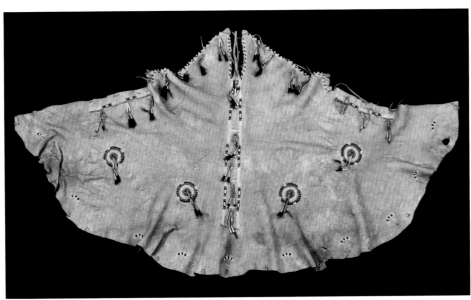

FIG. 1.10

PHOTO 1.6

PHOTO 1.6
LAKOTA GIRLS PLAY WITH THEIR TOY TIPIS, C. 1890

Smithsonian Institution, National Anthropological Archives, 43-126-G

Photographer unknown

The girls are playing with their miniature tipis, even though by 1890 they no longer lived in tipis.

BABY CARRIERS IN COLD AND WARM CLIMATES

PHOTO 1.7

PHOTO 1.7
INUIT WOMEN WEARING BEADED INNER PARKAS, 1903-04

A.P. Low Expedition, Photograph by Shoofly Coomer

Public Archives Canada, PA-53606

FIG. 1.11
WOMAN'S INNER PARKA (*ATIGI*), 1937

Central Eastern Inuit peoples

Padlimiut, Canadian Arctic

Native-tanned caribou skin, glass beads

Parka: 39 x 24 3/4 in. (99 x 63 cm); hood: 21 5/8 in. (55 cm)

The Manitoba Museum of Man and Nature, The Bishop Marsh Inuit Collection, (H5.21.25) 244.80

The hood of an Inuit woman's parka is exceptionally large, because Inuit mothers carry their babies in their hood from infancy until age two or three. Babies go everywhere with their mothers, creating a close bond between the two. According to scientific study, babies who are carried most of the time cry less. (Barr and Hunziker 1987: 197–98).

This style of parka is ideal for the severe climate of the Canadian Arctic, ranging from northwestern Alaska to Greenland. It has two layers—the outer layer with the fur facing outward and the inner layer, worn year-round, with the fur on the inside next to the bodies of the woman and her baby. As the baby grows, the mother can extend the size of the hood. The roominess of the parka also allows her to shift her baby around to nurse without leaving the warmth of the parka.

Beadwork is only embroidered on the inner layer of the parka (Fig. 1.11). With the availability of glass beads introduced through trade with whaling ships, Inuit women replaced the traditional protective amulets on their parkas with beads embroidered in conventionalized patterns. In a climate where survival is precarious, protective additives take on great significance. Some have suggested that beadwork took on the magico-religious work of the amulets, protecting both mother and child dressed in the parka. While the Inuit allowed for personal variation in beadwork designs, some patterns appeared on most parkas (Photo 1.7). For example, the beaded triangular motif likely replicates tattoo markings, which held deep religious significance for Inuit women, who could not enter the land of the blessed without them. A series of oval beaded shapes on the strip running down the hood may signify animal vertebrae, especially found in hunting cultures where pursuit of game was essential to life. Today only a few beadworkers continue this work, learning from relatives and vintage photographs. (Driscoll 1984: 43).

FIG. 1.11

FIG. 1.12
BABY CARRIER, EARLY TWENTIETH CENTURY

Aoheng peoples, Orang Ulu group, Kalimantan region, Borneo island, Indonesia

Cotton, leather cord, glass beads, metal, cowry shells, organic, wood

12³/₄ x 19¹/₂ x 13¹/₂ in. (12.8 x 49.5 x 34.3 cm)

David McLanahan Collection

"The beaded baby carrier has become something of a Borneo icon," says Borneo bead expert, Heidi Munan (2005: 50).

For an Orang Ulu baby, its cradle is not only a practical way to be carried, but it serves as a marker of the child's position in society and as a protective spiritual guardian. The finely woven rattan basket with a wooden seat has an opening on one side. The baby sits in the basket facing its mother's back with its legs wrapped around the adult at or near waist height. When the child is very young, the infant carrier might face the mother's front for nursing. From birth to two years or even longer, the child can be carried in its cradle.

The enclosed sides are decorated with a panel of beadwork and adorned with heirloom attachments. A female relative, generally the baby's grandmother, makes the beaded panel, starting several months before its birth, so that the complex panel will be ready for the infant's arrival. Preferred bead colors are black, white, and yellow, with smaller amounts of red, blue, green, etc., plaited using pineapple leaf fibers. In older pieces, such as this example, russet red is a favored bead color.

In the past, Orang Ulu societies were stratified, so the social rank of the baby and its family could be ascertained by the designs on the carrier's beaded panel. The use of certain designs was restricted for the aristocracy, others for the middle class, none of these for the lower class or the slaves. The motif of the displayed figure, likely a female, seen here, was reserved for the highest social class. Also called the "slave" motif, indicating that the family owned slaves, this motif has a long history in the region. The displayed female, known as the "heraldic woman" image, was used by cultures throughout the pan-Pacific region—from such disparate places as New Guinea, Peru, Canada, Borneo, and the northwest coast of the U.S. The meaning of the image was similar throughout—she is warding off evil. (Fraser 1966: 56–57, 80).

Other motifs reserved for the upper class included the leopard; the dragon; the hornbill, a magnificent bird of the region; and the tiger, remarkable because tigers are not indigenous to Borneo. The middle class had the rights to use scroll designs, stylized animals, and the human face or mask (Photo 1.8), but not a full figure. Traditionally, Orang Ulu people used only beaded designs that they were entitled to, else they would risk disaster in the form of illness or bad harvests. The symbolic designs used by the aristocracy were considered the most powerful of all designs.

These designs also served essential protective purposes. Orang Ulu people believed that the souls of infants were in transition and thus highly vulnerable to wandering, and that evil spirits were intent on stealing the baby's soul. In infancy their

FIG. 1.12

souls were not very well attached to their bodies, and thus failure of the soul to stay close was a cause of illness and even death. (Whittier and Whittier 1988: 54). The beaded panel of the baby carrier kept the infant healthy by being attractive to its soul, so that it would stay nearby.

The squatting female held potent magic to dispel evil spirits by the display of female genitalia. "The spirits, themselves sexless, are puzzled and repelled by such [an] incomprehensible" sight. (Munan 1995: 56). The tiger and other fierce images also frightened away evil spirits.

Special objects were attached to the carrier, such as heirloom beads, bells, shells, tiger or leopard teeth, coins, etc., creating noises that not only soothed the baby, but also repelled the evil spirits lurking around to steal the baby's soul. The carrier in Figure 1.12 is adorned with venerated beads, bells, and coins.

When the child outgrew the carrier, some of his/her vitality remained attached to it. Hence the carrier could not be disposed of, else the child might fall ill or die. Mothers stored it for the next child or removed the beaded panel from a worn-out carrier, but never sold the carrier to someone outside the family.

In the last 40 to 50 years, many of Borneo's young indigenous people have moved downriver to the coastal cities to find more opportunities. There the traditional social stratification system does not apply. Schooling and the introduction of Christianity have leveled these once strict class societies. Today beaded baby carriers are a popular item for the tourist market, where the buyers have no awareness of taboos. As in the past, the producers of the beaded panels are never at risk, only the users are.

FIG. 1.13

FIG. 1.13
BABY CARRIER PANEL, MID-TWENTIETH CENTURY

Kenyah peoples, Orang Ulu group, Borneo island, Indonesia / Malaysia

Cotton, glass beads, pineapple leaf fiber

12³/₁₆ x 10¹/₄ in. (31 x 26 cm)

Museum of International Folk Art, IFAF Collection, Gift of Diane and Sandy Besser, FA.2002.49.9

The displayed figure, likely a female, with opposing tigers is similar to the carrier on the mother's back seen in the photo (Photo 1.8). The tiger and full figure motifs indicate that this panel was reserved for a baby of the aristocrat class.

FIG. 1.14

FIG. 1.14
BABY CARRIER PANEL, LATE NINETEENTH CENTURY

Kenyah peoples, Orang Ulu group, east Borneo island, Indonesia

Cotton, glass beads, pineapple leaf fiber

James Barker Collection

The maker of this panel chose very fine beads to plait the hornbill motifs for the infant of an aristocratic family.

FIG. 1.15
BABY CARRIER PANEL, MID-TWENTIETH CENTURY

Kenyah peoples, Orang Ulu group, Borneo island, Indonesia / Malaysia

Cotton, glass beads, pineapple leaf fiber

12³/₁₆ x 13 in. (31 x 33 cm)

Museum of International Folk Art, IFAF Collection, Gift of Diane and Sandy Besser, FA.2002.49.5

The two mask motifs on this baby carrier panel indicate that this panel would be suitable for a baby of the middle class in the stratified Kenyan society.

FIG. 1.15

PHOTO 1.8

PHOTO 1.8
BORNEO WOMAN WITH HER BABY IN ITS CARRIER, 1988

Kenyah peoples, Orang Ulu group, Borneo island, Indonesia / Malaysia

Photograph by Bernard Sellato

CHILDREN ELSEWHERE

FIGS. 1.16A (FRONT) AND B (BACK)
CHILD'S HAT, C. 1950

Nuristan province, Afghanistan

Cotton, silk, glass beads, buttons, metal, embroidered applied trim

22³/₄ x 4³/₄ in. (58 x 12 cm)

Museum of International Folk Art, Gift of Ira and Sylvia Seret,
A.1990.80.2

Photographs by Addison Doty

Although these children's hats come from different parts of Asia,
they share the visible aspirations of their parents for their child's
enculturation, safety, health, and longevity. Use of dangling beads
and small metal disks on the Afghan hat (Figs. 1.16a and b) distracts
"the evil eye" away from the child, offering protection from harm.

The Chinese children's hats (Figs. 1.17 and 1.18) are decorated to
attract attention with their pom-poms and feathers and are heavily
covered in a variety of amulets and charms to ward off evil and bring
good fortune. The child's hat (Fig. 1.17) is covered with amulets of
Buddha to ensure survival and long life. The boy's tiger hat (Fig. 1.18)
calls upon the powerful tiger, the mount of benevolent deities, to
guard its wearer from evil spirits.

Before they are old enough to take up the veil, young Bani Malik
girls are enculturated into the feminine practice of covering their
head. In the mountainous Asir region of southwest Saudi Arabia
bordering Yemen, a girl's first headcovering is a beaded bonnet-like
hat called a *quba'a* (Figs. 1.19a and b and 1.20a and b). At age eight
or nine, she will exchange this bonnet for a woman's headdress and
ultimately a veil.

FIG. 1.17
CHILD'S HAT, TWENTIETH CENTURY

Bai peoples, Dali county, Yunnan province, People's Republic of
China

Cotton, silk, metal amulets and beads, buttons, yarn

Diameter: 6³/₄ in. (17 cm)

Museum of International Folk Art, IFAF Collection, FA.1992.104.10

Photograph by Addison Doty

FIG. 1.16A

FIG. 1.16B

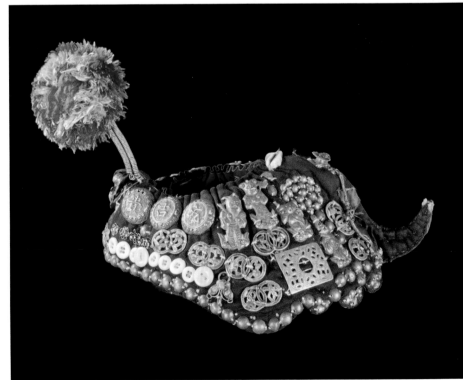

FIG. 1.17

FIG. 1.18

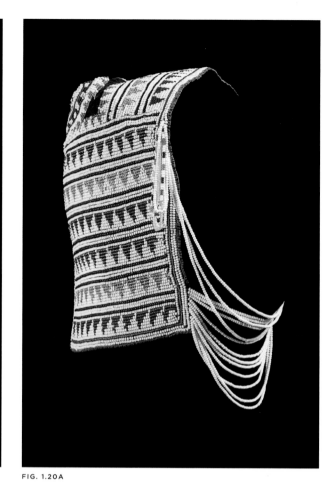

FIG. 1.20A

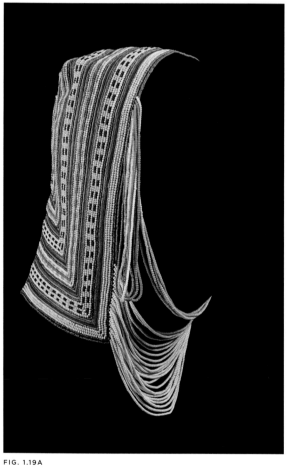

FIG. 1.19A

FIG. 1.19B

FIG. 1.20B

FIG. 1.21

FIG. 1.22

FIG. 1.18, *Opposite*
BOY'S HAT, TWENTIETH CENTURY

Bai peoples, Dali county, Yunnan province, People's Republic of China

Silk, cotton, metal beads and objects, feathers, yarn, embroidered appliquéd applied trim

Diameter: 5$1/2$ in. (14 cm)

Museum of International Folk Art, IFAF Collection, FA.1995.55.1

Photograph by Addison Doty

Made especially for Chinese boys ages one month to five years old, tiger hats ward off evil spirits. Mothers and grandmothers made these protective hats, which were common boys' attire among the Han people and the Chinese minority peoples.

FIGS. 1.19A (FRONT) AND B (BACK), *Opposite*
GIRL'S HEADCOVERING (*QUBA'A*), TWENTIETH CENTURY

Bani Malik peoples, Asir region, Saudi Arabia

Tanned leather, glass beads

Museum of International Folk Art, A.2015.48.2

FIGS. 1.20A (FRONT) AND B (BACK), *Opposite*
GIRL'S HEADCOVERING (*QUBA'A*), TWENTIETH CENTURY

Bani Malik peoples, Asir region, Saudi Arabia

Tanned leather, glass beads

Museum of International Folk Art, A.2015.48.1

FIG. 1.21
HANGING PARROT, C. 1970

Rabari peoples, Gujarat, India

Cotton, glass beads, shells

9$13/16$ x 11$13/16$ in. (25 x 30 cm)

Museum of International Folk Art, IFAF Collection, FA.1990.16.38 or 149

Fanciful beaded parrot toys are hung above a baby's cradle to attract their interest.

FIG. 1.22
TWIN FIGURES (*ERE IBEJI*), TWENTIETH CENTURY

Yoruba peoples, Nigeria

Wood, cotton, glass beads, string, metal, pigment

14$1/4$ in. (36 cm)

Fowler Museum at UCLA, X86.1085a, b

Photograph by Don Cole

These twin figures are not playthings for Yoruba children. They were made for a Yoruba mother who had twins, and, in this case, both twins died. The Yoruba people have one of the highest rates of twin births in the world, some 45 twin births out of every 1,000 births. (Pemberton 1989: 170). However often one, or both twins, fails to survive due to a high infant mortality rate and frailty due to twin birth.

Twins hold a unique status in the Yoruba world. Whether living or dead, they are considered powerful spirits who can bring good fortune to the parents who honor them and misfortune to those who do not. If a twin dies, the parents commission a memorial figure to commemorate that twin. If both twins die, then two figures are carved. The mother then cares for the twin figures in the same way that she would care for a living twin by carrying them everywhere, feeding, bathing and anointing them. On occasion, mothers will dress the figures in expensive beaded tunics.

"Through the process of ritual transformation, the carvings are no longer viewed by the mother, or the others in the family, as wooden memorial figures. As the loci of ritual activity, *ere ibeji* come to embody the living dead. The deceased child, whether having died at six weeks or after sixty years, is present to the living in, with, and through the *ibeji* figure. Indeed, the carvings themselves convey the *ase* [authority, power, and life force] of the twin child even in death." (Pemberton 1989: 175).

FIG. 1.23

FIG. 1.23
CHILD'S TEMPLE AMULETS, C. 1965

Vaghadia Rabari peoples, Samakhiali, Gujarat, India

Glass beads, organic

Diameter: 2 7/16 in. (6.2 cm)

Museum of International Folk Art, IFAF Collection, FA.1990.16.88v

FIG. 1.23
CHILD'S TEMPLE AMULETS, C. 1965

Vaghadia Rabari peoples, Samakhiali, Gujarat, India

Glass beads, organic

Diameter: 2 7/16 in. (6.2 cm)

Museum of International Folk Art, IFAF Collection, FA.1990.16.88v

Rabari mothers place a pair of lavishly beaded amuletic disks on each temple of their young children as a distraction against the evil eye and protection from misfortune. Children are particularly vulnerable and a child's head is especially so.

FIG. 1.24
BABY'S AMULETS, TWENTIETH CENTURY

Northern Afghanistan

Wool felt, cotton, glass beads

Left: 10 1/2 x 5 1/2 in. (26.7 x 14 cm); right: 11 1/2 x 5 1/2 in. (29.2 x 14 cm)

Anne and Bill Frej Collection

PHOTO 1.9
RABARI GIRL WEARING TEMPLE AMULETS, 1983

Vaghadia Rabari peoples, Gujarat, India

Photograph by Judy Frater

The most common amulet found in central Asia is the triangle form, generally made out of cloth decorated with embroidery and beads. These triangular amulets are tied to cradles to protect babies, who are especially vulnerable to evil spirits.

In addition to the pair of beaded amulets on her temples, the young Rabari girl is tattooed with a cross on her left cheek to prevent her from being too beautiful and thus attracting the attention of the evil eye.

FIG. 1.25

FIG. 1.25
CHILD'S BLOUSE PANEL, TWENTIETH CENTURY

Northern Afghanistan

Cotton, glass beads

15 x 13 in. (38 x 32.7 cm)

Anne and Bill Frej Collection

This vivid, fully beaded inset panel has blue beaded fringe, indicative of central Asia. The color blue protects its wearer from the evil eye.

FIG. 1.26
CHILD'S AMULETIC VEST (BACK), C. 1930

Nuristan province, Afghanistan

Cotton, glass beads, buttons, zipper, metal dangles, amulet with glass insets

11 x 12⁵⁄₈ in. (28 x 32 cm)

Museum of International Folk Art, A.1990.80.4

Both the front and back of this vest are covered with shiny buttons and metal dangles, giving it a highly decorative appearance. However these additives are intended to enhance the vest's protective capability against evil spirits. The attached amulet on the back adds a further measure of protection.

FIG. 1.27
BOY'S AMULETIC SHIRT, C. 1960

Turkmenistan

Wool, cotton, silk, metal, glass beads, shells

20 x 21 in. (50¹⁄₂ x 53 cm)

Museum of International Folk Art, Bequest of Lois Livingston and the Museum of New Mexico Foundation, A.1997.39.1

This boy's shirt is covered, front and back, with metal amulets with repoussé designs meant to protect its wearer.

FIG. 1.26

FIG. 1.27

LAKOTA CRADLES TODAY

Nothing is as precious to the Lakota people as a child, the future of their people. Indeed the same can be said about all of the world's peoples. Although Lakota babies are no longer routinely wrapped in fine beaded cradles as they once were, there are still exceptional Lakota beadworkers who have the skill to make these most complex of all traditional Lakota beaded objects. Some are motivated by the news of the coming of a new baby. Others are motivated by the desire to maintain an important tradition so closely associated with the identity of their people.

Thomas "Red Owl" Haukaas (b. 1950—Sicaŋġu Lakota/Creole) made a beaded cradle for his baby niece in 2001. By that time he had already made two fully beaded cradles. As a trained psychiatrist and an artist who identifies himself primarily with his Lakota heritage, Haukaas has spent much of his artistic career concerned about two issues: 1) maintaining the traditions and issues of identity of the Lakota as a people, and 2) social issues that confront his people, Native Americans at large, and the wider world.

As Haukaas recounts: "Beadwork was in my background throughout my life. My great-grandmother lost her husband early and supported her family by making pictographic and Lakota abstract floral beadwork. Some of her work remains with us . . . and are a source of family pride. . . . Like most Native practitioners, I did not have formal training. Rather, my skills are a result of the kindness and thoughtfulness of many generations of Lakota people. Learning beadwork often allows time for passing on family histories and myths as well as transmitting tribal values and narratives. One does not learn beadwork without a social context. These narratives, and more modern ones, inform our art at a deeper level, imbued with notions of tribe and spirituality." (Haukaas 2005: 142).

FIG. 1.28
ANIMISTIC CRADLE, 1992

Maker: Thomas "Red Owl" Haukaas (b. 1950, Sicaŋġu Lakota/Creole)

Brain-tanned elk hide, cotton, glass beads, thread, hawk bells

Marilyn Eber Collection

"This cradle was purposely designed and constructed for cultural exchange with people from other traditions. The Deer has been a dream symbol for many in our family. Like the Bison, it references love and caring for family. The Horse is my own dreamed figure obtained while falling asleep one night. I have taken it as a symbol that encourages me to adhere and honor Lakhota values and customs. My point is all people have these, and more, hopes for their progeny and future generations." (Haukaas 2017).

FIG. 1.28

FIG. 1.29

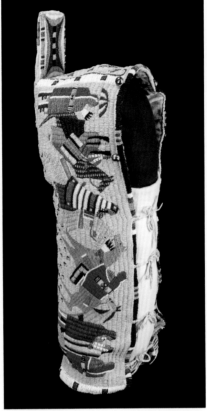

FIG. 1.30A

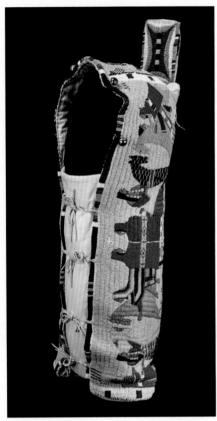

FIG. 1.30B

FIG. 1.29
CREATION STORY CRADLE, 1995

Maker: Thomas "Red Owl" Haukaas

Brain-tanned hide, wool, cotton, glass beads, thread

Denver Art Museum, Richard G. Conn Memorial Fund and the Volunteer Endowment Fund

"All cultures have creation narratives that detail a primordial physical form, during a timeless era, in a particular space. Before being tricked into emergence to the surface world by Iktomi the spider, we were a nation of bison living in the crystal caves in He Sapa, the Black Hills.

The design motivations were three-fold. One, can I make a classic half cradle that is visually balanced? Two, it was an outcome of years of discussion on the definition and value of the then nascent contemporary Native art movement with the late DAM curator Dick Conn. The final and most important motivation is a statement that Native Peoples have our own religions, values and perspectives. These must be respected." (Haukaas 2017).

FIGS. 1.30A (LEFT SIDE), AND B (RIGHT SIDE)
MITAKUYE OYASIN CRADLE, C. 2005

Maker: Thomas "Red Owl" Haukaas

Brain-tanned elk hide, cotton, glass beads, thread

27 x 9¼ x 12 in. (68.5 x 23.5 x 30.5 cm)

Marilyn Eber Collection

"This title translates as 'for all my friends and relatives,' at once a saying and a prayer. [This cradle] is a large, beaded pictographic ledger [with] figures that are different on each side. It's a crowd scene about the definition of family in many of our tribes. . . . There are different ways to define family relationships that are valid to our culture. Adoption via Hunka ceremony. Marriage, whether same gender or not. The community witnesses and supports these families." (Haukaas, August 17, 2015).

"The motivation was to contrast with the then raging DOMA [Defense of Marriage Act] movement and to illuminate that Native People have many differing ways of defining our roles and relationships within our tribes. I also wanted to note we have differing definitions of gender and gender roles." (Haukaas 2017).

FIG. 1.31
INTERCONNECTED CRADLE, 2007

Maker: Thomas "Red Owl" Haukaas

Brain-tanned elk hide, cotton, 76 different colors of glass beads, thread, brass bells

24 x 11 in. (61 x 28 cm)

Iris M-L Model Collection

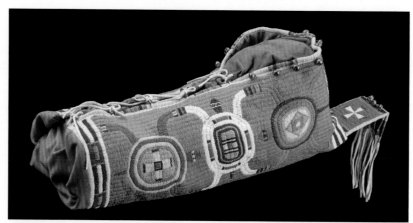

FIG. 1.31

"This is the one with three turtle designs on each side. Each of the turtles has one of the six directions as the primary color. . . . If you look at the composition from a distance, you can see it forms a DNA double helix. So both sides of the cradle represent the grandparents of the child contained within. Children are part of a larger family (*Tiyospaye*) that helps care for this child. . . . No small part of the underpinning for this cradle was that I was getting tired of artisans passing themselves off as Native or supposed Native work. For me, this was a comment that native works have an inherent content and context [that] reproductions and falsifications can't. They may be beautifully made, but they don't SPEAK about US. . . . The issue is more than technical ability." (Haukaas, May 15, 2015).

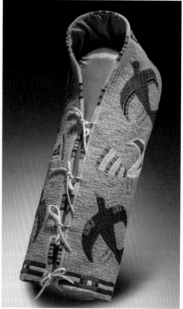

FIG. 1.32

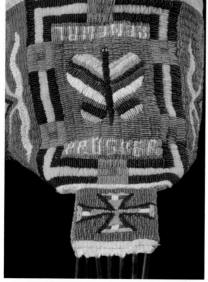

FIG. 1.33 DETAIL

FIG. 1.32
ECONOMIC CONUNDRUM CRADLE, 2010

Maker: Thomas "Red Owl" Haukaas

Brain-tanned elk hide, satin, glass beads, thread, hawk bells

Nerman Museum of Contemporary Art, Johnson County Community College, Overland Park, Kansas, Gift of Barton P. and Mary D. Cohen Charitable Trust

"The cradle is another sociopolitical allegory. The scattering birds speak to many peoples' reaction to the current economic downturn. No matter what, the birds know they will land on solid ground . . . eventually. Meantime, they look up and forward, even if in a helter-skelter fashion. The top of the cradle has one of those geometric *Iktomi* (trickster) designs and it means that we are in uncharted territory so we must look carefully and logically at proposed solutions. Some are not solutions but a continuance of the rapacious and greedy practices that got us where we are globally. The bottom line is this cradle asks: What have we learned and what will we do?" (Haukaas 2010).

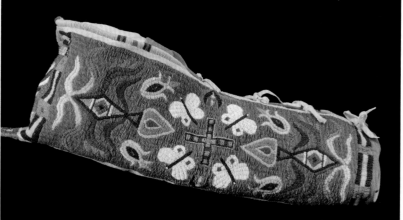

FIG. 1.33

FIG. 1.33 AND DETAIL, *Opposite*
FLORAL CRADLE, 2012

Maker: Thomas "Red Owl" Haukaas

Brain-tanned elk hide, cotton, glass beads, thread

27 x 10 in. (68.6 x 25.4 cm)

Private collection

"[My] penultimate cradle—it's a decision to acknowledge and promote one form [floral] of surface design the Lakhota historically used. One that is almost gone. The designs are based on over 40 years of research. My great-grandmother did this kind of work. She also did pictographic work. Clearly, my own work is a furtherance and continuation of a family tradition. . . . Since we were small children, our own father would draw Indian scenes and have us color them. Those are some of the most precious memories my siblings and I have of our early childhood in Puerto Rico, when dad was in the Navy." (Haukaas, May 15, 2015).

FIG. 1.34 AND DETAIL
KIMIMILA **(IMMIGRATION) CRADLE, 2014**

Maker: Thomas "Red Owl" Haukaas

Native-tanned hide, glass beads, brass bells

23 1/2 x 9 x 10 1/4 in. (59.5 x 22.5 x 26 cm)

Private collection

"My cradles are clearly meant for enticing dialogue. . . . The Monarch butterfly on top says it all. . . . So does the verbiage: 'We did not cross the border, the border crossed us'. . . . As a Native person, this makes great sense to me." (Haukaas, May 15, 2015).

As Haukaas was completing this cradle, he wrote: "The butterfly on the top will be a monarch butterfly, the symbol for immigration. The butterflies on the sides represent the usual themes of freedom, metamorphosis, and positive change. *Kimimila* is the Lakhota word for butterfly. It was our grandmother's favorite symbol and image. She told me she danced like a butterfly going through the hills. She did. Graceful." (Haukaas 2014).

PHOTO 1.10
THOMAS HAUKAAS HOLDS HIS JUST-COMPLETED
KIMIMILA CRADLE, 2014

Photograph by Marsha Bol

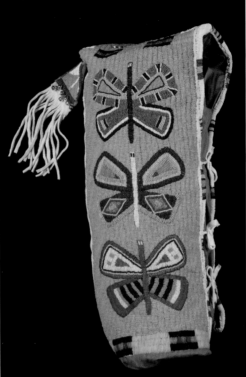

FIG. 1.34   FIG. 1.34 DETAIL

PHOTO 1.10

BECOMING AN
ADULT

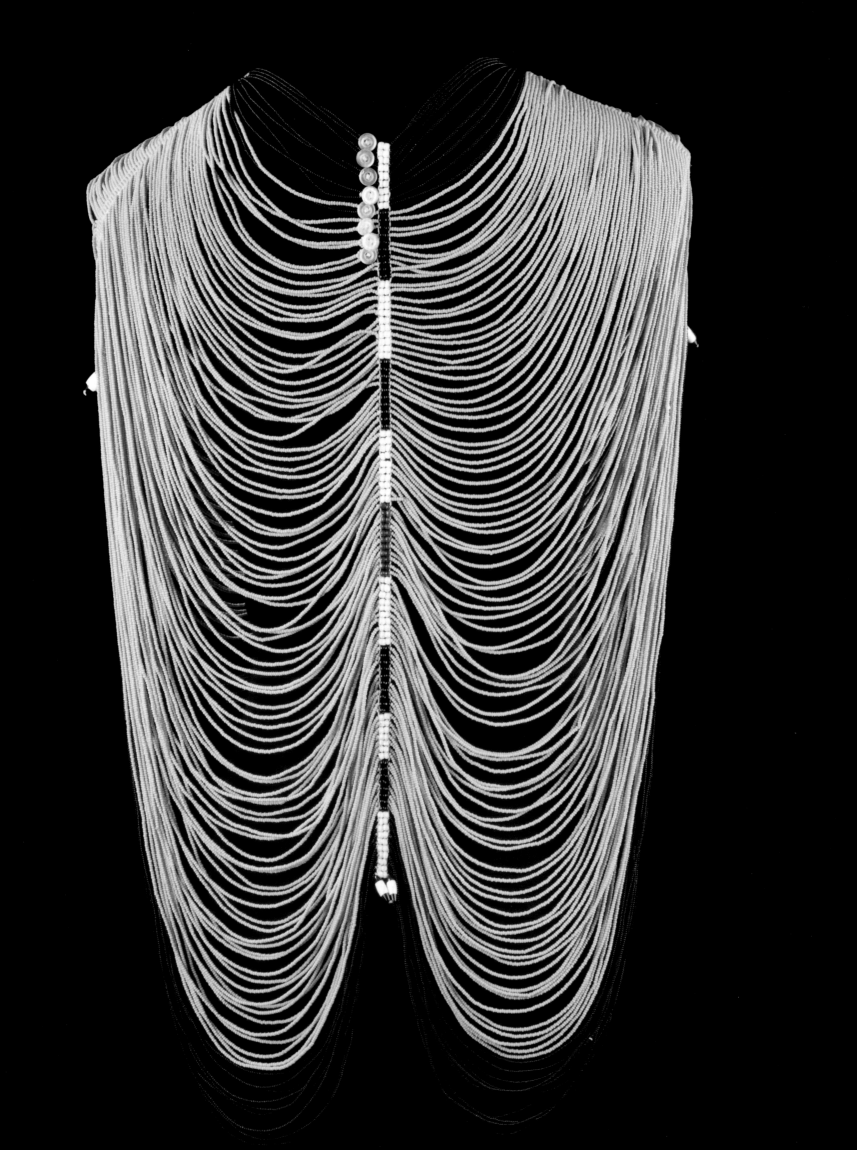

VERY HUMAN LIFE MOVES THROUGH A SERIES OF TRANSITIONS from one status to another, beginning with birth and ending with the grave. All societies publicly mark each individual's life transitions with special observances. "Possibly the most noteworthy of transitions, and one that is most frequently celebrated with works of art, is the move from childhood to adulthood." (Sieber and Walker 1987: 46).

One of the main goals of initiation into adulthood, also known as a coming-of-age rite of passage or puberty ceremony, is preparation for marriage. "One could say then that initiation is a ritual sanctification and preparation for marriage, and only when it is over may young people get married." (Mbiti 1969: 135). Eligibility for marriage often required that the young woman or man be able to demonstrate the skills and industry required to be a "good" spouse and member of society. Initiation is the time when the novices ritually learn to practice their society-defined, ideal domestic roles specific to their gender.

MBUKUSHU GIRLS' PUBERTY CEREMONY

In societies where beadworking figures as a major art form, beads generally play an important role in the initiation rites and newly acquired adult status of adolescents. Such is the case for the Mbukushu female initiates of the Okavango River Delta in the northwestern province, Ngamiland, Botswana. The river delta is a large, inland wetland, surrounded by the Kalahari Desert. The people of this numerically small tribe were somewhat isolated, though in contact with traders from other places, until the late 1960s.

"As soon as a young girl had her first menstruation called the *kohorama*, the ceremony commences and often would last for a month and even longer in some cases until her relatives had been able to provide for her all the garments, coiffure, and symbolic ornaments and jewelry which would mark her as the newly arrived woman who would take her place in the village and community." (Larson 2001: 132).

The initiate immediately went into seclusion at the edge of the forest, where a puberty hut was constructed for her. Much of her time was spent receiving instruction from her grandmothers. She was taught about household duties and adult feminine behavior, and given advice about sex. One of her grandmothers, using her own strand of beads, passed the beads ceremonially through the initiate's mouth, declaring that this act marked the changing status of the girl into a woman.

Once the new moon arrived, the initiate was bathed thoroughly. Then she received her new coiffure, composed of braided plant fibers from root bark, coated with fat and soot to blacken the fibers, with a roll of tree bark to frame the face, giving the appearance of long hair. Strings of large white beads decorating the crown and hanging down the back of the headdress were indicators of prosperity and wealth (Fig. 2.2).

On the final day of her initiation, she was reintroduced into her village as a woman. Now came the time for her to receive her new wardrobe from her senior female relatives, which would identify her as an initiated woman. Thereafter she could wear this precious outfit on important occasions.

FIG. 2.1, *Opposite* WOMAN'S UNDER-APRON (*MOJAMBORO*), C. 1950

Mbukushu peoples, Okavango Delta, Botswana

Impala or duiker hide, glass beads, ostrich eggshell beads

41⁵⁄₁₆ x 20 in. (105 x 50.8 cm)

Museum of International Folk Art, IFAF Collection, FA.2009.2.2

The new wardrobe for the newly made woman included the following:

1. An under-apron worn in back, made of impala hide or similar antelope skin, maintaining the shape of the animal, including the skin of the legs. The under-apron was decorated with strands of glass beads (Fig. 2.1).

2. A belt with pendant panels to be worn on top of the under-apron (Figs. 2.3, 2.4, 2.5), fully embroidered with black and white beads in strikingly bold patterns. When the belt had more than one pendant, each was usually beaded in a differing geometric design selected by its maker. The rarest type of these belts had round ostrich eggshell beads adorning the waist piece (Fig. 2.5). These eggshell beads were fashioned by hand and traded for from their Kalahari Bushmen neighbors, likely preceding the availability of glass beads.

3. A front apron fully beaded in graphically strong, black and white geometric designs (Figs. 2.6–2.12). Mbukushu women preferred to work in black, or dark blue, and white patterns of their own design. However these front aprons disappeared from sight early. "The older women . . . told us that the dress was traditionally not complete without the apron attached in front. No one could show us this piece, however, so we concluded that it must have gone out of fashion a very long time ago." (Lambrecht & Lambrecht 1977: 35). In 1970 American anthropologist Thomas Larson (2001: 20) found that a few of the rural girls were still undergoing the traditional puberty ceremony and receiving the traditional dress and ornamentation.

FIG. 2.2
WOMAN'S COIFFURE HEADDRESS (*THIHUKEKA*), C. 1960

Mbukushu peoples, Okavango Delta, Botswana

Plant bark fiber (*Terminalia Sericea*), leather, soot, various oils, glass beads

23 5/8 x 7 in. (60 x 18 cm)

Museum of International Folk Art, IFAF Collection, FA.2009.2.1

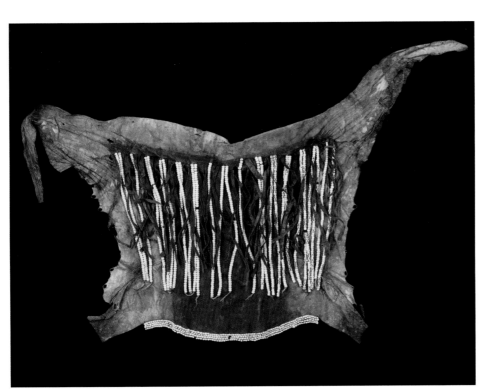

FIG. 2.1

FIG. 2.2

FIG. 2.3

FIG. 2.4

FIG. 2.5

FIG. 2.6

FIG. 2.3
WOMAN'S BACK BELT, C. 1950

Mbukushu (or Bayei) peoples, Okavango Delta, Botswana

Animal hide, glass beads, sinew

26 3/8 x 12 5/8 in. (76 x 32 cm)

Museum of International Folk Art, Gift of the Girard Foundation Collection, A.1982.30.583

FIG. 2.4
WOMAN'S BACK BELT, C. 1950

Mbukushu (or Bayei) peoples, Okavango Delta, Botswana

Animal hide, glass beads, ostrich eggshell beads

25 3/16 x 16 9/16 in. (67 x 32 cm)

Museum of International Folk Art, Gift of the Girard Foundation Collection, A.1982.30.584

Photograph by Addison Doty

FIG. 2.5
WOMAN'S BACK BELT, C. 1950

Mbukushu (or Bayei) peoples, Okavango Delta, Botswana

Animal hide, glass beads, ostrich eggshell beads

26 3/16 x 16 9/16 in. (66.5 x 42 cm)

Museum of International Folk Art, Gift of the Girard Foundation Collection, A.1982.30.582

FIG. 2.6
WOMAN'S FRONT APRON, EARLY TO MID-TWENTIETH CENTURY

Mbukushu peoples, Angola

Animal hide, glass beads

16 15/16 x 15 9/16 in. (43 x 39.5 cm)

Museum of International Folk Art, IFAF Collection, FA.2010.65.1

FIG. 2.7

FIG. 2.8

FIG. 2.9

FIG. 2.10

FIG. 2.11

FIG. 2.12

FIG. 2.7
WOMAN'S FRONT APRON, C. 1960

Mbukushu peoples, Okavango Delta, Botswana

Animal hide, glass beads

14 x 12^1/$_3$ in. (35.5 x 31.3 cm)

Museum of International Folk Art, Gift of the Girard Foundation Collection, A.1982.42.448

FIG. 2.8
WOMAN'S FRONT APRON, C. 1960

Mbukushu peoples, Okavango Delta, Botswana

Animal hide, glass beads

15^3/$_4$ x 14^3/$_{16}$ in. (40 x 36 cm)

Museum of International Folk Art, Gift of the Girard Foundation Collection, A.1982.42.451

FIG. 2.9
WOMAN'S FRONT APRON, C. 1960

Mbukushu peoples, Okavango Delta, Botswana

Animal hide, glass beads

15^1/$_5$ x 14^1/$_3$ in. (38.5 x 36.5 cm)

Museum of International Folk Art, Gift of the Girard Foundation Collection, A.1982.42.443

FIG. 2.10
WOMAN'S FRONT APRON, C. 1960

Mbukushu peoples, Okavango Delta, Botswana

Animal hide, glass beads

16 x 13^3/$_{16}$ in. (40.5 x 33.5 cm)

Museum of International Folk Art, Gift of the Girard Foundation Collection, A.1982.42.449

FIG. 2.11
WOMAN'S FRONT APRON, C. 1960

Mbukushu peoples, Okavango Delta, Botswana

Animal hide, glass beads

17^1/$_8$ x 14^3/$_4$ in. (43.5 x 37.5 cm)

Museum of International Folk Art, Gift of the Girard Foundation Collection, A.1982.42.450

FIG. 2.12
WOMAN'S FRONT APRON, C. 1960

Mbukushu peoples, Okavango Delta, Botswana

Animal hide, glass beads

14^3/$_4$ x 16^{15}/$_{16}$ in. (37.5 x 43 cm)

Museum of International Folk Art, Gift of the Girard Foundation Collection, A.1982.42.445

These front aprons are rarely found in museum collections. The Museum of International Folk Art is fortunate to have a sizeable collection of aprons, allowing for comparison of the differing designs worked out by each individual maker.

FIG. 2.13

FIG. 2.14

INITIATIONS ELSEWHERE

FIG. 2.13
CELESTIAL CROWN, NINETEENTH CENTURY

Mun division of Yao peoples, northern Laos

Silver, hair, wood, silk, cotton

Diameter: 9¹/₂ in. (24 cm)

Museum of International Folk Art, IFAF Collection, FA.2003.9.1v

Photograph by Addison Doty

A young Yao woman earns the right to wear a crown like this one after she has completed her puberty initiation. She places the central dome on top of her head of wound hair, inserting the silver pins into the disk surrounding the dome. Dragon pins and dangles hang from the outer rim of the crown. Thereafter she may choose to wear the crown daily or only on special occasions. When the crown is not in use, it is wrapped in a white cloth embroidered with blue Chinese poetry characters. For her wedding, she wears the crown wrapped in a red cloth.

FIG. 2.14
PUBERTY DRESS TOP, 1860–1900

Western Apache nation, Arizona, USA

Tanned buffalo calfskin, tin can tinklers, glass beads, sinew, dye, metal tacks, paper, cotton

25¹⁵/₁₆ in. (65.8 cm)

Museum of Indian Arts and Culture / Laboratory of Anthropology, 1860/12

Many Apaches still practice the girls' puberty rite. Preparations begin with the girl's female relatives sewing an elaborate two-piece dress for the initiate, meant to mirror the dress worn by White-painted Woman, the mythical creator of the womanhood ceremony.

ONE LAKOTA GIRL'S PUBERTY RITES

When a young Lakota girl experienced her first menses, she was isolated for four days in a separate dwelling, the menstrual lodge. She was instructed to stay inside the tipi at all times and not to look outside or go near any males. During her first seclusion (*išnati awicalowanpi*, which translates as: "They sing over the one dwelling alone"), the girl was considered to be at her most sensitive and impressionable time, so those activities and thoughts in which she engaged were of utmost importance to the direction of her future as a woman. Even though she likely already knew how to sew porcupine quills and glass beads, she was ritually instructed by a senior woman, generally her grandmother, to do quillwork, traditionally, and beadwork in more recent times. (Bol 1989: 178–82).

In 1925 on Rosebud reservation Nellie Star Boy Menard spent all four days of her seclusion learning and practicing the arts of quill- and beadwork. It was essential that she completed at least one top of a pair of moccasins. (Bol & Menard 2000: 28–29).

The Buffalo Ceremony was held shortly following a girl's first seclusion, if her family was affluent enough to so honor her. Conducted by a shaman, who had authority to do so, it was an opportunity to call upon the supernatural assistance of the buffalo spirit on her behalf and to announce that she had become a woman.

As Menard recalled: "They have a ceremony. They got a man to sing over you. And they pray for you and from there you're not a girl any more. You're going to the womanhood. So they pray for you that you'll lead a good life and . . . prepare to be a wife and a mother and what you should teach your children in the future. . . . And then you throw the ball." (Bol & Menard 2000: 32).

Accounts about the throwing of the beaded ball are quite rare (Fig. 2.15). Menard gave an account of her own experience: "When he gets done why then I took the [beaded] ball and then . . . they pick the girl to receive that, and so she comes up, and I had to throw that ball and she's to catch it. And if she drops it they say it's bad luck. What kind I don't know." (Bol & Menard 2000: 33).

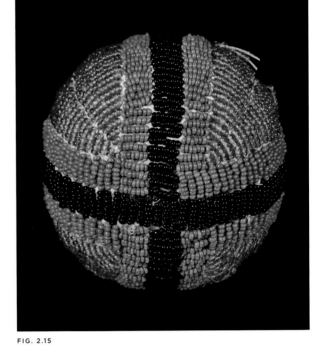

FIG. 2.15

FIG. 2.15
CEREMONIAL BALL, 1875–1925

Lakota nation, North or South Dakota, USA

Native-tanned hide, glass beads, sinew

Diameter: 2¼ in. (6 cm)

Museum of Indian Arts and Culture / Laboratory of Anthropology, 45643/12

PHOTO 2.1
OGLALA SIOUX MAN AND GIRL ON HORSE LADEN WITH BEADED MOCCASIN TOPS AND OTHER GIVEAWAY GOODS, 1906

Pine Ridge Reservation, South Dakota, USA

Brennan Collection

South Dakota State Historical Archives, FB 108

PHOTO 2.1

PHOTO 2.3
DIPO INITIATION CEREMONY,
TWENTY-FIRST CENTURY

Krobo, Ghana

Photograph by Cedi Djaba

PHOTO 2.2
NOMODA EBENEZER (CEDI) DJABA
AT THE SANTA FE INTERNATIONAL
FOLK ART MARKET, 2011

Odumase Krobo, Ghana

Photograph by Bob Smith, courtesy
of the International Folk Art Alliance

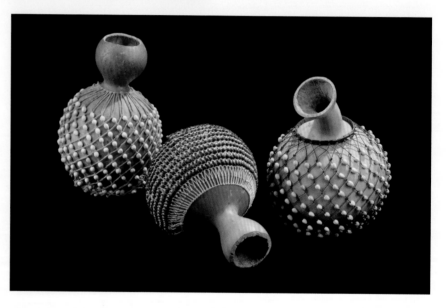

FIG. 2.16
RATTLES, C. 1963

Krobo peoples?, Ghana; and Yoruba peoples, Nigeria

Gourd, cotton string, seeds

Left: 10$^{1}/_{16}$ in. (25.5 cm); middle: 10$^{1}/_{16}$ in. (25.5 cm);
right: 10$^{1}/_{4}$ x 7$^{7}/_{8}$ in. (26 x 20 cm)

Museum of International Folk Art, left: IFAF Collection, FA. 1965.28.23;
middle: A.1975.12.38; right: Gift of Lloyd E. Cotsen and the Neutrogena
Corporation, A.1982.1.840.

PHOTO 2.4
STRINGS OF BEADS MADE FROM
RECYCLED GLASS, 2016

Maker: Nomoda Ebenezer (Cedi)
Djaba (b. 1969), Cedi Beads Industry,
Odumase Krobo, Ghana

Photograph by Marsha Bol

As the senior women are arraying the Dipo girls in their multiple strings
of beads during the closing initiation ceremonies, they play these musical
instruments, while dancing and singing to the beat.

MASTER CEDI DJABA AND BEADS FOR THE KROBO DIPO
INITIATION CEREMONY IN GHANA

Nomoda Ebenezer Djaba, better known as "Cedi," is a descendant of many generations of Krobo beadmakers in southeastern Ghana. He has been making beads from recycled glass since he was seven years old, working alongside his family. As "Ghana's most internationally renowned glass bead artist," Cedi Djaba says: "My work represents my culture, because everyone in Africa associates beads with Odumase Krobo [village]." (Stewart & Wallach 2011; Gott 2014:25). Cedi heads his workshop, which supports both his family and 24 families of the artists who work there. They make beads using five different processes and use glass recycled from bottles, broken window panes, broken beads, and such.

These strings of beads serve an important purpose during the adolescent girls' initiation ceremony, known as *Dipo*, among the Krobo people of southeastern Ghana in West Africa. "No other ritual, in the life of a female Krobo, is of greater importance than—or even equal to—the dipo. Through it the girl officially enters adulthood and obtains full status in the tribal community. . . . There is the conviction, dating from ancient times, that no Krobo girl can ever become a mature Krobo woman and a wife worthy of a Krobo man, unless she can show on her body and on her hand the visible marks of her initiation." (Huber 1963: 165).

The Dipo season begins each February. In the past the ceremony took many months, but today its duration has been shortened to three days to a week. The ceremony is expensive for the parents, who "usually start collecting beads as soon as the girls are born. . . . My family has provided the beads for these celebrations for many generations." (Djaba 2003: 105).

Sometimes younger girls in the family (ages six to eighteen) also go through the ceremony, along with their older sisters, as it is less costly if the younger ones go through with their elder sisters. "Frequently another reason for having the girls initiated in their early age is the wish of the parents to present their daughters for baptism in a Christian church. The nature of the ritual . . . is held repugnant to Christian beliefs. So most churches forbid their baptized members to pass dipo." (Huber 1963: 166).

Throughout their several-day confinement, the girls are ritually instructed in feminine domestic tasks—such as cooking, sweeping, and washing clothes—and the correct behavior of a Krobo woman. Following rites of cleansing and purification, the initiates arrive at the closing celebrations, where they are richly adorned in clothes and beads.

"Whatever a 'house' can afford in the ancestral treasures and new acquisitions and borrowings, is put on display in this final stage of the daughters' initiation. It is the women's business to tie the strings of beads around the girls' necks, wrists, arms, waists and legs." (Huber 1963: 183-84).

Cedi Djaba says about beads and the Dipo ceremony: "For us, the Krobos, beads are almost everything. . . . So you see that we use beads during the Dipo. . . . So if you have a lot of beads or if you have very important beads, it's like you are a rich man or a woman. That's why the Dipo girls, they wear a lot of beads. They want to show that they are wealthy. Or their family wants to show how important they are." (Stewart and Wallach 2011).

NDEBELE BEADWORK MARKS LIFE CHANGES

Among South African peoples, beginning in the mid- to late nineteenth century, beaded adornment became the primary means of expressing identity, be it gender identity, group membership, or to mark the movement of an individual through life's stages. The Ndzundza, or Southern, Ndebele women, living in the sparse southern Transvaal region of South Africa, sew beadwork and paint house murals, which share common styles, motifs and colors, as their signature arts.

History played a pivotal role in the florescence of Ndzundza Ndebele beadwork. We know that during the 1860s and 1870s, they were a prosperous and powerful people. Subsequent power struggles with surrounding neighbors culminated in a devastating siege and defeat by the Boers in the Mapoch War of 1882–83. Ndzundza villages were destroyed, and the people were removed from their land. The Boers imposed a system of five years indentured service, which lasted much longer, on the Ndzundza Ndebele people, scattering them among white farmers distant from their homeland. The full effect was devastating, but rather than sinking into total demoralization and assimilation, the Ndzundza reacted by reclaiming their ethnic identity. "It is significant that in reaction to being divided socially and geographically, a stronger consciousness of identity developed and was expressed in the material culture." (Davison 1985: 19; see also Delius 1989). Male initiation, the *wela*, was resurrected in 1886 even while the people were indentured. Traditionally upon return from their training, the initiates wore beadwork, one of the few occasions when males wore beads, and also mothers of the initiates wore a special form of beadwork—long pendants of sewn beads that hung from their heads to the ground, termed "long tears" (*umlingakobe*), as a sign of their sons leaving the fold and becoming men (Photos 2.8 and 2.9). Likely female initiation continued as well, although it was less noticeable since the girl's seclusion took place in her home. This was the time when young maidens learned the arts of beadwork and house mural painting from their female elders, so necessary to the continuation of these traditions. "One of the crucial ways in which the Ndzundza fought back was through their attempts to regroup and to revive key social institutions. . . . " (Delius 1987: 18).

"Thus, given the historical factors of the late 1800s, it is possible that the beadwork was, at the least, reintroduced, and extended, to fulfill an increased need to express identity in dress when no longer living as a unified Ndebele community." (Davison 1985: 19). "Production and use of beadwork has continued to the present day. It is likely that, while simultaneously establishing other levels of meaning, the beadwork has continued to serve the important function of defining ethnic identity. . . . " (Levy 1989: 28).

As Ndebele women continue to make and wear on special occasions the beaded garments for which they are renowned, every member of Ndebele society is still able to identify the life stage of an Ndebele female simply by looking at her traditional beaded clothing. (Levy 1989: 25). The form and decoration of her clothing identifies her as a child, a pubescent girl, a bride, or a married woman:

- A child, more usually female than male (until he soon moves into trousers), wears a small apron, little more than a beaded band with fringe (Fig. 2.17). As she grows, the too-small apron is replaced with a larger one.

- When a young girl reaches puberty, she goes into seclusion, where she is ritually taught the art of beadwork and house mural painting by her mother and grandmothers. (Pemberton 2008: 27–28).

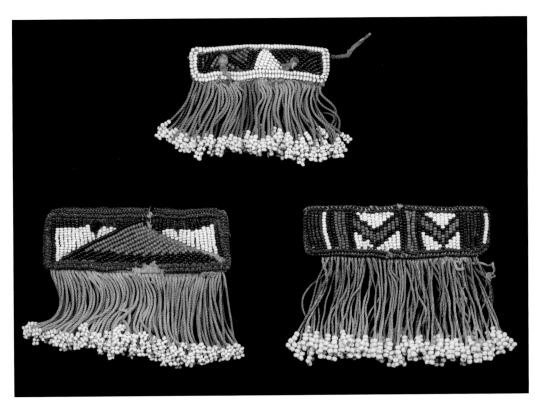

FIG. 2.17
CHILD'S APRONS (*LIGABI*),
C. 1970

Ndzundza Ndebele peoples,
Transvaal region, South Africa

Cotton, glass beads

4.3 x 5.7 in.; 4.7 x 5.7 in.; 3.1 x
4.3 in. (11 x 14.5 cm; 12 x 14.5 cm;
8 x 11 cm)

Museum of International Folk
Art, Gift of Rosina Lee Yue,
A.1996.34.5–7

FIG. 2.18
MAIDEN'S APRON (*ISIPHEPHETHU*), C. 1950

Ndzundza Ndebele peoples, Transvaal region, South Africa

Pounded goatskin, glass beads

15 3/8 x 16 15/16 in. (39 x 43 cm)

Museum of International Folk Art, Gift of Rosina Lee Yue,
A.1996.34.2

FIG. 2.19
MAIDEN'S APRON (*ISIPHEPHETHU*), C. 1970

Ndzundza Ndebele peoples, Transvaal region, South Africa

Canvas, glass beads

12 11/16 x 15 7/8 in. (32.3 x 40.4 cm)

Museum of International Folk Art, Gift of the Girard
Foundation Collection, A.1982.30.540

FIG. 2.20

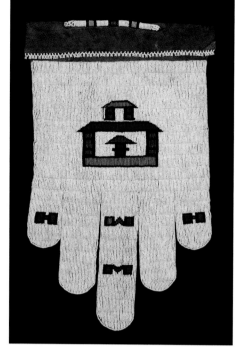

FIG. 2.21

FIG. 2.22

FIG. 2.25

FIG. 2.20
BRIDE'S APRON (*IJOGOLO*),
C. 1950

Ndzundza Ndebele peoples,
Transvaal region, South Africa

Goatskin, glass beads

24 x 19⁵/₁₆ in. (61 x 49 cm)

Museum of International Folk
Art, Gift of Rosina Lee Yue,
A.1996.34.1

FIG. 2.21
BRIDE'S APRON (*IJOGOLO*),
C. 1950

Ndzundza Ndebele peoples,
Transvaal region, South Africa

Goatskin, glass beads

25¹³/₁₆ x 15³/₁₆ in. (65.5 x
38.5 cm)

Museum of International
Folk Art, Gift of the Girard
Foundation Collection,
A.1982.30.541

FIG. 2.22
BRIDE'S APRON (*IJOGOLO*),
C. 1950

Ndzundza Ndebele peoples,
Transvaal region, South Africa

Goatskin, glass beads

24⁷/₁₆ x 17¹/₈ in. (62 x 43.5 cm)

Museum of International
Folk Art, Gift of the Girard
Foundation Collection, A.
1982.30.592

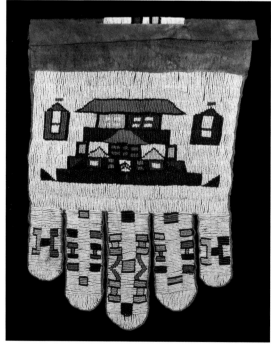

FIG. 2.23

FIG. 2.24

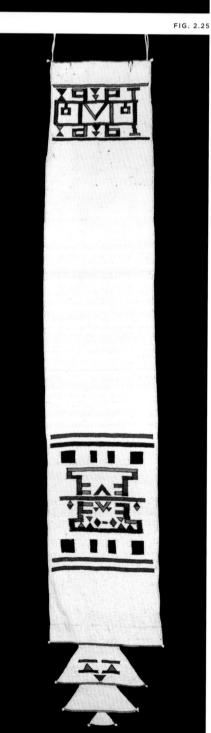

She wears a rectangular-shaped front apron, made by her mother, on her coming-out day along with other beaded ornaments that she made during her seclusion. The apron identifies her as pubescent and thus old enough for proposals of marriage (Figs. 2.18–2.19).

- After her initiation, a young woman is eligible for marriage. Her future mother-in-law makes her a five-paneled beaded apron (Figs. 2.20–2.24), which signals her as a bride and married woman. She keeps this apron to wear on ceremonial occasions after her wedding. The bride may also wear a long beaded train hanging down her back and trailing along the ground (Figs. 2.25–2.26), and a beaded veil (Fig. 2.27).

- After the first few months as a married woman, she is eligible to wear an apron with a central area of beaded fringes bordered by beaded side panels (Figs. 2.28–2.31). This apron is for a married woman's everyday use.

- One of the treasures of a married woman is her beaded wool blanket, heavily encrusted with rows of beadwork sewn onto a brightly colored multi-striped trade blanket. With the large number of extremely costly glass beads, the blanket is very heavy, weighing as much as twenty-two pounds (Figs. 2.32–2.34). Not all married women are fortunate enough to have a heavily beaded blanket. As Esther Mahlangu, an Ndebele elder (Photo 2.5), says about Figure 2.34: "This woman must have had an important husband to provide her with such an elaborate blanket! The more beadwork, the more important the husband. A married woman does not pass her blanket to her daughter, because it is only for a married woman." (Mahlangu 2012).

- Before the availability of woolen trade blankets, women made a cape from animal skins elaborately embellished with a large white beaded panel and edged in white beads. Brides wore these capes for their weddings and later for special occasions (Photo 2.6).

Until about 1970, these age-related garments were stitched with a large field of white seed beads as the background with a few geometric designs in limited colors sparsely floating in the field. Beginning in 1970, bead color preferences changed suddenly, moving away from the predominant white field to a palette of dark blue, green, purple, and black beads. (Priebatsch & Knight 1978: 25).

Both the women's beaded designs and painted house murals share design similarities. From the 1920s to the 1970s abstracted designs referred to the domestic space—a woman's home, courtyard, the cattle corral, and the *kraal* (compound housing one or several families) (Figs. 2.18, 2.21, and 2.23). Beginning in the 1970s, design choices broadened to include the wider world. Designs, such as airplanes (Fig. 2.19) and letters of the alphabet (Fig. 2.33), popular more for their shapes than their meaning, found their way into the beaded aprons, trains, and blankets. These innovations help to keep the tradition dynamic and relevant in a contemporary world.

FIG. 2.23, *Opposite*
BRIDE'S APRON (*IJOGOLO*),
C. 1970

Ndzundza Ndebele peoples,
Transvaal region, South Africa

Goatskin, glass beads

23 13/16 x 16 9/16 in. (60.5 x 42 cm)

Museum of International Folk Art, Gift of the Girard Foundation Collection, A. 1982.30.595

FIG. 2.24, *Opposite*
BRIDE'S APRON (*IJOGOLO*),
C. 1970

Ndzundza Ndebele peoples,
Transvaal region, South Africa

Goatskin, glass beads

24 3/16 x 15 3/4 in. (61.5 x 40 cm)

Museum of International Folk Art, Gift of the Girard Foundation Collection, A.1982.30.593

FIG. 2.25, *Opposite*
BRIDE'S TRAIN (*INYOGA*), C. 1950

Ndzundza Ndebele peoples,
Transvaal region, South Africa

Glass beads, thread

59 1/16 x 9 13/16 in. (150 x 25 cm)

Museum of International Folk Art, Gift of the Girard Foundation Collection, A.1982.30.549

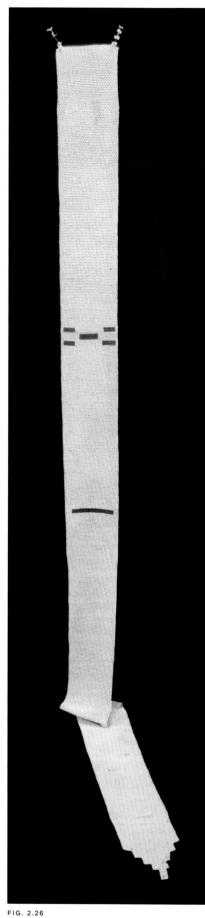

FIG. 2.26

FIG. 2.27A

FIG. 2.27B

FIG. 2.26
BRIDE'S TRAIN (*INYOGA*), EARLY TO MID-TWENTIETH CENTURY

Ndzundza Ndebele peoples, Transvaal region, South Africa

Glass beads, thread

89³/₄ x 4³/₄ in. (228 x 12 cm)

Museum of International Folk Art, Gift of Rosina Lee Yue, A.1996.34.3

FIGS. 2.27A (FRONT) AND B (BACK)
BRIDE DOLL, EARLY 2000S

Mopani Crafts, Ndzundza Ndebele peoples, Transvaal region, South Africa

Cloth, glass beads

Santa Fe International Folk Art Market, New Mexico

"This doll is in the traditional dress of an Ndebele bride. The five panels of her apron are symbolic of the deposit of five head of cattle toward the *lobolo* (bride price). She wears a beaded train (*inyoga*) which hangs from her shoulders. Her face is covered by a beaded veil called an *isiyaya*."
(Mopani Crafts label)

FIG. 2.28

FIG. 2.29

FIG. 2.30

FIG. 2.31

FIG. 2.28
MARRIED WOMAN'S APRON
(*LIPOTHO*), C. 1935

Ndzundza Ndebele peoples, Transvaal
region, South Africa

Goatskin, glass beads

22³/₈ x 20 in. (8.8 x 7.9 cm)

Museum of International Folk Art, Gift
of the Girard Foundation Collection,
A.1982.30.542

FIG. 2.29
MARRIED WOMAN'S APRON
(*LIPOTHO*), C. 1950

Ndzundza Ndebele peoples, Transvaal
region, South Africa

Goatskin, glass beads

21¹/₂ x 25¹/₂ in. (8.5 x 10 cm)

Museum of International Folk Art, Gift
of Lloyd E. Cotsen and the Neutrogena
Corporation, A.1995.93.94

FIG. 2.30
MARRIED WOMAN'S APRON
(*LIPOTHO*), C. 1970

Ndzundza Ndebele peoples, Transvaal
region, South Africa

Goatskin, glass beads

21¹/₁₆ x 17¹/₂ in. (53.5 x 44.5 cm)

Museum of International Folk Art, Gift
of the Girard Foundation Collection,
A.1982.30.545

FIG. 2.31
MARRIED WOMAN'S APRON
(*LIPOTHO*), C. 1970

Ndzundza Ndebele peoples, Transvaal
region, South Africa

Cotton, glass beads

22¹/₁₆ x 21⁵/₈ in. (56 x 55 cm)

Museum of International Folk Art, Gift
of the Girard Foundation Collection,
A.1982.30.548

FIG. 2.32

FIG. 2.33

FIG. 2.32
MARRIED WOMAN'S BLANKET (*IRARI*), MID-TWENTIETH CENTURY

Ndzundza Ndebele peoples, Transvaal region, South Africa

Wool, glass beads

61½ x 65½ in. (156.21 x 166.37 cm)

Natalie Fitz-Gerald Collection

FIG. 2.33
MARRIED WOMAN'S BLANKET (*IRARI*), C. 1960

Ndzundza Ndebele peoples, Transvaal region, South Africa

Wool, glass beads

34¹/₁₆ x 54³/₄ in. (86.5 x 139 cm)

Museum of International Folk Art, Gift of the Girard Foundation
Collection, A.1981.42.440

"It is quite common to see the letters 'TP,' which are the first characters
of the Pretoria motor vehicle license plate." (Priebatsch & Knight 1978: 25)

PHOTO 2.5
ESTHER MAHLANGU (B. 1935) DISCUSSING A BEADED NDEBELE
WOMAN'S BLANKET, 2012

Ndzundza Ndebele, Transvaal region, South Africa

Museum of International Folk Art, Santa Fe, New Mexico, USA

Photograph by Marsha Bol

FIG. 2.34, *Opposite*
MARRIED WOMAN'S BLANKET (*IRARI*), C. 1970

Ndzundza Ndebele peoples, Transvaal region, South Africa

Wool, glass beads

106 x 150.1 in. (269.2 x 381.2 cm)

Museum of International Folk Art, A.2012.65.1

PHOTO 2.5

FIG. 2.34

PHOTO 2.6

PHOTO 2.7

PHOTO 2.6
SOUTHERN NDEBELE BRIDE WEARING A BEADED CAPE (*LINAGA*), 1923

Mokopane (Potgietersrust), Limpopo, South Africa

McGregor Museum, Kimberley, South Africa

Photograph by Alfred Duggan-Cronin, DC1717

This Ndebele woman, dressed as a bride, is wearing a lavishly beaded cape and other ornaments. However, she is not wearing the traditional bride's apron. Rather she wears a train on the front rather than on her back. She holds a beaded doll, a very early Ndebele example. There is some evidence that the photographer owned the cape and the doll, carrying them as props to dress his indigenous models when photographing them, in order to lend a more "authentic" look to the photos. (Schneider 1998: 139–141).

The practice of early photographers, when traveling into native locales, of bringing their own props in order to dress indigenous people in traditional clothing (which in some cases they no longer wore), rather than allowing any presence of Western wear, has been uncovered in similar circumstances in other parts of the world. Edward S. Curtis is known for using this same technique when photographing American Indians in the western United States in the first third of the twentieth century.

PHOTO 2.7
YOUNG NDEBELE WOMAN STANDING AT DOORWAY, 1936–1949

Transvaal region, South Africa

Smithsonian Institution, National Museum of African Art, Eliot Elisofon Photographic Archives

Photograph by Constance Stuart Larrabee, EEPA_1998_060439

The young woman dressed in her pubescent apron and multiple beaded arm, leg, ankle, and waist rings stands in the doorway of an Ndebele house displaying painted murals. She may have made her beaded rings during her puberty seclusion. The rings are constructed of coils of grass wound tightly with strings of beads.

PHOTO 2.8

**PHOTO 2.8
NDEBELE WOMAN IN DOORWAY (FRONT),
1936-1949**

Transvaal region, South Africa

Smithsonian Institution, National Museum of
African Art, Eliot Elisofon Photographic Archives

Photograph by Constance Stuart Larrabee,
EEPA_1998_060526

This woman is dressed in her finest, wearing the
five-paneled apron signifying that she is now
a married woman. She is wrapped in a beaded
hide cape and wears the "long tears" as the
mother of a male initiate who is returning from
his training and will now leave his mother's
home. She holds a beaded dance wand.

PHOTO 2.9

PHOTO 2.10

**PHOTO 2.9
NDEBELE WOMAN (BACK), 1936-1949**

Transvaal region, South Africa

Smithsonian Institution, National Museum of African Art, Eliot Elisofon
Photographic Archives

Photograph by Constance Stuart Larrabee, EEPA_1998_060531

**PHOTO 2.10
MARRIED NDEBELE WOMEN AND CHILDREN, 1936-1949**

Transvaal region, South Africa

Smithsonian Institution, National Museum of African Art, Eliot Elisofon
Photographic Archives

Photograph by Constance Stuart Larrabee, EEPA_1998_060610

Two married Ndebele women are dressed in their daily aprons and brass rings,
while a youngster wears her/his small fringed apron with beaded rings around
the ankles.

FIG. 2.35

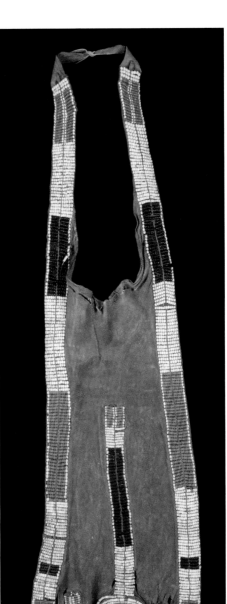

LIFE STAGE IDENTIFIERS ELSEWHERE

FIG. 2.35
MARRIED WOMAN'S APRON, TWENTIETH CENTURY

Turkana peoples, Kenya

Gazelle or goat hide, glass beads

16 9/16 x 9 1/4 in. (42 x 23.5 cm)

Museum of International Folk Art, Bequest of Greg LaChapelle, A.2011.20.29

PHOTO 2.11
YOUNG UNMARRIED WOMAN, 1973

Turkana peoples, Lodwar, Kenya

Smithsonian Institution, National Museum of African Art, Eliot Elisofon Photographic Archives

Photograph by Herbert M. Cole, Image no. 2000-080209

Turkana female age groups are identifiable by their aprons. Married women wear gazelle or goatskin aprons decorated along the sides with metal bells, while unmarried women and marriageable age girls wear aprons decorated with large beads. Little girls also wear small beaded aprons. (Best 1993: 95–102). The preferred bead palate is generally limited to red, white, and black/blue colored beads.

FIG. 2.36
UNMARRIED WOMAN'S APRON, TWENTIETH CENTURY

Turkana peoples, Kenya

Gazelle or goat hide, glass beads

38 11/16 x 11 7/16 in. (98.3 x 29 cm)

Museum of International Folk Art, Bequest of Greg LaChapelle, A.2011.20.39

PHOTO 2.11

FIG. 2.36

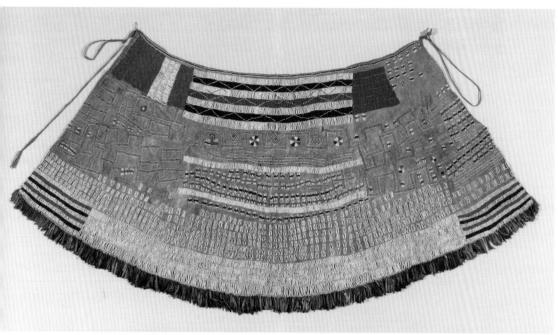

FIG. 2.37

FIG. 2.37
MAIDEN'S INITIATION SKIRT, TWENTIETH
CENTURY

Iraqw peoples, Tanzania

Tanned hide, glass beads, bast fiber

28 1/2 x 70 in. (72.4 x 177.8 cm)

Fine Arts Museums of San Francisco, Gift of Diane
and Sandy Besser, FAMSF #2008.49.1

During her initiation seclusion, an Iraqw girl beads
an elaborate hide skirt, converted from the leather
cape that she arrived in, as part of her preparation
for womanhood and marriage. In this example,
the young woman has used the conventional red,
white, and blue beads. While she is allowed a
certain degree of freedom in her designs, the red,
white, and blue stripes at the top and the band of
white at the bottom are standard. Although the
initiation ceremony was outlawed in 1930 by the
government, the beaded skirt continues to be worn
at group rituals. (Wada 1984:195).

PHOTO 2.12

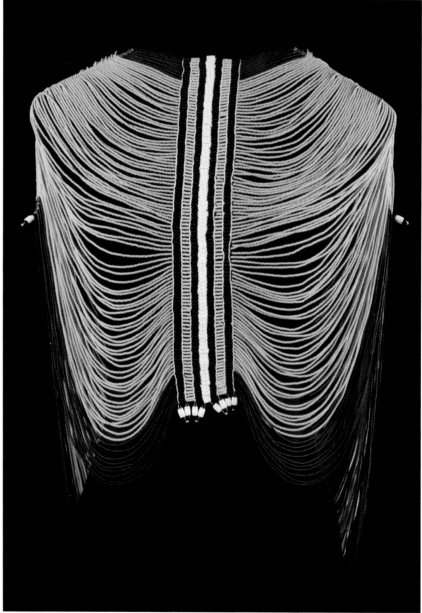

FIG. 2.38A

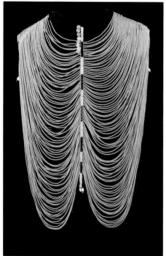

FIG. 2.38B

FIG. 2.39

FIG. 2.39 DETAIL

FIGS. 2.38A (FRONT) AND B (BACK), *Opposite*
UNMARRIED WOMAN'S CORSET, 2012

Maker: Mary Padar Kuojok Athac (Dinka), Yirol West County, Lakes State, Bahr el Ghazal Region, Republic of South Sudan

Cotton, glass beads, plastic buttons

40 3/4 x 19 7/8 in. (103.5 x 50.5 cm)

Museum of International Folk Art, IFAF Collection, FA.2012.48.1

PHOTO 2.12, *Opposite*
MARY PADAR KUOJOK ATHAC, 2012

Dinka peoples, Yirol West County, Lakes State, Bahr el Ghazal Region, Republic of South Sudan

Photograph by Bob Smith, courtesy of the International Folk Art Alliance

---

These striking corsets are worn by marriageable Dinka girls. Their bead colors signify the girls' age groups—yellow for pubescent girls, light blue for ages 16–18 (Fig. 2.38), and red for older unmarried girls aged 18 or older. The remarkable maker of this corset, Mary Padar (Photo 2.12), spent from 1984 to 2010 working as a cook for the Sudanese People's Liberation Army during the devastating civil war between north and south Sudan that killed more than two million people, turning south Sudan into a disaster area. Finally, in 2011, the Republic of South Sudan became the world's newest nation state when it declared its independence.

When the war ended, Padar, only a young girl when it broke out, remembered how to make the beaded corsets that signal a Dinka girl's readiness for marriage. Now she makes them for the girls in her village and teaches her daughters how to make the corsets. Padar is a member of the non-profit ROOTS Project of South Sudan, for "women crafting a new nation together." Founder of ROOTS, Anyieth D'Awol (2013), says that "some girls are beginning to wear them [the corsets] again in some villages . . . on special occasions and they now use buttons or zips to be able to remove them." In the past, both Dinka men and young unmarried women wore beaded corsets tightly stitched in place. A young woman wore her corset until her wedding, when it was cut open and removed. (Fisher 1984: 50).

FIG. 2.39 AND DETAIL
UNMARRIED GIRL'S SKIRT (*RAHAT*), C. 1900

Sudan or Egypt

Hide fringe, glass/metal/and ceramic beads, shells

16 9/16 x 27 3/16 in. (42 x 69 cm)

Museum of International Folk Art, Gift of Florence Dibell Bartlett, A.1955.86.907

Photograph by Addison Doty

This is an ancient style of an unmarried girl's skirt. Similar examples have been recovered from archaeological excavations in both the Sudan and southern Egypt. In the past the skirt was worn by girls in various ethnic groups of the region, including the Nubians and the Shilluk people. When the girl married she exchanged her fringed skirt for a white cotton dress and perhaps a veil, depending on the culture.

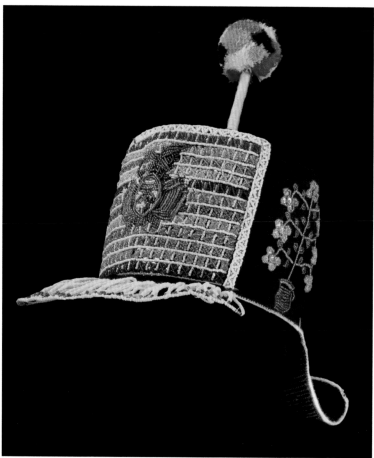

FIG. 2.40

FIG. 2.40
UNMARRIED WOMAN'S HAT, 2012

Maker: Natividad Flores (Quechua), Candelaria, Chuquisaca
Department, Bolivia

Cotton, glass beads, other

11 x 11 x 9^{13}/$_{16}$ in. (28 x 28 x 25 cm)

Museum of International Folk Art, IFAF Collection,
FA.2012.52.2

FIG. 2.41
MARRIED WOMAN'S HAT, 2012

Maker: Santusa Quispe (Quechua), Candelaria, Chuquisaca
Department, Bolivia

Rawhide, glass beads, metal sequins

7^{7}/$_{8}$ x 7^{1}/$_{2}$ x 9^{7}/$_{16}$ in. (20 x 19 x 24 cm)

Museum of International Folk Art, IFAF Collection,
FA.2012.52.1

In the Andean highlands of Bolivia, the indigenous peoples'
status, gender, and tribal ethnicity are identifiable by their
special headwear. Both of the Quechua-speaking makers
of these hats are members of an artisan cooperative, Unay
Pallay Asociación de Tejedoras Indígenas de Candelaria,
owned and operated by the artisans themselves, with the
proceeds from the sales of their arts going to support their
families, their cooperative, and the community museum.

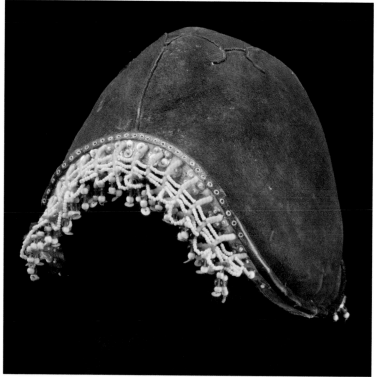

FIG. 2.41

FIG. 2.42

FIG. 2.42
UNMARRIED GIRL'S CROWN, C. 1890

Russia

Cotton, paper, metal, glass beads, pearls

8^{1}/$_{16}$ x 3^{9}/$_{16}$ in. (20.5 x 9 cm)

Museum of International Folk Art, Gift of H. L. "Bud" and
Katherine Hagerman in memory of Governor Herbert J.
Hagerman, second secretary to the American Embassy at
St. Petersburg, 1889–1901, A.2009.18.1

FIG. 2.43

FIG. 2.43
ADULT WOMAN'S HEADDRESS,
TWENTIETH CENTURY

Loimi Akha peoples, Burma

Bamboo, wood, cotton, wool, silver alloy,
glass beads

Private collection

Among the Akha people of Burma, Laos,
Thailand, and Yunnan, China, the women
are known for their striking headdresses.
Beginning as a baby, a girl child wears
first a cap, then graduates around age 12
to a headdress, to which she begins to
add silver beads, balls, coins, and strands
of glass beads. As an adult, an Akha
woman attaches a silver repoussé plate to
the back of her headdress, which by now
is completely covered with silver beads
and coins, and many strings of beads.
The coins are an indicator of status and
wealth, usually made from large silver
rupees from the era of British India. As
an essential element of an Akha woman's
identity, she wears her headdress every
day, even while working and sleeping.

FIGS. 2.44A (FRONT) AND B (BACK)
ADULT WOMAN'S HEADDRESS,
TWENTIETH CENTURY

Akha peoples, Burma

Bamboo, silver alloy

15 3/4 x 10 3/5 x 9 4/5 in. (40 x 27 x 25 cm)

Private collection

FIG. 2.45
UNMARRIED MAN'S BASKET HAT
(SOKLONG), EARLY TWENTIETH
CENTURY

Non-Christian Gaddang peoples, northern
Luzon, Philippines

Rattan, wood, giant clam shell, glass
beads, human hair

Basket diameter: 2 3/4 x 8 1/4 1 2/3 in. (7 x 21
x 4.3 cm)

Shari and Earl Kessler Collection

Bachelors wear this heavily decorated
basket hat on the back of their head. The
fine cord worn under the front bangs
holds the small basket in place. When
the bachelor marries, he replaces this
highly decorated example for a simple
undecorated basket.

FIG. 2.44A

FIG. 2.44B

FIG.2.45

FIG. 2.46

FIG. 2.47

FIG. 2.48A

FIG. 2.48B

FIG. 2.46
MARRIAGEABLE GIRL'S HAT,
TWENTIETH CENTURY

Turkmen, northern Afghanistan

Cotton, silver, carnelian, glass
beads

16 x 9¼ x 5½ in. (40.6 x 23.5 x
14 cm)

Anne and Bill Frej Collection

FIG. 2.47
MARRIAGEABLE GIRL'S HAT,
TWENTIETH CENTURY

Turkmen, northern Afghanistan

Cotton, silver, glass beads

15 x 7 in. (38.1 x 17.8 cm)

Anne and Bill Frej Collection

FIGS. 2.48A (FRONT) AND B
(BACK)
MARRIAGEABLE GIRL'S HAT,
TWENTIETH CENTURY

Lakai, Uzbekistan

Cotton, silver, buttons, glass
beads

31½ x 12½ x 8¾ in. (80 x 31.8 x
22.2 cm)

Anne and Bill Frej Collection

ZULU COURTSHIP

From the time that young men and women are eligible to marry, they spend much of their time preparing for and seeking their mate. This includes making themselves attractive to as many potential mates as possible. In many societies, the dress that both males and females wear contains cultural signals, sending messages of their readiness to select or be selected as a life mate.

For Zulu-speaking peoples, the use of "beadwork reaches its peak at courtship time." (Carey 1986: 55). From the time of puberty to marriage, young Zulu-speaking women spend much of their time making a great variety of beaded rectangular panels, necklaces, anklets and wristlets, bands for bandoliers, and aprons (Figs. 2.49 and 2.50), for adorning themselves to attract eligible young men (Photo 2.13). These beaded objects tend to be multifunctional, that is to say that an ornament can be worn in different ways—around the neck, the head, the arm, the wrist, the ankle, or the waist. "The range of Zulu beadwork forms is perhaps the largest found in one tribal group [in South Africa]," according to Carey (1986: 50). Unmarried girls spend almost as much time making beadwork gifts for potential sweethearts as they do for themselves.

"In a tradition that has been carried into contemporary times, when a young woman decides to tell a young man that she wants him for a sweetheart, she does not use words but instead uses beads." (Boram-Hays 2005: 44). At the time when young Zulu-speaking men become old enough to go courting, they "wear more beadwork than at any other time" in their lives. (Carey 1986: 55). Since all beadwork is made by women, each of the beaded ornaments that young men wear is made by one or more maidens who are expressing their admiration (Fig. 2.51, Photo 2.14). The beadwork gifts hold no pledge of engagement, so a young man, if he is fortunate enough to receive gifts from several girls, can wear all of these pieces at the same time. As he dresses to go courting, he wears as many beaded ornaments as possible in order to display the high esteem he holds among various girlfriends (Photo 2.15).

One type of these gifts, recognizable by its form as a small beaded panel, has been termed a "love letter," containing an encoded message from a girl to her boyfriend (Figs. 2.52 and 2.53). These love letters have become popular tourist items, with buyers making the assumption that complex messages are beaded into the panel much like a written letter. In reality, "there is sufficient agreement on the symbolic meaning of colour and bead placement to make the communication of a general message feasible. What is not possible is the conveying of a complex and detailed message." (Preston-Whyte & Thorpe 1989: 127–29). According to Boram-Hays (2005: 93 nt. 17): "These messages are conveyed by proverbs that are associated with bead colors."

Working glass beads does not have a lengthy history among Zulu-speaking peoples, although it is still an important part of contemporary life, especially

PHOTO 2.14

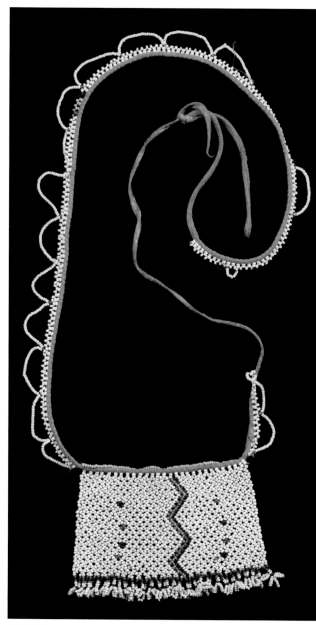

FIG. 2.49

FIG. 2.49
**COURTING-AGE ADOLESCENT GIRL'S
APRON (*ISIGEGE*), C. 1930**

Zulu-speaking peoples, region unknown,
South Africa

Tanned hide, glass beads

3 1/8 x 4 3/4 in. (8 x 12 cm)

Museum of International Folk Art,
Gift of Girard Foundation Collection,
A.1982.1.874

FIG. 2.50
**COURTING-AGE ADOLESCENT GIRL'S
APRON (*ISIGEGE*), C. 1960**

Zulu-speaking peoples, Nongoma region,
KwaZulu-Natal province, South Africa

Cotton, glass beads, amalosi seeds

9 1/16 x 9 13/16 in. (23 x 25 cm)

Museum of International Folk Art, IFAF
Collection, Gift of Diane and Sandy
Besser, FA.2006.77.9

FIG. 2.51
**BANDS FOR WRISTS, ANKLES, OR
NECK, C. 1960**

Zulu-speaking peoples, Nongoma region,
KwaZulu-Natal province, South Africa

Cotton, glass beads

2 3/4 x 12 5/8 in. (7 x 32 cm)

Museum of International Folk Art, IFAF
Collection, Gift of Diane and Sandy
Besser, FA.2006.77.10 & 11

FIG. 2.52, *Opposite*
**"LOVE" LETTERS (THREE PENDANTS)
(*UBALA ABUYISE*), PRE-1893**

Zulu (Xhosa?)-speaking peoples, South
Africa

Cotton, glass beads

Diameter: 7.8 in. (19.8 cm)

The Field Museum, Image no.
A114545_04d, Cat. No. 29016

Photograph by John Weinstein

FIG. 2.53, *Opposite*
**"LOVE" LETTERS (FIVE PENDANTS)
(*UBALA ABUYISE*), PRE-1893**

Zulu (Xhosa?)-speaking peoples, South
Africa

Cotton, glass beads

Diameter: 6.3–7.8 in. (16–19.8 cm)

The Field Museum, Image no.
A114546_03d, Cat No. 29023

Photograph by John Weinstein

FIG. 2.50

FIG. 2.51

visible during major events, such as the religious Nazareth Baptist Church celebration, and the spectacular annual Umhlanga, or Reed Dance, celebrated at the royal capital.

Its origin can be clearly identified. When Shaka Zulu (reign 1817–1828), who along with his mentor, Dingiswayo, formed the Zulu kingdom at the end of the eighteenth century (still in existence today and located in KwaZulu-Natal province, South Africa) from among independent clans in the region, the king strictly controlled the import and circulation of glass beads as a prestige item, reserving them only for himself, his wives and the female court, and high-ranking officials. A visitor to the court in the mid-nineteenth century, George French Angas, observed: "On grand occasions the amount of beads worn by the King's women is almost incredible, a single dress having been known to consist of fifty pounds weight of these highly valued decorations, so as to render it a matter of some difficulty as well as personal inconvenience for the wearer to dance under the accumulated weight of her beads." (Angas 1849: 63). Around this same time, the third Zulu King Mpande began to loosen the restrictions on European traders, thus providing an opportunity for others beyond the king's court, who could afford these expensive items, to have access to glass beads. By the late nineteenth and early twentieth centuries, beadworking became more generally practiced by the wider population.

PHOTO 2.15
YOUNG ZULU MEN DRESSED FOR COURTING, C. 1900

South Africa

Missionaries of Mariannhill, Reimlingen, Germany, 001.Mariannhill

Photographer unknown

FIG. 2.52

FIG. 2.53

COURTING ELSEWHERE

FIG. 2.54

FIG. 2.54

FIG. 2.54
COURTING LEDGER DRAWING,
1995

Thomas "Red Owl" Haukaas (b.
1950), Sicaṅġu (Brulé) Lakota/
Creole

Paper, lead and colored pencils,
commercial dye

12³/₄ x 6³/₄ in. (32.5 x 16.7 cm)

Carnegie Museum of Natural
History, 36099-1

The traditional Lakota Indian system of courtship was recorded in drawings on ledger paper by male artists. When a young man went courting, he took his blanket to wrap around the girl of his interest, so that they might hold a private conversation, concealed from the prying eyes of the community. If the young woman was popular, as is the girl in this drawing, several suitors would wait in line for their opportunity to woo her.

A few Plains Indian artists have revived the art of ledger drawing, which was the product of a rapidly changing world in the last quarter of the nineteenth century. Drawn with colored pencils, crayons, watercolors, or inks on lined paper, many of the scenes nostalgically recall cherished pre-reservation lifeways.

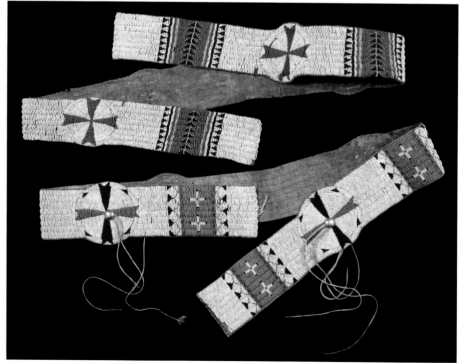

FIG. 2.55

FIG. 2.55
PAIR OF COURTING BLANKET STRIPS,
LATE NINETEENTH CENTURY

Lakota nation, South Dakota, USA

Native-tanned hide, glass beads, sinew

67¹/₂ x 4 in. (171.5 x 10.1 cm)

Museum of Indian Arts and Culture /
Laboratory of Anthropology, 16122/12,
14387/12

Young Lakota men prized their trade cloth blankets with beaded strips, which they used when courting young women. Beaded for a young man by his elder sister, the courting blanket enhanced his ability to attract and capture a woman's interest.

PHOTO 2.16

PHOTO 2.16
BEN REIFEL PLAYS THE
COURTING FLUTE, C. 1925

Rosebud Reservation, South
Dakota, USA

Nebraska State Historical
Society, RG2969-01-88

Photograph by John A.
Anderson

A young Lakota suitor plays
a flute while wrapped in his
courting blanket to charm the
lady of his choice. The sound of
the flute resembles the bull elk's
bugle that attracts females to
his side.

PHOTO 2.17
MIAO WOMEN DRESSED IN
TRADITIONAL OUTFITS, 2014

Xijiang Qianhu Miaozhai,
southeast Guizhou province,
People's Republic of China

Photograph by Marsha Bol

FIG. 2.56
COURTSHIP ENSEMBLE,
TWENTIETH CENTURY

Miao peoples, Guizhou province,
People's Republic of China

Silver

Crown: 7 in. (18 cm); necklace:
28 3/4 x 9 1/16 in. (73 x 23 cm)

Museum of International Folk
Art, IFAF Collection, crown:
FA.1996.36.94; JoAnn and Bob
Balzer purchase prize, necklace:
A.2014.48.2

Miao silversmiths continue to
make these elaborate silver
ensembles, just as they have
for ages past. Miao parents
purchase the silver sets, costing
roughly a family's annual wages,
for their daughters' courtship
and wedding. These ensembles
form the major portion of a
young woman's dowry.

PHOTO 2.17

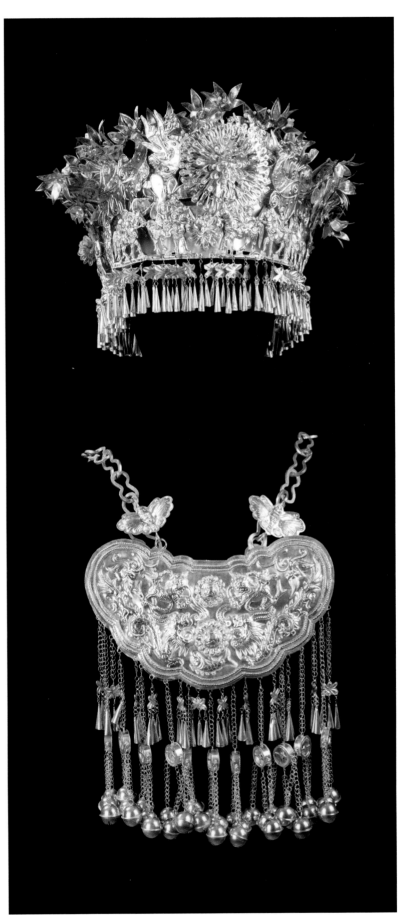

FIG. 2.56

65

UMOJA UASO WOMEN'S VILLAGE, KENYA

In northern Kenya, among Samburu peoples, "beads are perhaps the essential component of dress. For a woman of one of these peoples to be seen without beads, indeed without several pounds of beads around the neck, would constitute . . . one of the most serious of social breaches . . . Beads constitute clothing." (Cole 1975: 29). This is as true today as it was in 1975.

The Samburu people, like most of their neighbors, are semi-nomadic pastoralists, who own cattle and follow their herds in search of grazing and water. Their nomadism demands that they carry only essential possessions as they travel their vast hot, arid, and sparse environment. Thus the human body has become the center of display for their possessions. The age and status changes of a woman are displayed in the beadwork that she wears day and night—masses of multicolored beads strung on wires around her neck and shoulders, piled high to her chin, which click when she walks and bounce (and "whoosh") when she dances, from puberty until well into child-bearing years.

Girls shave their heads, giving more prominence to their accumulation of neck beads, many of which are gifts from male admirers. When young women marry, they will give away some of their glass bead necklets to younger sisters in exchange for a married woman's set of necklaces, made from flexible thin splints of dark wood or elephant tail, which overlays the remaining beaded necklaces. "Altogether it is not uncommon for a [married] woman to wear ten or more pounds of beads and other ornaments." (Cole 1979: 96). As they age, Samburu women begin to remove and give away various necklets to their daughters and granddaughters to aid them in amassing their own stack of neck beads.

In the early 1990s, a group of 15 Samburu women, led by Rebecca Lolosoli, opted to form a cultural village, named Umoja Uaso, for Samburu women victims of rape and domestic violence, away from their husbands. This village where "no men are allowed" has attracted international attention, but has not been without its controversy and challenges. In the Samburu culture there is a precedent, termed *kitala*, "that sanctions the practice of women running away from abusive or negligent husbands. While kitala, women may live with older children or relatives, have sexual affairs, and demand that their case against their husbands be adjudicated. And whether kitala or within successful marriages, Samburu women have the right to run their own businesses and make decisions about the proceeds." (Straight 2013: 137).

The village, located on the way to the nearby Samburu National Game Reserve, proved successful as a tourist attraction, where the women charged a small entry fee for tourists to visit their village and purchase beaded necklaces made by the women, similar to those that they wear daily. At its height, Umoja housed 60 women and their children. Through the years, splinter groups have departed, forming new settlements, so that currently about 20 women reside in Umoja.

Through the years the village residents have found that they can't depend on the uncertainty of tourism and market demand for their beadwork sales. So in 2008 the Samburu women of Umoja, and those who have left, partnered with a joint U.S. nonprofit/Kenyan NGO, called the BOMA Project. This Project's objective is to offer an innovative training program that provides the tools women need to start small businesses in their communities, leading to a sustainable income.

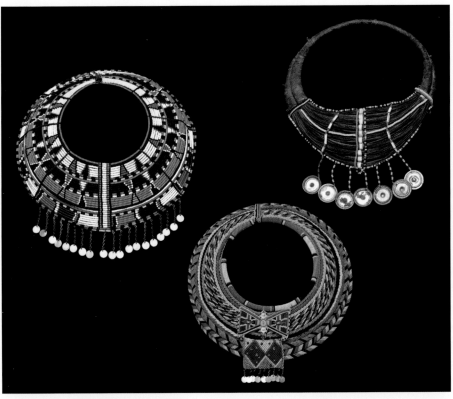

FIG. 2.57A

FIG. 2.57C DETAIL

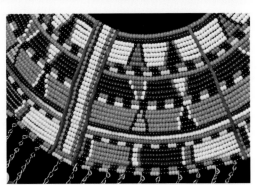

FIG. 2.57B DETAIL

PHOTO 2.18

FIGS. 2.57A (3 NECKLACES), B (DETAIL MIDDLE), AND C (DETAIL LEFT)
UMOJA WOMEN'S NECKLACES, 2010

Samburu peoples, Umoja Uaso, northern Kenya

Left: Unmarried woman's necklace (*drapo*), made by Mandilan, A.2017.57.3

Metal, rubber, glass beads

2⁷/₈ x 13¹/₄ x 14¹/₂ in. (7.3 x 33.7 x 36.8 cm)

Middle: Unmarried woman's necklace, made by Maparasoroi Lekarimwai, A.2017.57.1

Plastic, metal, glass beads, thread

2⁵/₈ x 14¹/₂ x 14¹/₂ in. (6.7 x 36.8 x 36.8 cm)

Right: Married woman's necklace (*mparo*), made by Ntipayon Lemariketo, A.2017.57.2

Sheepskin, Palm tree root, glass beads, metal

1¹/₄ x 10³/₄ x 14 in. (3.2 x 27.3 x 35.6 cm)

Museum of International Folk Art

PHOTO 2.18
UNMARRIED UMOJA UASO WOMEN GREETING VISITORS TO THEIR VILLAGE, 2008

Samburu peoples, Umoja Uaso, northern Kenya

Photograph by Stephanie Mendez

PHOTO 2.19
MARRIED WOMAN WEARING HER *MPARO*, 1973

Samburu peoples, Barseloi, northern Kenya

Smithsonian Institution, National Museum of African Art, Eliot Elisofon Photographic Archives

Photograph by Herbert M. Cole, Image no. 2000-080114

PHOTO 2.19

FOSTERING LIFE'S
CONTINUITY

CONTINUITY IS ONE OF THE MOST IMPORTANT CONCERNS of any society. Its future depends upon the current generation of adult couples to produce the children for the next generation. Hence, human fertility takes center stage as an essential asset for families and societies the world over.

ENSURING FERTILITY

THE TSONGA DOLL

Grow up, grow up you child
Now you are a woman
This doll shows
That you have grown up
It shows you can perform your
Tasks in marriage

Tsongan bridal song (Dederen 2007: 111)

Dolls, when viewed by those outside the culture, are often dismissed as mere playthings for the entertainment of children, especially girls. In many societies, however, they have a serious side. Girls play with dolls to rehearse for their future adult roles. These dolls may also represent the desired fertility status of their female owners and even aid in achieving that status to bear children after becoming a married woman.

Tsonga-speaking women of the Transvaal Lowveld region of South Africa make a distinctive beaded doll, which figures in the maturity and fertility of a Tsonga woman (Fig. 3.1). Once a Tsonga girl has completed her initiation, she receives a beaded doll (n'wana, meaning "child") made by her paternal aunt, or, according to some informants, the girl makes the doll herself. "Mamaila Maswanganyi said after attending initiation school each girl had to make a doll, which . . . was taken to her new home when she married." (Becker 1998: 123).

The bride brings the doll as a part of her dowry to the groom's family home at the end of the wedding ceremonies. "The presence of the doll confirms that its 'mother' has been fully prepared through initiation and discussion with her aunt and older female relatives. She is ready for her new home. . . . The doll lives with the newlyweds, who treat it like their child, until a baby is born, at which point the baby replaces the doll. At the first signs of pregnancy, the wife and doll move to the living quarters of the mother-in-law. If the baby is a boy, some of the beads can be used on his arms, waist, and ankles. In the case of a girl, the doll is kept intact so that she can play with it when she gets older." (Dederen 2007: 111–12).

FIG. 3.1

FIG. 3.1
DOLL / CHILD FIGURE (*N'WANA*),
MID-TWENTIETH CENTURY

Tsonga-speaking peoples, Transvaal
Lowveld region, South Africa

Metal, cloth, glass beads, plastic
beads, thread, buttons

7 x 9 1/2 in. (17.8 x 24.1 cm)

Museum of International Folk Art,
Purchased with MNMF Acquisition
Purchase Funds, A.2015.46.1

PHOTO 3.1
TSONGA WOMEN AT THABINA,
EARLY 1930S

Limpopo province, South Africa

The McGregor Museum, Kimberley,
South Africa, DC2531

Photograph by Alfred Duggan Cronin

The shape of the doll only minimally looks human. The bulky cylinder is usually formed from an empty tin can filled with dirt and fully wrapped with strings of beads. With the addition of a ruffled dance skirt decorated with beaded panels, the doll becomes a female figure (Fig. 3.1). The doll's skirt is a miniature replica of a married Tsonga woman's festival skirt, which is pleated or gathered from as much as 20 yards of salempore (colored cotton cloth made for export to Africa), thus adding substantial bulk to the pelvic area of a woman's figure (Photo 3.1). As Nettleton (2007: 88) suggests, this conspicuous abundance of cloth, which doubles the size of the woman's pelvic region, "emphasizes the reproductive region of the woman's body. . . . Despite their being called 'child' (*n'wana*) these figures replicate the imagery of a fertile woman decked out in beaded finery in a manner that defines her as able to bear children. . . . The figure may represent a child in the way it is used, but visually, it encodes an ideal image of a grown woman." (Nettleton 2007: 93).

Tsonga dolls are now also made for sale to tourists without any conflict in values. As "Forisa Makhubela commented that like a child, from which the dolls take their Tsonga name, dolls are meant to make the owners happy." (Becker 1998: 125–127).

PHOTO 3.1

FIG. 3.2

FIG. 3.3

FERTILITY MATTERS ELSEWHERE

FIG. 3.2
DOLL (*UMNDWANA*), MID-TWENTIETH CENTURY

Ndzundza Ndebele peoples, Transvaal region, South Africa

Textile?, glass beads, thread, grass

7³/₄ x 4¹/₄ in. (19.7 x 10.8 cm)

Museum of International Folk Art, IFAF Collection, FA.2015.42.1

Cone-shaped Ndebele dolls can be traced back at least to a 1923 photograph taken by Alfred Duggan-Cronin of an Ndebele bride holding a bottle-shaped doll (Photo 2.6). The dolls are easily identified as Ndebele-made because of the grass-filled graduated beaded rings that form their bodies. The rings are a signature item of Ndebele traditional women's dress, worn on their arms, legs, and neck, to mark an Ndebele woman's adult status. The dolls' "arms" are indicated by a beaded braid loop with small rings attached and no legs. The colors are the typical Ndebele color palate with a predominance of white beads.

Stories differ about the function of these dolls (Schneider 1998: 147; Gianturco and Tuttle 2004: 107), but, as seen in a photograph by Constance Stuart Larrabee (1936–1949), a pubescent-age Ndebele girl is making a beaded ring doll, perhaps as a part of her initiation. Photographer Constance Larrabee also documented a cottage industry, which developed around these and other beaded items when Ndebele villages became a tourist attraction, encouraged by the South African government, because of their vivid mural house paintings and the women's traditional beaded attire. Ndebele women sold small dolls, beaded jewelry, gourds, and bottles on the roadside in front of their painted house compounds. The women still make dolls for themselves and to sell as a supplemental income. "Johannah Anna Mahlangu learned doll making at fifteen. Today, she can finish three dolls a day and earns more money than her husband does as a house painter." (Gianturco and Tuttle 2004: 116).

FIG. 3.3
DOLL, C. 1970

Ndebele peoples, Transvaal region, South Africa

Cloth, grass, hide, glass beads

6⁷/₈ x 3⁹/₁₆ x 1⁹/₁₆ in. (17.5 x 9 x 4 cm)

Museum of International Folk Art, Gift of the Girard Foundation Collection, A.1981.42.85

This Ndebele doll with its arms and legs is a variation on the cone-shaped ring doll. Purchased by a collector around 1970, it was a predictor of the heyday to come during the 1980s and '90s for Ndebele dolls in more naturalistic forms for tourists. (Schneider 1998: 145–47). Dolls, in particular, have a ready market with Westerners, who find the representation of "the people" in miniature an attractive collectible.

FIG. 3.4, *Opposite*
DOLL / CHILD FIGURE (*IKOKU*), TWENTIETH CENTURY

Turkana peoples, Kenya

Doum-palm fruit, goat hide, antelope hooves, bottle caps, wild banana seed, cowrie shells, glass beads, ostrich eggshell beads, vegetal fiber

Smithsonian Institution, National Museum of African Art, Gift of Daniel Collier, 75-34-5

FIG. 3.4

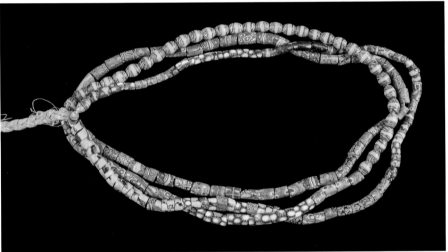

FIG. 3.5

PHOTO 3.2
TURKANA UNMARRIED WOMAN
WITH DOLL, 1973

Lorigumu, Kenya

Smithsonian Institution, National Museum of African Art, Eliot Elisofon Photographic Archives

Photograph by Herbert M. Cole, Image no. 2000-080214

PHOTO 3.2

These dolls are used exclusively for fertility by young Turkana women of marriageable age, brides, and childless married women. Reflecting the shape of male genitalia, yet dressed in women's aprons, the doll emphasizes the interaction between the woman and her male partner. (Cameron 1996: 31). Decorated with beads supplied by her lover or husband via his best friend, the doll is named after the best friend and treated by the couple as their son.

The woman wears the doll daily around her neck and at night hangs it inside her house. After a successful childbirth, the doll is no longer needed and is passed on to a younger sister. It has proven efficacious and thus is considered lucky to own.

FIG. 3.5
WAIST BEADS (*TOMOMA*), N.D.

Ghana or Nigeria, Africa

Glass trade beads, cotton string

Diameter: 14$\frac{1}{2}$ in. (37 cm)

Museum of International Folk Art, IFAF Collection, FA.1973.11.3

FIG. 3.6
DOLLS (*NGIDE*), 1960–64

Turkana peoples, Kenya

Wood, organic, glass beads, fiber

Various dimensions

Museum of International Folk Art, Gift of the Girard Foundation Collection, A.1981.13.e388-390, 403v–408

FIG. 3.6

Objects other than dolls can similarly be used to enhance the fertility of women. Among the Asante peoples of Ghana, women wear up to six strands of waist beads hidden beneath the layers of their clothing, where no one but their husband or lover can see them. The beads adorn the most private, sexually explicit part of their body, the hips and buttocks, where the physical contact of the woman's body or the touch of the husband or lover activates the beads' potential to ensure fertility. "One older Asante woman explained the reasoning behind the practice: 'If you put on beads, they will make you heavy so that your buttocks are made beautiful' . . . —referring to waist beads' capacity to 'grow curves' through physical contact, or the power of touch, in order to enhance female fertility, sexuality, and childbearing." (Gott 2007: 86).

As soon as a young Turkana woman reaches maturity, she receives a second type of doll, carved by her father and dressed by her mother, which looks more like her. This doll also serves to ensure fertility but focuses more on the girl's readiness to properly mother the child doll. "These dolls are used exclusively by girls past puberty and by married women without children for role play games as mother and child. The Turkana are of the opinion that role play for married women, either alone or in a group, can help them become pregnant and give birth to a healthy child." (Best 1993: 162).

MARKERS FOR MARITAL STATUS

"Marriage is a crucial event the whole world over. In many societies it is one of the most significant indications that the adult state has been attained." (van Dongen, et. al., 1987: 43). Entry into marriage is the beginning of life's most productive and reproductive years. Although the bride and groom are the center of the events, this is not simply a celebration between two people. A wedding creates an alliance between two families and involves many extended family members in the weeks, months, and sometimes even years of wedding preparations, including accumulation of the banquet food, the gifts, the dowry, the bride wealth, and the decorations.

Lengthy preparations for the wedding by both the bride's and groom's families usually result in an exchange of gifts and finery between the two families, which are displayed during the wedding events. Such finery often centers on the splendid adornment of the bride and the groom.

RABARI WEDDINGS

Multiple weddings take place on the same night in the pastoralist Rabari villages of Kutch, Gujarat, India. In 1977 in one village alone, 56 weddings took place on Krishna's birthday. (Elson 1979: 21). However, each couple's wedding takes place separately, officiated by a Brahman. The groom is the center of attention, resplendent in his finery, while the bride is shyly veiled throughout.

Although the wedding ceremony only takes about an hour, the preparations leading up to the ceremony start months ahead of time. The bride's family has the responsibility to assemble her dowry. Her parents give her jewelry to adorn her ears, nose, neck, arms, and ankles. Upon engagement, the groom's family gives her a necklace with a central embossed gold medallion for her to wear on her wedding day (Fig. 3.7). Her mother and female relatives provide her with a new wardrobe plus textiles and pots for her new home in the groom's village. "Because of its embroidered ornamentation, the Rabaris consider the blouse their most important art form. The blouse conveys information about the occasion for which it is worn and about the age of the wearer." (Elson 1979: 100). One of these very special blouses will be worn for the wedding (Fig. 3.7).

Although ornamental embroidery is the favored art form among rural India, beads play an enhancing role as borders and attachments on textiles, fine jewelry with silver and gold beads, and glass-beaded jewelry. Women spend a great deal of time each day on their needlework. The female relatives of the groom's family must prepare his special clothing for the upcoming wedding. Dressed in his finery emulating a king (Fig. 3.8), the groom leads his wedding party to the village of his bride where the ceremony will take place. As the procession arrives, "women of the *vas* [Rabari section of the village], also sparkling in festival dress, ceremonially stop the groom. They give him money, touch the beaded coconut he holds [Fig. 3.9], bless him and sing songs in his praise. He gives them *supari* [betel nut] from an embroidered *pothu* [purse] [Fig. 3.10] returning a wish for good luck." (Frater 1995: 165).

FIG. 3.7

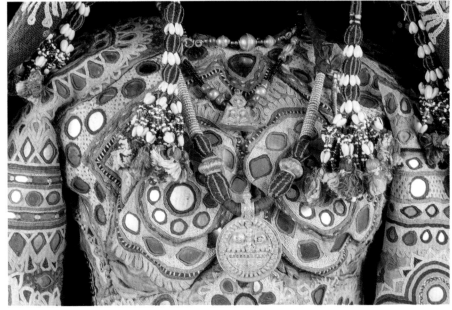

FIG. 3.7 DETAIL

FIG. 3.7 AND DETAIL
BRIDE'S DRESS ENSEMBLE, C. 1975

Vaghadia Rabari peoples, Samakhiali village, eastern Kutch district, Gujarat state, India

Museum of International Folk Art, IFAF Collection, FA.1990.62. 65, 66, 83, 84, 207, 209, 215

This bride's blouse (*kanchali*), made by Himaben, is the most elaborate type of this Rabari subgroup. She receives it as a part of her dowry to wear for her wedding and then later for festivals. For the wedding, the bride also wears a silk and cotton skirt (*mashru*) and her engagement necklace.

Dress serves as an ethnic identifier among Rabari people, as well as an indicator of the stage of life of the wearer. Each Rabari subgroup has its own distinct dress, readily identifiable by other Rabaris.

PHOTO 3.3

PHOTO 3.3
GROOM ON THE NIGHT OF HIS WEDDING, 1983

Vaghadia Rabari peoples, Gujarat state, India

Photograph by Judy Frater

Around midnight, the Vaghadia Rabari groom, who traditionally wears an outfit of brilliant red, sits waiting for his bride to arrive and the wedding ceremony to begin. He holds high his wedding sword covered in beadwork, which he must keep up during the entire ceremony. His beaded turban ornament continues a generations-long tradition, and he wears beaded anklets. All of his finery has been lovingly crafted by his female relatives, as befitting his ceremonial status.

**FIG. 3.8 AND DETAIL
GROOM'S DRESS ENSEMBLE, C. 1965 AND 1980**

Kachi Rabari peoples, Bhuj area, western Kutch district, Gujarat state, India

Museum of International Folk Art, IFAF Collection, FA.1990.16.20, 21, 22, 23, 33; FA.1992.78.16

Photograph by Addison Doty

The jacket (*angadi*), pants, and sash (*bukani*) were made by a Kachi woman named Ranakiben for her brother's wedding. The beaded turban ornament (*mors*) was made in the 1960s by Ranakiben's mother, Lassuben. Very few turban ornaments have been made since the 1960s. Instead they are handed down through the generations to be worn by the male family members.

FIG. 3.10, *Opposite*
**GROOM'S PURSE
(*POTHU*), C. 1975**

Vaghadia Rabari people, Samakhiali, Kutch, Gujarat state, India

Silk, mirrors, buttons, beads, tassels

11 x 11¹/₂ in. (28 x 29 cm)

Museum of International Folk Art, IFAF Collection, FA.1990.16.84

FIG. 3.8

76

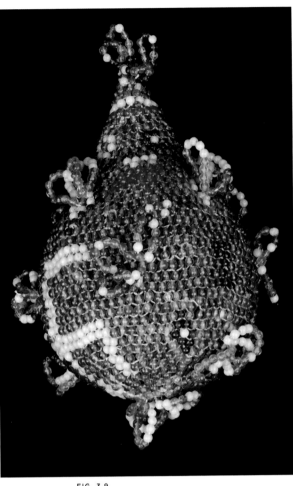

FIG. 3.9

FIG. 3.9
GROOM'S COCONUT
(NARIYAL), C. 1975

Sorathi Rabari peoples,
Saurashtra district,
Gujarat state, India

Cotton, beads, organic

6 11/16 x 10 5/8 in. (17 x
26.6 cm)

Museum of International
Folk Art, IFAF Collection,
FA.1990.16.147

A Rabari groom carries
a beaded coconut in the
wedding processional
that makes its way
to his bride's village.
He continues to hold
the coconut, a sign of
his vitality, as he sits
waiting for his bride to
be carried to the place
under the canopy where
they will marry.

FIG. 3.11
GROOM'S TURBAN/CHIN
WRAP (BUKANI), C. 1980

Maker: Ranakibehn

Kachi Rabari peoples,
Bhujodi, Kutch district,
Gujarat state, India

Cotton, glass beads,
rickrack

8 1/2 x 73 in. (21.5 x
185.5 cm)

Museum of International
Folk Art, IFAF Collection,
FA.1990.16.20

Traditionally this garment, a
prescribed part of a groom's outfit,
was worn over the turban and around
the chin and mouth as a protection
for the groom from the sandy winds
as he traveled on an adorned camel
through the desert to his new bride's
village. Today with painted public
carrier trucks and other transportation
available, the groom no longer arrives
by camel. His *bukani* can also be
worn as a shoulder cloth or a sash.
Glass beads border the wrap, with an
abstracted temple motif dominating
both end panels.

FIG. 3.11

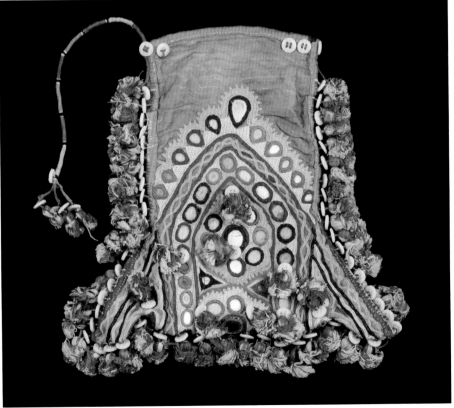

FIG. 3.10

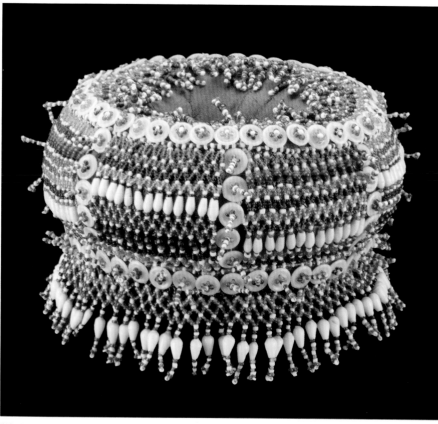

FIG. 3.12

FIG. 3.12
**WOMAN'S HEADRING (*INDHONI*),
TWENTIETH CENTURY**

Rabari peoples, Kutch district, Gujarat
state, India

Cotton, fiber, glass beads, buttons

7$\frac{1}{2}$ x 3$\frac{1}{2}$ in. (19 x 9 cm)

Museum of International Folk Art, IFAF
Collection, FA.2012.72.1

PHOTO 3.4
**RABARI WOMAN BEARING BRASS
POTS ON HER HEADRING, 1983**

Vaghadia Rabari peoples, Samakhiali,
Kutch district, Gujarat state, India

Photograph by Judy Frater

The heavily beaded headrings are
only used for festival occasions, such
as weddings. During these occasions
women balance brass pots filled
with auspicious coconuts and leaves
on these headrings as a ceremonial
welcoming of guests from other
villages (Frater 1995: 79).

PHOTO 3.4

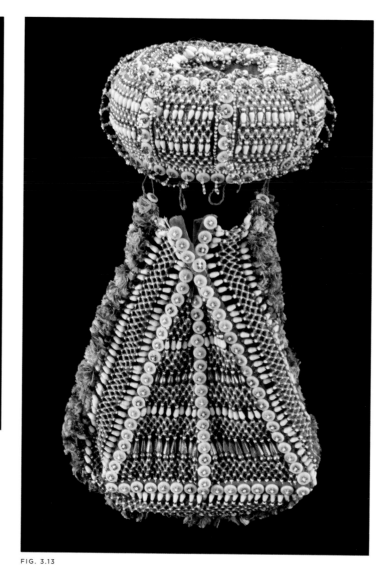

FIG. 3.13

FIG. 3.13
WOMAN'S HEADRING (*INDHONI*), TWENTIETH CENTURY

Rabari peoples, Kutch district, Gujarat state, India

Cotton, fiber, glass beads, buttons

7$\frac{1}{2}$ x 17 in. (19 x 43 cm)

Museum of International Folk Art, IFAF Collection, FA.2012.72.2

Rabari people bead special items, such as this woman's headring
used as a stand for a ceremonial vessel during the wedding
ceremony. Such lavish headrings are used for festival occasions,
whereas more modest examples are used daily by women and
girls to balance and cushion water jars on their heads.

FIG. 3.14

FIG. 3.14
GAME BOARD, C. 1960

Kathi peoples, Saurashtra district, Gujarat state, India

Silk, cotton, glass beads

24 1/8 x 24 1/8 in. (61.2 x 61.2 cm)

Museum of International Folk Art, Gift of the Girard
Foundation Collection, A.1981.22.325

Chopat is a traditional Indian game played on this
beaded game board that is often associated with
marriage. It assists the newlyweds to become better
acquainted. The sixteen game pieces, also covered in
beads, are stored in a pocket under one arm of the
board.

FIG. 3.15
HANGING (*TORAN*) (DETAIL), PRE-1930S

Kathi peoples, Saurashtra district, Gujarat state, India

Burlap, glass beads

75 3/16 x 5 1/2 x 2 3/8 in. (191 x 14 x 6 cm)

Museum of International Folk Art, Gift of the Girard
Foundation Collection, A.1980.1.733

Beaded hangings for their homes were made by Kathi
women to be hung on auspicious occasions, such as
for the bride and groom on their wedding night. In
this detail from a very long hanging is a depiction in
beads of the bride and groom on their nuptial bed.

FIG. 3.15

BANJARA WEDDING REGALIA

The nomadic Banjara people roam throughout much of the subcontinent of India, identifiable by the colorful outfits of the women, predominantly dressed in red and wearing plentiful jewelry. Traditionally they owned herds of bullocks, which they used to transport cargo throughout the country. These nomadic people have maintained strong cultural values, including the importance of their arts of embroidery and other adornment.

Even the remaining bullocks in their care are adorned for ceremonies. The mother of a bride stitches a set of ornaments to decorate a bullock for her daughter's departure. The bride stands on the bullock weeping and singing mourning laments upon leaving her parents' home. These bullock ornaments for the forehead and horns are adorned with cowrie shells (Figs. 3.18a, b, c, d, and e), a ceremonial and valuable trade item found on many of the objects associated with Banjara weddings.

A special square ceremonial wedding cloth (Fig. 3.19) is a marker of a Banjara bride, which she embroiders in preparation for her wedding to wear atop pots (Photo 3.5). The bride carries a small ceremonial bag (Fig. 3.20) to her new home, filled with tooth-cleaning sticks that she gives to each home in her new husband's community. She also gives her groom a traditional four-pocketed wedding bag (Fig. 3.16), which may be used to carry his betel nut supplies or her spices, which she brings for her new kitchen.

When a Banjara woman marries, she has the right to wear a dress that marks her as a married woman (Fig. 3.17). The backless blouse with its pairs of flaps, ornamented with tassels with lead and glass beads, on the shoulders and chest identify her as such. It is heavily adorned with mirrors, tassels, and beads. If she becomes widowed or divorced, she can no longer wear this blouse with its flaps. (Fisher 1993: 149, 164). Her three sets of armlets worn at her elbows (Fig. 3.17 detail), which she first wore as a bride, combine yarn tassels, cowrie shells, and lead and glass beads. A similar married woman's blouse (Fig. 3.21) allows a closer look at the various types of ornament found on these blouses.

FIG. 3.16, *Opposite*
GROOM'S WEDDING BAG, C. 1986

Banjara peoples, Wadi, Gulbarga, Karnataka state, India

Cotton, cowrie shells, metal

19 3/8 x 12 in. (49 x 30.5 cm)

Museum of International Folk Art, IFAF Collection, FA.1989.48.81

FIG. 3.17 AND DETAIL, *Opposite*
MARRIED WOMAN'S DRESS, C. 1974

Makers: Ranakiben, Lassu Kanabhai, and others, Banjara peoples

Fiber, glass beads, lead beads, mirrors

Museum of International Folk Art, IFAF Collection, FA.1992.78.12vx; FA.1989.48.82, 84, 85, 87, 88v, 89v, 90v, 94

PHOTO 3.5
YOUNG WOMAN PREPARING FOR MARRIAGE, 1989

Banjara peoples, Karakucha farming compound, Chikmagalur and Shimoga Hills districts, Karnataka state, India

Photograph by Nora Fisher

PHOTO 3.5

FIG. 3.16

FIG. 3.17 DETAIL

FIG. 3.17

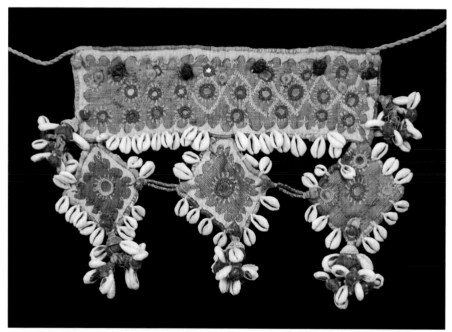

FIG. 3.18A

FIG. 3.18B

FIG. 3.18C

FIG. 3.18D

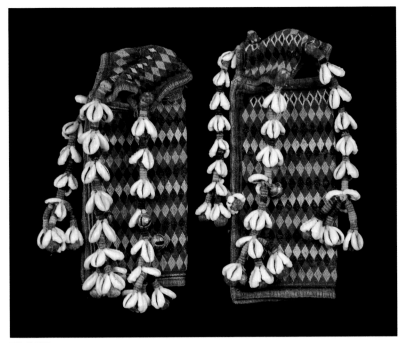

FIG. 3.18E

FIG. 3.19

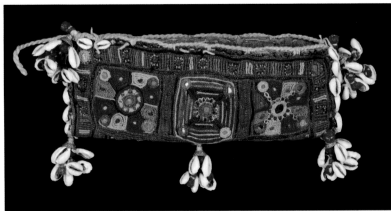

FIG. 3.20

FIGS. 3.18 A, B, C, D, *Opposite,* **AND E**
BULLOCK FOREHEAD AND HORN ORNAMENTS

Banjara peoples

a and b: Maker: Laxmi Yadi, Shimoga district, Karnataka state, India, c. 1970

Wool, cowrie shells, metal beads

Horn ornaments: 6 x 3¹⁄₄ in. (15 x 8 cm)

Museum of International Folk Art, IFAF Collection, FA.1989.48.96v

c: Wadi, Gulbarga, Karnataka state, India, c. 1980

Fiber, cowrie shells, metal

10¹⁄₄ in. (26 cm)

Museum of International Folk Art, Gift of Celia Drake, A.1990.25.6

d: Maker: Rathnibal Naik, Tukkuguda village, Rangareddi, Andhra Pradesh state, India, c. 1986

Fiber, cowrie shells

12¹⁄₄ x 4³⁄₄ in. (31 x 12 cm)

Museum of International Folk Art, IFAF Collection, FA.1989.48.42v

e: Chalisgaon, Khandesh region, Maharashtra state, India, c. 1950

Cotton, cowrie shells, metal bells

3⁹⁄₁₆ in. (9 cm)

Museum of International Folk Art, Gift of Barbara M. Goodbody, A.1990.33.2v

FIG. 3.19
BRIDE'S CEREMONIAL CLOTH, C. 1930

Banjara peoples, Khandesh region, Maharashtra state, India

Fiber, cowrie shells

19⁵⁄₁₆ x 19⁵⁄₁₆ in. (49 x 49 cm)

Museum of International Folk Art, IFAF Collection, FA.1990.65.17

FIG. 3.20
BRIDE'S BAG FOR TOOTH-CLEANING STICKS (*KOTLI***), C. 1930**

Maker: Laxmi Yadi, Banjara peoples, Malagoppa village, Shimoga district, Karnataka state, India

Fiber, cowrie shells

11³⁄₁₆ x 3¹⁄₄ in. (30 x 8 cm)

Museum of International Folk Art, IFAF Collection, FA.1989.48.95

FIG. 3.21

FIG. 3.21
MARRIED WOMAN'S BLOUSE (*KACHALI*), C. 1968

Maker: Romali Naik, Banjara peoples, Nellisara village, Shimoga district, Karnataka state, India

Fiber, glass and lead beads, mirrors

$20^7/_8$ x $21^1/_4$ in. (53 x 54 cm)

Museum of International Folk Art, IFAF Collection, FA.1989.48.9

FIG. 3.22

PHOTO 3.6

FIG. 3.22
GROOM'S WEDDING HEADDRESS, 1949

Marwada Meghwal peoples, Dinara village, Kutch district, Gujarat state, India

Fiber, glass beads

$13^3/_8$ in. (34 cm)

Museum of International Folk Art, IFAF Collection, FA.1989.48.60

PHOTO 3.6
HEADDRESS MADE BY A MARWADA MEGHWAL WOMAN FOR HER SON IN 1949, 1989

Banjara peoples, Dinara village, Kutch district, Gujarat state, India

Photograph by Nora Fisher

This groom's beaded facepiece was made by his mother for his wedding. The Marwada Meghwal peoples are one of several rural culture groups residing in the district of Kutch.

IBAN BRIDAL DRESS

The Iban people are the largest indigenous group in Sarawak, in the Malaysian section of Borneo. The majority of the population still lives an egalitarian life, living communally in longhouses along rivers, with the exception of those who have moved to urban centers to work. The women are best known for their accomplished warp-woven (*ikat*) textiles.

Beads play the leading role in most Iban weddings, although since World War II, many wedding couples have adopted westernized wedding clothing or choose to have the best of both worlds—both traditional and western ceremonies. (Munan 2005: 59). A traditional Iban bridal outfit includes an open-work overdress composed of large carnelian and glass beads (Fig. 3.25), an elaborate wedding crown with strings of beads dangling from its framework (Fig. 3.27), and a long beaded train (Fig. 3.24) culminating in brass "frog" bells that trail behind the bride making a tinkling sound. After wearing this dress at her wedding, the married woman has the right to wear it at future festivals.

In the nineteenth century, a traveler described witnessing an Iban woman dressed in this type of beaded outfit, saying: "from the neck to the hips [the women] were covered over with large agate beads, string of them was heaped on string, till many of the women were cuirassed an inch thick in solid stone before and behind . . . ." (F. Boyle as quoted in Munan 2005: 100). These beaded dresses alone could weigh up to 33 pounds. Understandably, some Iban women tired of wearing such heavy outfits and began to opt for wearing a beaded-net yoke with pompom tassels in its place (Fig. 3.26).

Carnelian and glass beads were never made in Borneo. They were imported from elsewhere, valued by their owners, and passed down through the generations. Since ancient times in East Java, carnelian was present and worked into beads. Some carnelian beads are probably from India, if "the perforations of the beads are small and fine which could only have been made with diamond drills invented and used in India before BC." (Adhyatman and Arifin 1993: 21).

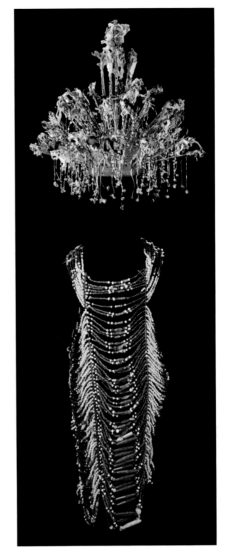

FIG. 3.23

FIG. 3.23
WEDDING OUTFIT (*ULU* RAJANG), TWENTIETH CENTURY

Iban peoples, Sarawak state, Borneo island, Malaysia

David McLanahan Collection

PHOTO 3.7
BRIDE IN WEDDING OUTFIT, TWENTIETH CENTURY

Iban peoples, Sarawak state, Borneo island, Malaysia

Sarawak Museum, Kuching

Photograph by Heidi Munan

PHOTO 3.7

85

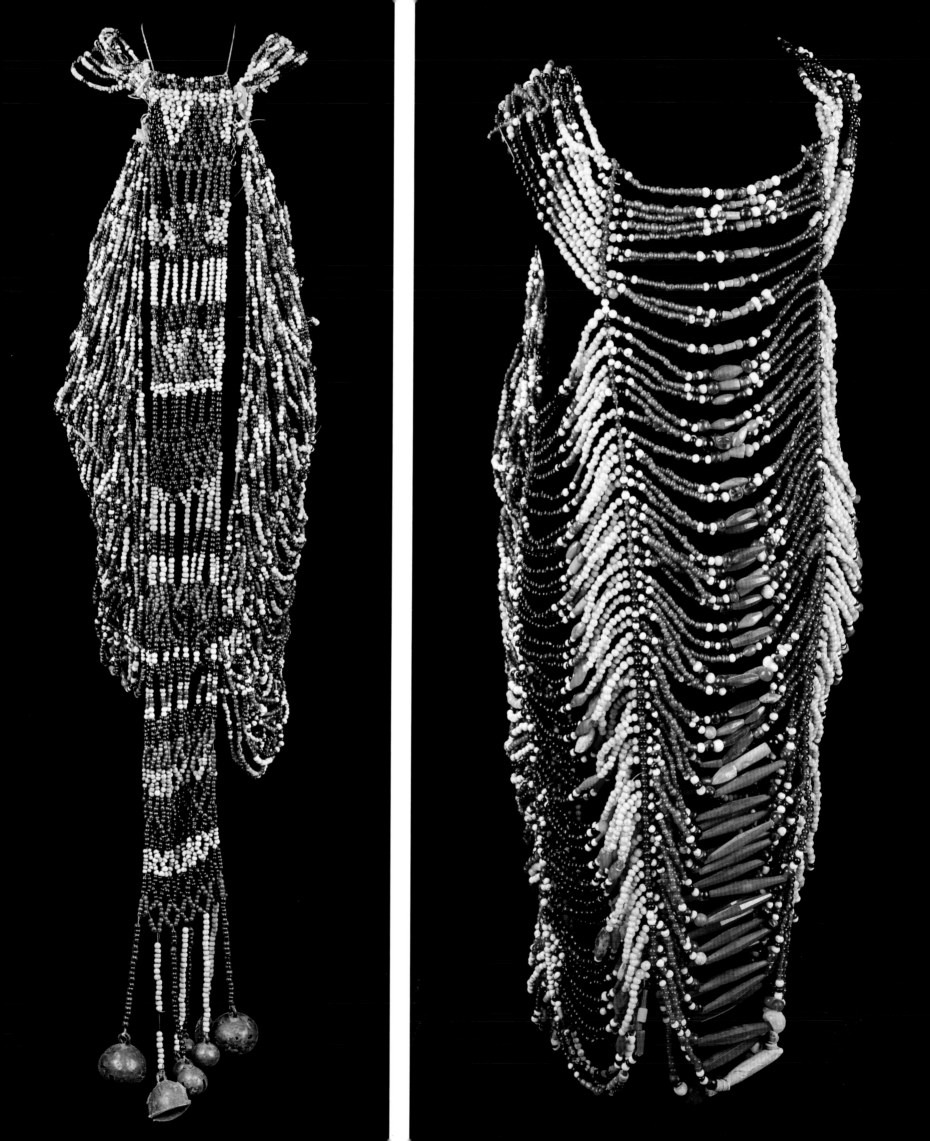

FIG. 3.24, *Opposite left*
WEDDING TRAIN,
TWENTIETH CENTURY

Iban peoples, Sarawak state,
Borneo island, Malaysia

Stone, glass and shell beads,
brass bells

51 x 13½ in. (129.5 x 34.3 cm)

David McLanahan Collection

FIG. 3.25, *Opposite right,*
AND DETAIL
WEDDING DRESS,
TWENTIETH CENTURY

Iban peoples, Sarawak state,
Borneo island, Malaysia

Stone, glass and shell beads

30½ in. (77.5 cm)

David McLanahan Collection

PHOTO 3.8
BRIDE WITH BEADED TRAIN,
MID 1960S

Iban peoples, Sarawak state,
Borneo island, Malaysia

Sarawak Museum, Kuching

Photograph by Heidi Munan

FIG. 3.26
WEDDING YOKE, TWENTIETH
CENTURY

Iban peoples, Sarawak state,
Borneo island, Malaysia

Cotton, glass beads

8½ x 27 in. (21.6 x 68.6 cm)

David McLanahan Collection

FIG. 3.27
WEDDING HEADDRESS,
TWENTIETH CENTURY

Iban peoples, Sarawak state,
Borneo island, Malaysia

Wood, paper, glass beads,
cotton, sequins

15 x 24 in. (38.1 x 61 cm)

David McLanahan Collection

PHOTO 3.8

FIG. 3.27

FIG. 3.26

FIG. 3.25 DETAIL

FIG. 3.28

FIG. 3.28 DETAIL

FIG. 3.29A DETAIL

FIG. 3.29B DETAIL

FIG. 3.29C

MARITAL MARKERS ELSEWHERE

FIG. 3.28 AND DETAIL, *Opposite*
WOMAN'S TWO-PIECE
HEADDRESS, C. 1960

Kalash peoples, Bumburet Valley,
Chitral, Pakistan

Wool, glass beads, buttons, cowry
shells, metal

12 1/16 in. (30.6 cm)

Museum of International Folk Art,
IFAF Collection, FA.1980.47.5 a & b
(detail), & FA.1980.47.6

A girl is given the right to wear
this headdress as soon as she is
betrothed. It has two parts: 1) the
visible outer part is covered in glass
beads, cowries, buttons, bells, and
other ornaments; and 2) the inner
part has a headband, which supports
the outer piece, with a long back flap
also covered with similar ornaments.

FIGS. 3.29A, B (DETAILS, *Opposite*),
AND C
WEDDING TUNIC (*JUMLO***), C. 1880**

Swat River Valley, Northwest Pakistan

Cotton, buttons, metal, glass beads

33 7/8 in. (86 cm)

Museum of International Folk Art,
IFAF Collection, FA.1988.44.1

This woman's wedding tunic has
very long sleeves and dozens of
gores, or triangles, stitched into the
skirt to make it extremely full. The
bodice is covered with a multiplicity
of buttons, zippers, dangles, glass
beads, and brooches.

FIG. 3.30
CLOVE WEDDING NECKLACE
(*UGUD KRUNFUL*), C. 1910

Bedouin peoples, historic Palestine

Metal, cloves, glass beads

50³/₄ in. (129 cm)

Museum of International Folk Art,
IFAF Collection, FA.1981.48.133

A Bedouin bride wore this type of
necklace, made of whole cloves
and a variety of old and new glass
beads, on her wedding day. The
necklace is dipped into water before
the wedding to enhance the aroma
of the cloves, which adds to its
amuletic power.

FIG. 3.31
BRIDAL HEADDRESS (*WUQAYAT AL-DARAHEM*),
C. 1850

Southern Judean Hills, Hebron region, historic Palestine

Cotton, silk, wool, silver, white metal, coral, glass beads

Diameter: 6¹/₄ in. (16 cm)

Museum of International Folk Art, Gift of Florence Dibell
Bartlett, A. 1955.86.919

Photograph by Addison Doty

A Palestinian bride from the Hebron region wore this
headdress for her wedding ceremony. Since it was a
very valuable item, most brides borrowed one from
their patrilineal kin group, if the kin group owned one,
or rented one from its owner. "The lending or renting
of expensive marriage crowns was customary in many
parts of the Arabic-speaking world." (Stillman 1979: 62).
The coral and blue glass beads plus the numerous silver
talismanic hands protected the bride against the Evil Eye.
This type of headdress continued to be used by village
brides up until the mid-twentieth century.

PHOTO 3.9
YOUNG WOMAN IN HER
BRIDAL HEADDRESS, LATE
NINETEENTH OR EARLY
TWENTIETH CENTURY

Historic Palestine

Photograph in American
Colony in Jerusalem
Collection, reproduced in
Peoples of All Nations, 1922,
vol. 6, p. 3948

A special high value coin of
gold dangles from the end of
this young bride's chin chain.
This coin was likely purchased
by her father, using some of
the funds from the groom's
obligatory gifts to the bride's
family.

FIG. 3.32

FIG. 3.32
MARRIED WOMAN'S HAT (*SHATWEH*),
C. 1900

Bethlehem, historic Palestine

Cotton, silk, gold, silver, coral, white metal

Diameter: 5¹⁄₈ in. (13 cm)

Museum of International Folk Art, Gift of
Florence Dibell Bartlett, A.1955.1.589

Photograph by Addison Doty

Married Palestinian women in Bethlehem
and surrounding villages wore this
distinctive conical hat daily. It was
embellished with rows of coral beads and
gold and silver coins from the wearer's
bride wealth, the more coins, the greater
the woman's prestige and wealth. However,
when going outdoors, the hat was covered
completely with a veil so that only the
tinkling sound of the coins could be heard
but not seen. Hooked to each side of the
hat is an amulet-shaped silver triangle from
which hang five chains ending in crescent
moons. The crescent moon, the number five,
and the triangle are all strong protection
against the Evil Eye. (Stillman 1979: 38).

PHOTO 3.10

PHOTO 3.10
MARRIED WOMAN DRESSED IN HER HAT WITH CHIN CHAIN, BEFORE 1922

Historic Palestine

Photograph by Donald McLeish, reproduced in Peoples of All Nations, 1922, vol. 6, p. 3929.

FIG. 3:33
MARRIED WOMAN'S HAT (*SMADEH*), C. 1860

Ramallah, historic Palestine

Cotton, silver

10⁶/₈ in. (27 cm)

Museum of International Folk Art, Gift of Florence Dibell Bartlett, A.1955.1.276

Married women wore this distinctive hat as daily wear in Ramallah, Samaria, and Lower Galilee into the twentieth century. By the late 1970s, it was seen worn by traditional women only in Ramallah. The row of 100 Ottoman coins plus the 60 smaller coins on the inner rim are the wearer's bride wealth and are kept as a cash reserve. "Sometimes you see a gap in the row of coins and you guess that a doctor's bill has had to be paid, or the husband in America has failed to send money." (Crowfoot and Sutton 1935: 37).

FIG. 3.34
CHIN CHAIN (*IZNAQ*), C. 1900

Historic central Palestine

Silver, glass beads

14¹/₂ in. (36.5 cm)

Museum of International Folk Art, Gift of Florence Dibell Bartlett, A.1955.86.732

FIG. 3.34

The chin chain was attached to the various types of Palestinian women's hats to keep them firmly in place. The five chains and the blue glass beads protect the wearer from the Evil Eye.

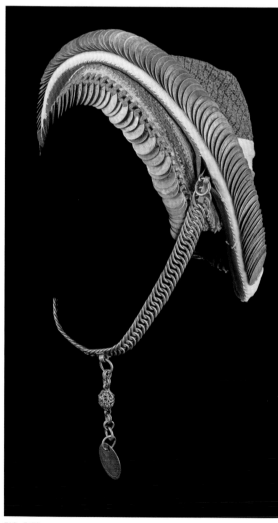

FIG. 3:33

FIG. 3.35

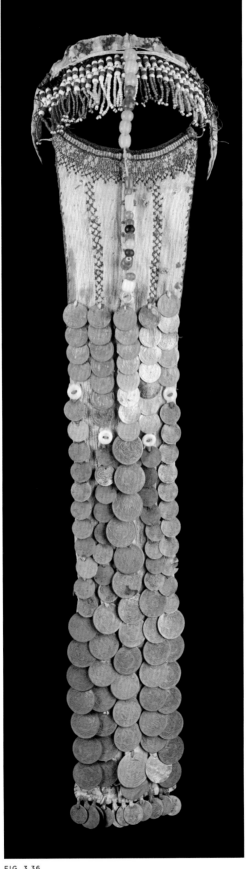

FIG. 3.35
MARRIED WOMAN'S FACE VEIL
(*BURQAH*), C. 1900

Bedouin peoples, Sinai Peninsula, Egypt

Cotton, silver, glass beads

16 9/16 x 13 3/16 in. (42 x 33.5 cm)

Museum of International Folk Art, IFAF Collection, FA.2010.66.1

PHOTO 3.11
BEDOUIN WOMEN AND CHILDREN, 1961

Abu Sir, Egypt

Smithsonian Institution, National Museum of African Art, Eliot Elisofon Photographic Archives,

Photograph by Eliot Elisofon, EEPA_EENG_005 71

Married Bedouin women in Arab countries wear several different types of face veils. The coins are from their bride dowries. Looking at the two veils, clearly one of the women had a larger dowry than the other.

FIG. 3.36
MARRIED WOMAN'S FACE VEIL
(*NIQAB*), N.D.

Bedouin peoples, Egypt

Cotton, synthetic fiber, wool, metal coins and chains, glass beads, plastic buttons

29 1/8 x 7 1/16 in. (74 x 18 cm)

Museum of International Folk Art, Gift of David B. and Bonnie Naifeh Smith, A.2011.33.3

PHOTO 3.11

FIG. 3.36

FIG. 3.37

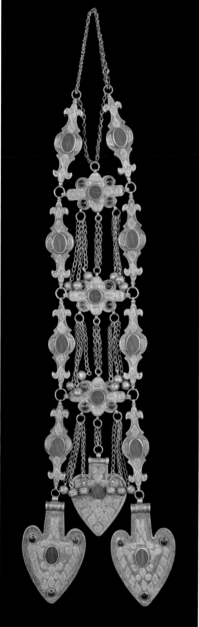

FIG. 3.38

FIG. 3.38 DETAIL

A Turkmen bride's dowry consists of carpets, which she makes herself, clothing, and jewelry.
"However this is not all the wedding jewellery, because some of the bride price which the
bridegroom has to pay also consists of jewellery." (Schletzer 1983: 52). "Jewelry played a very
important role in Turkman wedding ceremonials, not only to adorn the bride, but also as a dowry
and as wedding gifts for the bridal party." (Diba 2011: 36). Among the nomadic Turkmen peoples,
jewelry, made from high-grade silver coins, was a portable way to carry their wealth. Worn almost
exclusively by women, they adorned themselves more elaborately with jewelry as they aged.

A distinctive heart-shaped pendant form, representing the "anthropomorphic female form"
(Fig. 3.37), is presented to the bride by the groom's parents, which she wears at her wedding in
the groom's house. (Schletzer 1983: 216–18). This pendant was still being worn in the early 1980s.

After the wedding, the new bride enters into the married woman's age group, which is
identifiable by a change of hairstyle, headgear, jewelry, and clothing. She plaits her hair into
braids down her back to which she attaches a lavish hair ornament (Figs. 3.38 and 3.39).

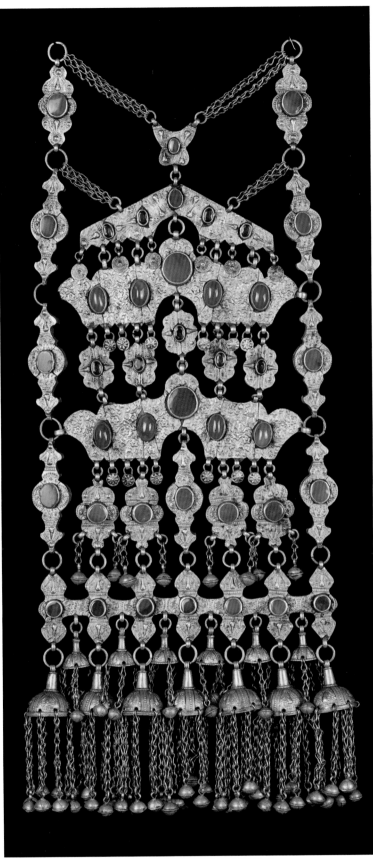

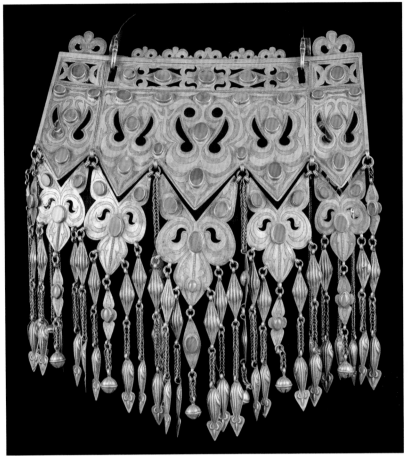

FIG. 3.40

FIG. 3.39

FIG. 3.39
MARRIED WOMAN'S HAIR ORNAMENT (*SACMONDZŬK*), C. 1900–1930S

Western Yomut Turkmen peoples, Central Asia or Iran

Silver, gilt, carnelian, glass

22⁷/₁₆ x 9⁷/₁₆ in. (57 x 24 cm)

Museum of International Folk Art, long-term loan from Monir Farmanfarmaian, IL.1999.582.3

FIG. 3.40
MARRIED WOMAN'S NECKLET, LATE NINETEENTH OR EARLY TWENTIETH CENTURY

Teke Turkmen peoples, Central Asia or Iran

Silver, gilt, carnelian, glass

13³/₁₆ x 10¹¹/₁₆ in. (33.5 x 27.2 cm)

Museum of International Folk Art, long-term loan from Monir Farmanfarmaian, IL.1999.582.2 & 44

This silver "collar" band with attached elaborate pectoral pendant (*bukov*) worn on the woman's chest was counterbalanced by the heavy hair ornaments worn on her braids in back. Thus she was protected from the Evil Eye on all sides.

FIG. 3.41

FIG. 3.42

FIG. 3.41
GROOM'S PECTORAL ORNAMENT,
NINETEENTH CENTURY

Yomut Turkmen peoples, Central Asia
or Iran

Gold, silver, gilt, turquoise, carnelian,
glass

20¹/₁₆ x 6¹/₂ in. (51 x 16.5 cm)

Museum of International Folk Art, long-
term loan from Monir Farmanfarmaian,
IL.1999.582

Some early observers reported that the
"bow and arrow"–shaped ornaments
were worn by grooms in Turkmen
weddings. (Diba 2011: 118).

FIG. 3.42 AND DETAIL
WEDDING HEADDRESS (*SOUALEF*),
NINETEENTH CENTURY

Tétouan city, northern Morocco

Silk, cotton, pearls, gold, stones

6⁵/₁₆ x 12¹/₈ in. (16 x 30.8 cm)

Museum of International Folk Art,
Gift of Florence Dibell Bartlett,
A.1955.86.757

Photograph by Addison Doty

Married Jewish women wore this
ancient style of headdress. When
going out, they would cover their hair,
so that only the false braids attached
to the headdress were visible. Today
few Jews remain in Morocco because
most moved to Israel after it became a
country in 1948.

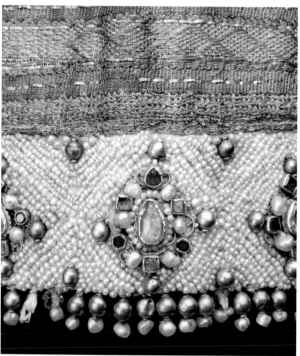

FIG. 3.42 DETAIL

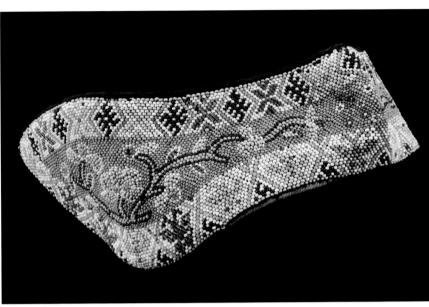

FIG. 3.43

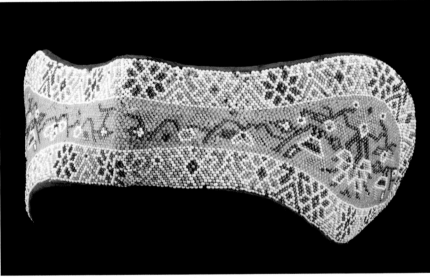

FIG. 3.44

FIG. 3.45

FIG. 3.43
WEDDING HEADBAND (*FA-LAP*), PRE-1949

Punti peoples, Hong Kong, People's Republic of China

Cotton, glass beads

3⁹/₁₆ x 7⁷/₈ in. (9 x 20 cm)

Museum of International Folk Art, IFAF Collection, FA.2013.18.2

FIG. 3.44
WEDDING HEADBAND (*FA-LAP*), PRE-1949

Punti peoples, Hong Kong, People's Republic of China

Cotton, glass beads

3⁵/₈ x 15³/₈ in. (9.2 x 39 cm)

Museum of International Folk Art, IFAF Collection, FA.2013.18.1

These beaded headbands were worn by Punti women on their wedding day in Hong Kong.

FIG. 3.45 AND DETAIL
PILLOW, LATE NINETEENTH CENTURY

Peranakan Chinese peoples, Palembang, Sumatra, Indonesia

Cotton, wooden frame, glass beads, metallic lace and wire

6¹/₂ x 13 x 2³/₄ in. (16.5 x 33 x 7 cm)

Museum of International Folk Art, IFAF Collection, Gift of Sandy and Diane Besser, FA. 2003.37.34

The Peranakan Chinese peoples, who migrated to Sumatra, Java, and the Malay Peninsula, became acculturated within their new homelands, developing a new style of beadwork as seen on this pillow, which was displayed at weddings and other festive occasions. Yet they retained Chinese designs and motifs like the peony.

FIG. 3.45 DETAIL

FIG. 3.46

FIG. 3.46
WEDDING BASKET, 1930-1960

Lampung Bay, Sumatra, Indonesia

Bamboo, glass beads, shell

5⁷⁄₈ x 7¹⁄₂ x 7¹⁄₂ in. (15 x 19 x 19 cm)

Museum of International Folk Art, Gift of Ronald and Vicki Sullivan, T.2015.90.9

In the past colorfully beaded gift baskets filled with food or cloth were given to the newlyweds on the occasion of their wedding.

FIG. 3.47 AND DETAIL
GROOM'S WEDDING OUTFIT, C. 1900

Bagóbo peoples, Mindanao Island, Philippines

Abacá (banana leaf-stems fiber), glass beads, cotton, metal bells, sequins, feathers

Jacket: 69⁵⁄₁₆ in. (176 cm); pants: 41³⁄₄ in. (106 cm);
bag: 10⁵⁄₈ in. (27 cm)

Museum of International Folk Art, IFAF Collection, FA.1979.34.1–3

PHOTO 3.12
YOUNG BAGÓBO MAN, EARLY TWENTIETH CENTURY

Mindanao Island, Philippines

The Field Museum, Chicago, Illinois, USA, Image # CSA21394

FIG. 3.47

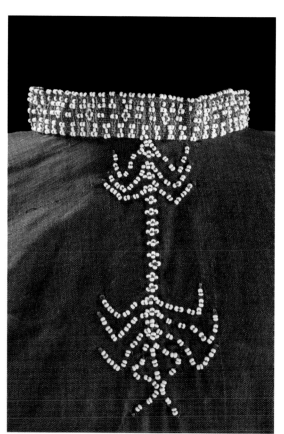

FIG. 3.47 DETAIL

PHOTO 3.12

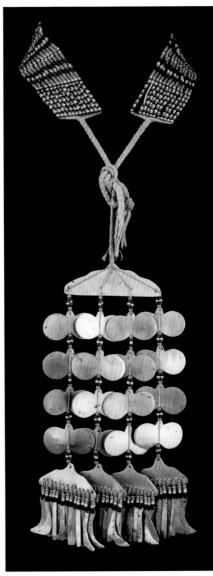

FIG. 3.48

FIG. 3.48
BRIDE PRICE CHEST ORNAMENT (*SIPATTAL*), EARLY TWENTIETH CENTURY

Isneg peoples, Apayao province, northern Luzon, Philippines

Fiber, glass beads, mother-of-pearl shell

17.9 x 4.5 in. (45.4 x 11.5 cm)

Shari and Earl Kessler Collection

These precious neck and chest ornaments, exclusive to the Isneg people, are passed down from generation to generation. Mothers may pass them to their son to give to his bride's family as compensation to her parents for their loss of their daughter.

FIG. 3.49
MARRIAGE EXCHANGE APRON (*SIREU*), EARLY TWENTIETH CENTURY

Ambai Island, Papua province, New Guinea (Indonesia)

Commercial cotton, glass beads, bark fiber thread

26 x 19 in. (66 x 48.2 cm)

Museum of International Folk Art, IFAF Collection, Gift of Diane and Sandy Besser, FA.2008.74.384

FIG. 3.50
MARRIAGE EXCHANGE APRON (*SIREU*), EARLY TWENTIETH CENTURY

Ambai Island, Papua province, New Guinea (Indonesia)

Commercial cotton, glass beads, bark fiber thread, feathers

31⁷/₈ x 22¹/₁₆ in. (81 x 56 cm)

Museum of International Folk Art, IFAF Collection, Gift of Diane and Sandy Besser, FA.2002.49.13

These beaded aprons have been made only on the island of Ambai off the New Guinea mainland, since at least the late eighteenth century. They are considered precious heirlooms and continue to be used within the community and traded to nearby islands and coastal communities for similar use, and more rarely to the outside world for cash. The apron is one of three items, including a shell bracelet and a beaded necklace, which plays an important role in a wedding exchange. The prospective groom promises these items to his bride. He obtains an apron either through inheritance from a female relative or by commissioning one to be made. "The exchange of the traditional items is still generally considered to be essential for the marriage to be legitimate." (Howard 2002:97).

FIG. 3.49

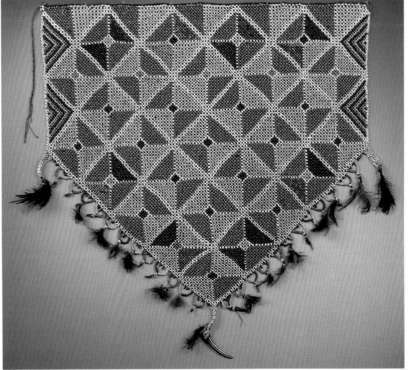

FIG. 3.50

FIG. 3.51

FIG. 3.51
BETROTHAL BASKET, 1630–70

England

Metal wire, glass beads

25³⁄₄ x 23¹⁄₄ x 5 in. (65.5 x 59 x 12.7 cm)

Corning Museum of Glass, 53.2.4

These seventeenth-century beaded baskets are believed to have been made by English women to celebrate a betrothal. The iconography supports this theory with a couple in the center, the gentleman holding his hat as he woos his intended, surrounded by fruits and flowers, which allude to fertility. The basket was used to hold sprigs of rosemary to give to the wedding guests.

FIG. 3.52
WEDDING HEADDRESS, C. 1920

Somogy county, Hungary

Silk, cotton, glass beads, sequins

Diameter: 8¹⁄₄ in. (21 cm)

Museum of International Folk Art, Gift of Florence Dibell Bartlett, A.1955.1.559

Photograph by Addison Doty

"On her wedding day, a [Hungarian] bride donned a special hat or wedding crown that she wore for a day, a few days, or a few years, depending on the region. As she had children and grew older, she changed her headwear." (Sumberg 2010: 90).

FIG. 3.52

FIG. 3.53 DETAIL

**FIG. 3.53 AND DETAIL
WEDDING DRESS, 1920S**

USA

Silk, waxed glass beads

New Mexico History Museum, NMHM-2011.31.1

The large beads on this flapper-style wedding dress were made of waxed glass beads, intended to look like pearls, but more affordable.

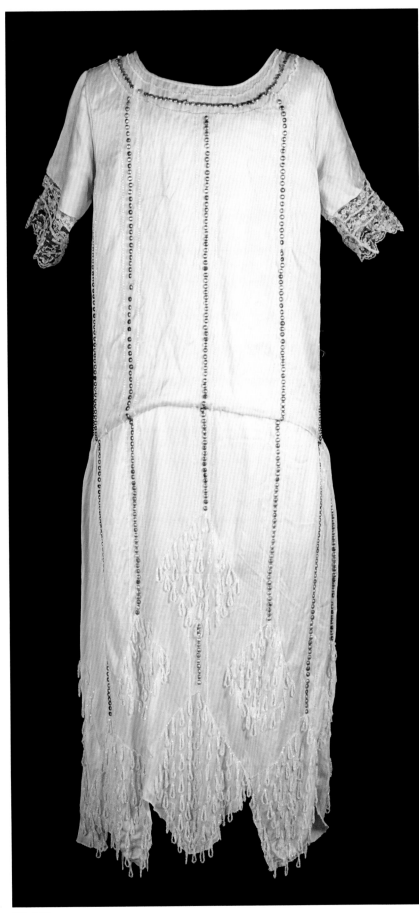

FIG. 3.53

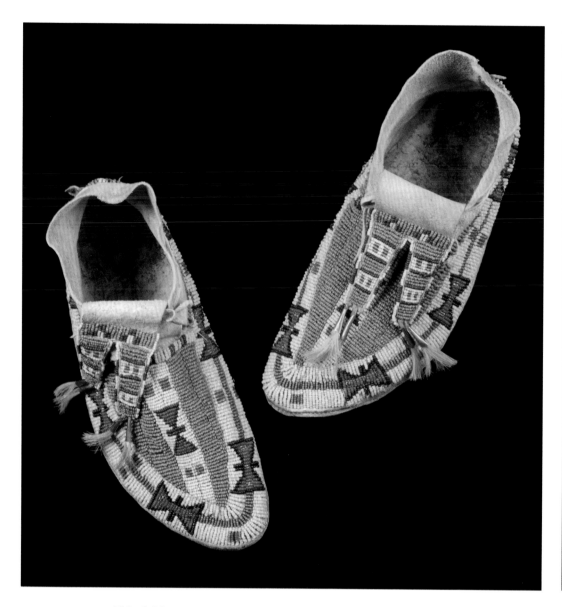

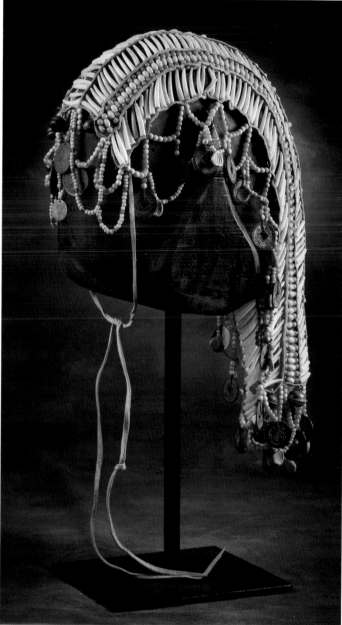

FIG. 3.54
WEDDING MOCCASINS FOR BRIDE'S IN-LAWS, C. 1930

Lakota peoples, North or South Dakota, USA

Tanned hide, glass beads

10¹/₂ in. (26.7 cm)

Museum of Indian Arts and Culture / Laboratory of Anthropology, MIAC 3689 a&b

Traditionally a Lakota woman's art was an important vehicle in confirming and maintaining kinship relationships. When a Lakota bride arrived at her mother-in-law's tipi for the first time, her first task was to make a pair of beaded moccasins to demonstrate her abilities as a good wife and daughter-in-law. "These were socially important gifts that a bride made with her own hands for her husband's parents; handsome moccasins for both. . . . People were inordinately proud of such gifts and were reluctant to give them away. Many a woman kept against her burial the moccasins which her son's wife made for her." (Deloria n.d.: 131).

FIG. 3.55
BRIDE'S HEADDRESS, LATE NINETEENTH CENTURY

Yakama peoples, Washington, USA

Tanned hide, glass beads, *dentalium* shells, Chinese coins

12¹/₂ in. (32 cm)

Bob and Lora Sandroni Collection

Photograph by LA High Noon, Inc.

Multiple rows of valuable *dentalium* shells proclaim the wealth of the Yakama bride's family in her wedding headdress. Likely the Chinese coins were acquired during the fur trade in the mid-nineteenth century. (Conn 1979: 258).

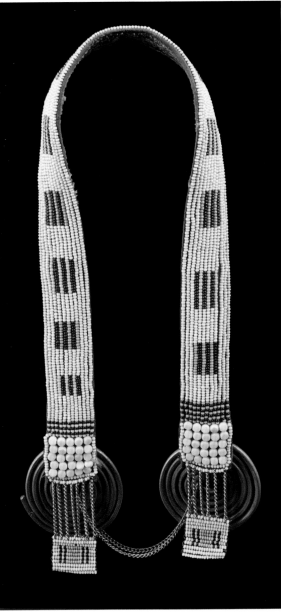

FIG. 3.56

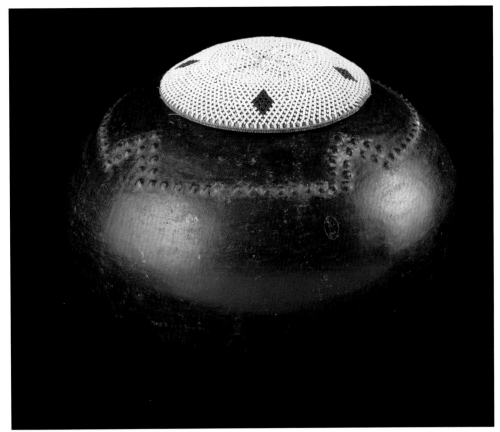

FIG. 3.57

FIG. 3.58

FIG. 3.56
MARRIED WOMAN'S NECKLACE,
C. 1930

Maasai peoples, Tanzania

Leather, metal, glass beads

27⁹/₁₆ x 1³/₁₆ in. (70 x 3 cm)

Museum of International Folk Art,
IFAF Collection, Gift of Sandy and
Diane Besser, FA.2003.37.40

Maasai women wear this type of
necklace as a sign of their martial
status.

FIG. 3.57
BEER POT WITH LID (*IZIMBENGE*),
TWENTIETH CENTURY

Zulu peoples, KwaZulu-Natal, South Africa

Pot: clay; lid: grass, glass beads

Pot: 11¹/₄ x 14¹/₄ in. (28.6 x 36.2 cm);
lid: 7¹/₄ in. (18 cm)

Pot: Museum of International Folk Art,
A.2001.41.17; lid: Private collection

A young Zulu bride must demonstrate her
commitment to her new in-laws through
the execution of specific services, including
the specialized task of brewing Zulu beer
(*umqombothi*). (Wells, et. al. 2004: 76). The
beer-brewing ritual honors the ancestral spirits.

FIG. 3.58
MARRIED WOMAN DOLL, 2004

Maker: Lobolile Ximba (Zulu)

Durban, South Africa

Cotton, glass beads

15³/₄ in. (40 cm)

Museum of International Folk Art, Gift of the
International Folk Art Market, A.2005.13.5

Married Zulu women can be identified by their
broad-brimmed red hats.

IN MEMORIAM

"MANY CULTURES REGARD LIFE AND DEATH AS OPPOSITE BUT COMPLEMENTARY SEGMENTS OF THE TURNING WHEEL OF TOTAL EXISTENCE." (TURNER 1982: 134)

BURIAL CLOTHING

In most cultures, the dead are dressed in their best clothing to carry them to the next world. Some are also surrounded by their worldly belongings. Among Asante women of Ghana, "gifts of *tomoma*, or waist beads . . . continue to be presented at funerary rites for an Asante woman as a farewell gift to accompany the deceased on her departure into the afterlife and ancestral realm. According to Akan customary beliefs, an ancestress guards the entrance to the ancestral world to ensure that all women who enter are wearing waist beads" (Fig. 3.5). (Gott 2007: 91).

Traditionally Lakota people of the central Plains did not bury their dead in graves. Rather they erected wooden scaffolds on a high hill where they laid their dead to rest, open to the sky. The deceased were dressed in their finery, including a fine pair of moccasins, which were sometimes beaded even on the soles (Fig. 4.1).

FIG. 4.1
MEN'S MOCCASINS
WITH BEADED SOLES,
LATE NINETEENTH
CENTURY

Lakota peoples, North or South Dakota, USA

Native-tanned hide, wool cloth, glass beads

10½ in. (26.7 cm)

Museum of Indian Arts and Culture, 9822/12ab

FIG. 4.1

According to Ella Deloria, who was Yankton Sioux but grew up on a Lakota reservation: "For rich or poor, the all-important item was creditable footwear. . . . It was a minor tragedy to be buried unshod or with shabby moccasins. . . . Even old people, ordinarily indifferent to finery, managed to keep on hand the best moccasins they could acquire, against their burial. Many carried theirs in a little sack hitched to the belt in the back, under their wrap. 'These I shall lie wearing' they said." (Deloria n.d.: 161).

In early twentieth century Sumba island, eastern Indonesia, a noblewoman was buried in a ceremonial skirt to identify her status when she arrived in the spirit world. The skirt is decorated with a powerful ancestral male figure, who will guide her to the next world, surrounded by stars, insects, and other figures (Fig. 4.2). The skirt's name, *Lau Hada*, describes it as a screen against the moon and protection against the sun.

FIG. 4.2
NOBLEWOMAN'S CEREMONIAL SKIRT (*LAU HADA*), EARLY TWENTIETH CENTURY

Sumba island, East Nusa Tenggara province, Indonesia

Cotton, beads, shells

57 x 22 in. (144.78 x 55.88 cm)

Museum of International Folk Art, gift of Lloyd E. Cotsen and the Neutrogena Corporation, A.1995.93.1147

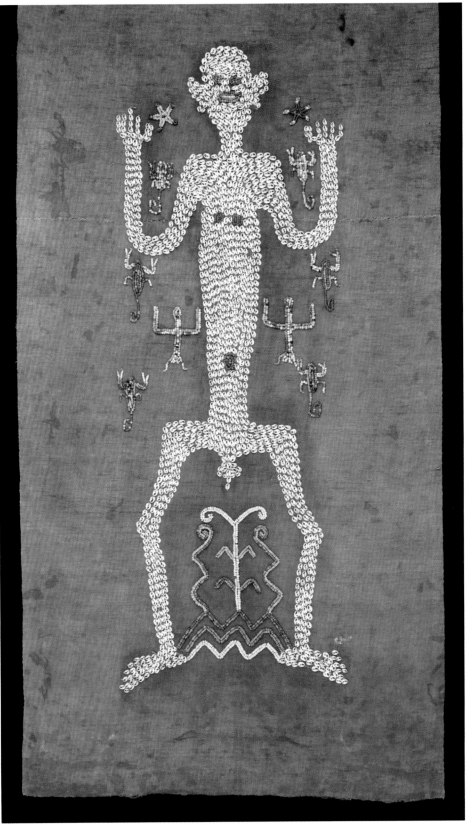

FIG. 4.2

FIG. 4.3

FIG. 4.4

FIG. 4.5

MEMORIALS

In many parts of the world, special ornaments are made to memorialize the dead at their resting place. When glass beads are incorporated into these memorials, the beads not only provide a beautiful decorative adornment but offer an everlasting quality.

FIG. 4.3, *Opposite*
GRAVE WREATH, C. 1880

France

Ceramic, glass beads, wire

$32^6/8$ x $29^1/2$ x $4^7/8$ in. (83 x 75 x 12.5 cm)

Museum of International Folk Art, Gift of the Girard Foundation Collection, A.1981.1.387

FIG. 4.4, *Opposite,* **AND DETAIL**
GRAVE WREATH, 1880

Père Lachaise Cemetery, Ville de Paris, France

Ceramic, glass beads, wire

$29^1/2$ x $22^1/4$ x $6^1/8$ in. (75 x 56.5 x 15.5 cm)

Museum of International Folk Art, Gift of the Girard Foundation Collection, A.1981.1.388

FIG. 4.5, *Opposite*
BOUQUET, C. 1880

Italy

Glass beads, wire

$2^9/16$ x $11^9/16$ x $6^{13}/16$ in. (6.5 x 29.3 x 17.3 cm)

Museum of International Folk Art, Gift of the Girard Foundation Collection, A.1984.153.514

During the Victorian era, wreaths constructed of glass beads were laid on graves in French cemeteries as "everlasting" memorials, termed *immortelles*, to loved ones. This wreath (Fig. 4.4) of beaded flowers graced a grave in Père Lachaise Cemetery, the largest cemetery in the city of Paris.

The art of making beaded flowers originated in rural France in the 1500s where peasants made and sewed the flowers onto ball gowns and men's jackets for the French royalty. By the 1800s, beadworkers combined multiple flowers to create funerary and grave wreaths for French Catholic cemeteries.

Spreading to Italy and England, the floral units were combined to create other forms, such as decorative Italian bouquets (Fig. 4.5) and English betrothal baskets (Fig. 3.51). After going into decline in the first half of the twentieth century, the art of making beaded flowers experienced a revival in the United States in the 1960s and continues today, aided by the connections beadworkers are able to make via the internet. (National September 11 Memorial & Museum).

FIG. 4.4 DETAIL

FIG. 4.6
NEW YORK 9/11 MEMORIAL WREATH, 2006

Made by bead hobbyists in the USA, Canada, England, Australia, Italy, France, and Switzerland

New York City, New York, USA

Glass beads, wire

42 x 35 x 8 in. (106.8 x 88.9 x 20.4 cm)

Collection 9/11 Memorial Museum, Gift of the Internet French Beaded Flower Group

Photograph by Matt Flynn

This wreath, assembled from hundreds of hand-beaded flowers made and donated by beadworking hobbyists from around the world, commemorates the victims of the 9/11 terrorist attack on the World Trade Center and on flights 11 and 175. Two additional hobbyist-made glass-bead wreaths commemorate the attacks on the Pentagon and United Flight 93. The mid-twentieth-century revival of making beaded flowers combined into wreaths has its roots in the French and Italian tradition of creating everlasting tributes to the dead.

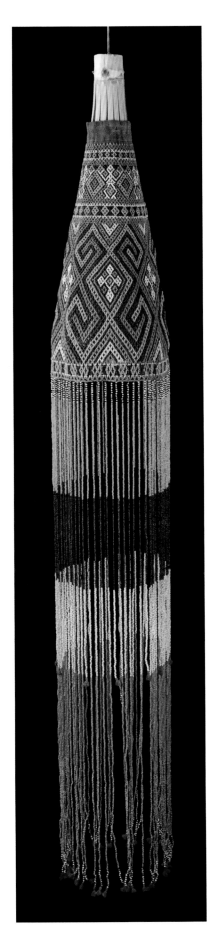

**FIG. 4.7 AND DETAIL
CEREMONIAL ORNAMENT (*KANDAURE*),
C. 1925**

Sa'dan Toraja peoples, South Sulawesi, Indonesia

Fiber, bamboo, glass beads

55 in. (139.7 cm)

Museum of International Folk Art, IFAF
Collection, Gift of Diane and Sandy Besser,
FA.2006.70.44

The Toraja peoples hold elaborate funeral
rites that are their most important social
occasions, attended by hundreds of
people and lasting for several days. The
valued *kandaure* stands on a pole next to
the *tongkonan*, the traditional house of
an extended family. The family owns the
kandaure, which they lend out to the male
family members of the deceased to wear
during the mortuary rituals.

GENDER IN BEADWORK

AMONG SOCIETIES WORLDWIDE, UNTIL RECENTLY, A division of labor existed between women and men. Men almost exclusively were the game hunters, went to war, and controlled the political and religious arenas, while women accomplished the domestic tasks of child-rearing, cooking, and other family and household tasks. Men dominated the public sphere outside of the village or camp, women controlled the domestic domain of the home place. It took both male and female working as a team to sustain a livelihood for their family.

This gender division of labor can also be seen in societal designations of particular industries to women or to men. In 1973, anthropologists George Murdock and Caterina Provost surveyed 185 societies throughout the world regarding the gender assignments of 50 technological tasks, which encompass artistic activities. (Murdoch and Provost 1973). Briefly stated, males tend to be assigned activities involving materials which are hard or tough, such as metalworking, woodworking, stone working, or work in bone, horn or shell. Women on the other hand are assigned the tasks associated with soft or pliable raw materials, such as basket-making, pottery making, spinning, weaving, and the manufacture of clothing. Murdoch observed that there are specific activities that are strictly masculine, and certain activities that remain generally, although not absolutely, feminine.

Notably, many of these assigned tasks or skills are related to the gender tasks that men and women are traditionally responsible for within their societies. For example, men make the tools and weapons that they use in hunting, war and ritual, while women make the objects necessary in caring for their families.

Most of the objects in this book have been and continue to be produced according to a division of labor by gender. However feminist scholarship has contributed new thinking to this concept. Rozsika Parker (1989: 2–3) contends: "Femininity, the behavior expected and encouraged in women, though obviously related to the biological sex of the individual, is shaped by society. . . . It is a crucial aspect of patriarchal ideology, sanctioning a rigid and oppressive division of labour. Thus women active in the upsurge of feminism which began in the 1960s set out to challenge accepted definitions of the innate differences between the sexes, and to provide a new understanding of the creation of femininity."

WOMEN'S WORK

In most societies beadwork has been designated a woman's art, primarily associated with ornamentation in dress and household objects. For example, "In most of eastern and southern Africa, beadworking is done by women and is, with a few exceptions, very much defined by gender. In southern Africa, for instance among

FIG. 5.1
AWL CASE, C. 1900

Cheyenne peoples, Wyoming or Oklahoma, USA

Rawhide, Native-tanned hide, glass beads, paint

9 x 1³/4 in. (22.9 x 4.4 cm)

Museum of Indian Arts and Culture / Laboratory of Anthropology, 26314/12

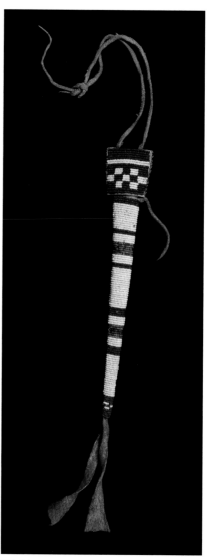

FIG. 5.1

the Zulu, if a young man wants to give a beaded message to his fiancée [Fig. 2.52], he has to get a sister or other female relative to make it for him, as the rule is so strong that [only] women do beadwork." (Carey 1998: 87).

Iban daughters of Borneo learn beadworking from their mothers. "Not only are men not encouraged to help, they are kept away from the whole 'women's business' quite firmly." (Munan 1995: 60). After mastering the art, Iban beadworkers can then dream their new designs. Women receiving new designs through dreams is found throughout other cultures. Rosalie Little Thunder, a gifted Lakota beadworker, said that Lakota beadworkers with exceptional skill are considered *waksupi ihanble*, literally to "dream beadwork" or "to dream and it becomes you." (Little Thunder 1993).

On the U.S. Plains, beadwork was a major activity reserved for Lakota Indian women, who made and ornamented clothing, spending many hours applying glass beads to Native-tanned hide in order to dress their families in the finest attire. Using a basic tool, called an awl, which they carried in a special case (Figs. 5.1 and 5.2) attached to their belt, the women stitched the beads to the hide backing. It significantly added to the prestige of a woman's family if the members were dressed in fine beaded clothing (Fig. 5.3). Her beadwork functioned as a major criterion for judging a Lakota woman's worth and differentiating her rank and prestige among others in her society.

FIG. 5.2
AWL CASE, C. 1900

Mescalero Apache peoples, southern New Mexico, USA

Native-tanned hide, glass beads, wood, tin tinklers

10 in. (25.4 cm)

Museum of Indian Arts and Culture / Laboratory of Anthropology, 36965/12

FIG. 5.3
BOY'S SHIRT, C. 1893

Lakota peoples, North or South Dakota, U.S.A.

Native-tanned hide, glass beads

14 1/8 x 20 7/8 in. (36 x 53 cm)

Museum of Indian Arts and Culture / Laboratory of Anthropology, 1797/12

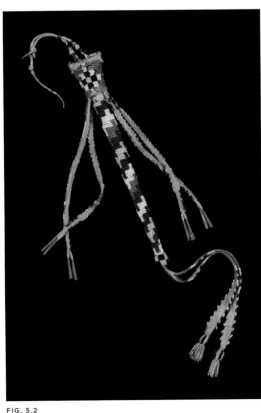

FIG. 5.2

FIG. 5.3

FIG. 5.4
HORSE MASK, 2000

Maker: Joyce Growing Thunder Fogarty (b. 1950),
Assiniboine/Sioux, Fort Peck Reservation, Montana

Wool, cotton muslin backing, glass beads, turkey feathers,
metal discs and beads, plastic rings, thread

16¹/₂ x 17¹/₂ in. (41.9 x 44.4 cm)

Ralph T. Coe Center for the Arts

PHOTO 5.1, *Opposite*
THREE GENERATIONS (LEFT TO RIGHT): JOYCE GROWING
THUNDER FOGARTY (MOTHER), JESSA RAE GROWING
THUNDER (GRANDDAUGHTER), AND JUANITA GROWING
THUNDER FOGARTY (DAUGHTER), 2016

Assiniboine/Sioux, Fort Peck Reservation, Montana

Photograph by Marsha Bol

THREE GENERATIONS OF GROWING THUNDER WOMEN

If traditions are to be carried forward, it has always been up to the older generation to teach the upcoming generation, who then has the responsibility to pass on the knowledge to the next. In the past century, with many competing attractions for the younger generation's interest, the passing of the torch of tradition has also required the interest of the younger folk.

Three living generations of women from the Growing Thunder family are carrying forward the Assiniboine beadworking tradition in an exemplary manner. The elder Joyce Growing Thunder learned beadworking from her grandmothers who raised her on the Fort Peck Reservation in Montana. As Joyce says: "I really have done this so the next generations can carry on," pointing to her granddaughter, Jessa Rae. (*The New Mexican,* August 29, 2016: A-4). Jessa Rae notes: "They [her great grandmothers] were really traditional women. And being traditional women, beadwork and quillwork are an important part of that identity. They would have a fully beaded women's buckskin top spread across the bed, and they would all be sitting at different corners working and talking. . . . [Now] we're all working side by side, and even though we may not always be working on the exact same piece at one time, we're able to kind of recreate that bonding experience. . . . [At age six] I thought everyone's mom and grandma woke up before the sunrise and sat there and beaded and quilled all day until dinnertime. I thought that was normal. . . . I'm still learning, and to be able to have that learning experience with my family— that's amazing . . . to be able to do that as three generations." (Indian Market Guide 2015: 64).

Juanita, Joyce's daughter and Jessa Rae's mother, notes: "It [beadwork] strengthens us as a family, because it gives everyone a purpose and self-worth, culture, and identity. We know what our background is, and it ties us to the culture." (Logan n.d.: 10).

The three Growing Thunders, plus additional family members, are veteran artists at the annual Santa Fe Indian Market held each August. The elder Joyce Growing Thunder has won Best of Show three times, and both daughter Juanita and granddaughter Jessa Rae have won many ribbons in the Beadwork category. As Joyce says: "I continue to do my work to inspire the younger generations to carry on our culture and tradition. I'll carry on my work as long as I'm able." (*Indian Market Guide* 2012: 69).

PHOTO 5.1

SARAGURO WOMEN'S BEADWORK COOPERATIVE

Women's artisan cooperatives are developing the world over as an organizational solution toward meeting the needs of their communities, while at the same time preserving their traditional arts. The United Nations declared 2012 as the International Year of Cooperatives. Not limited to only artisan coops, the declaration was intended to "raise public awareness of the invaluable contributions of cooperative enterprises to poverty reduction, employment generation and social integration. The Year also highlight[ed] the strengths of the cooperative business model as an alternative means of doing business and furthering socioeconomic development."

In the southern highlands of Ecuador, at an altitude of 8,500 feet on the eastern slopes of the Andes, indigenous Saraguro women have developed beadworking cooperatives, working together to make and market their netted-bead collars and necklaces, bracelets, and earrings. For several generations, all Saraguro girls and women have been making and wearing this bead jewelry to adorn their own daily traditional dress, composed of

a black pleated skirt with underskirt, an embroidered blouse, black shawl, and fedora-style hat.

In 2010, five separate women's beadmaking organizations joined together into one mega-size cooperative, which they named La Mega Cooperativa Artesanal de los Saraguros in order to market their beadwork internationally. Although each individual cooperative has its own internal organization, they share much in common. All have officers, a bank account, and the goal to improve the quality of life for the members, their families, and their communities. All of the earnings go directly to the cooperative, and after the coop's expenses are covered, the balance of the funds is variously used by the coops. Two coops use their earnings to make microloans to the members. Members use the funds to send their children to school, for health care, to construct an artisan center or open a sales shop, and in one case to support a women's shelter. Anywhere from 20 to 60 percent of their family's annual income comes from the beadwork earnings.

PHOTO 5.2

PHOTO 5.2
MEMBERS DISCUSSING PRICING
AT A LA MEGA MEETING, 2010

La Mega Cooperativa Artesanal de
los Saraguros, Ecuador

Photograph by Sue Ellen Kingsley

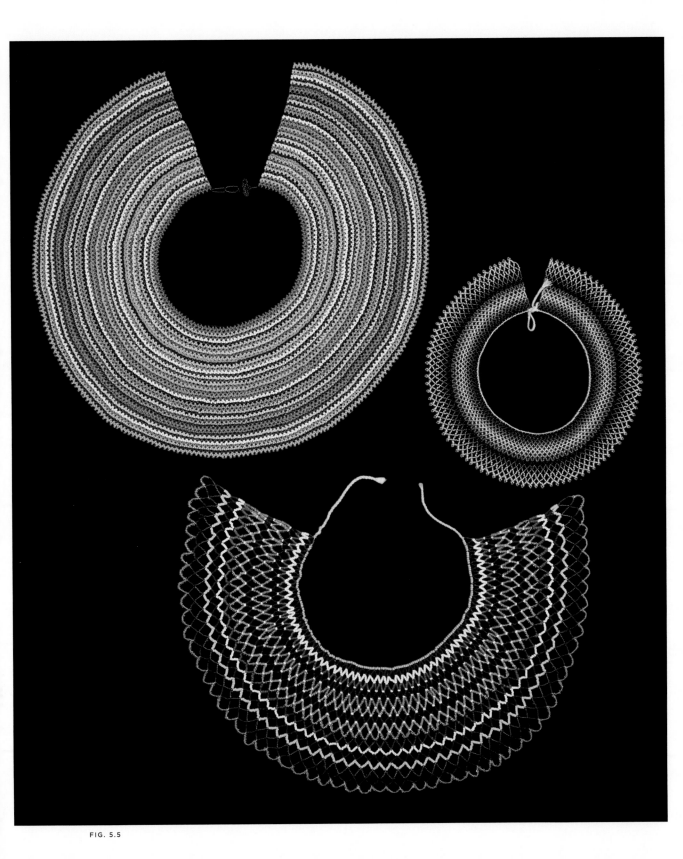

FIG. 5.5

FIG. 5.5

FIG. 5.5
COLLARS, 1963, 2013

Saraguro peoples, Ecuador

Glass beads, nylon thread

Top: 4⁵/₈ x 14⁹/₁₆ in. (11.7 x 37 cm); middle: 1⁷/₈ x 8⁷/₈ in. (4.7 x 22.5 cm); bottom: 5¹/₈ x 16 in. (13 x 40.7 cm)

Museum of International Folk Art, IFAF Collection, FA.2013.58.1–3

Indigenous Saraguro women do not go out of the house without wearing one of their beaded collars. The beads add striking color to the traditional black and white dress of the women. The beaded-net collar (bottom) is an early example that was purchased in 1963. The smaller collar (middle right), made in 2013, is a traditional wedding collar with the rainbow pattern, which represents fertility. According to Linda Belote, anthropologist: "Back in the '60s when I was still single, I would be warned, along with all the other single women, to go inside when a rainbow appeared, because it could make one pregnant!" (Belote 2013). Today the large multicolored collar (top left), made in 2013, is supplanting the rainbow collar in weddings.

WOMEN WORKING IN GROUPS

When women are embroidering beads, they tend to do so in groups as a social activity, thus allowing for conversation and design sharing. Group aesthetics developed and were shared between women as they worked together in groups, resulting in identifiable tribal or ethnic styles.

Visitors to Lakota Indian camps noted seeing women working in groups. Anthropologist Alice Fletcher observed in 1881: "I was glad to join the mother and daughter as they sat under a shade made of boughs. . . . Here the women sewed and chatted." (Fletcher 1887: 37). In the 1930s, Ella Deloria (n.d.: 79) also recorded the custom of Lakota women sitting in a group behind the tipi "to chat and do fancywork." Beadwork, referred to here as "fancywork," was a favored topic of discussion for Lakota women embroidering beads in groups and on other group occasions. (Deloria n.d.: 28).

Central Plains Indian tribes, such as the Lakota, Arapaho, and Cheyenne, developed women's societies devoted to producing ritually decorated objects. These sacred societies were originally devoted to porcupine quillwork embroidery, but when glass beads became available, beadworker societies based upon the same principles, appeared among some Cheyenne bands. (Coleman 1980: 62).

From nineteenth-century European historical novels, readers have learned that in elite households, when the hosts and guests retired from the dinner table, the men went off to smoke cigars and enjoy after-dinner drinks in the library, while the women settled into working on their embroidery or other needlework arts in the drawing room. Although beaded objects appeared in northern Europe as early as the mid-seventeenth century, bead embroidery became a widespread phenomenon in the late eighteenth century lasting into the late nineteenth century in Great Britain, France, and Germany, followed somewhat later by Russia. "Thousands of resourceful women in numerous European homes started laboring earnestly on various kinds of beadwork." (Yurova 2003: 5).

MEN DO BEADWORK, TOO!

Under certain circumstances or for special reasons, men do work beads in various parts of the world. For example, beads and royalty are closely linked in Africa. In the royal courts of Central and West Africa, male professional beadworkers are the only artists permitted to make beaded objects for the kings and members of the court. These master artists create splendid beaded crowns, tunics, thrones and other symbols of royal office for the king and his court (Fig. 5.7). Carey (2001: 88) suggests "the reasoning [for men doing the beadwork] may be that since royal or religious regalia are things of such power, they can only be made by men, because the power in women's bodies might have a bad effect on them, and hence on the divinity of the kingship or cult. On the other hand, women's bodies and their all-important fertility might be harmed."

During and after World War I, Turkish prisoners-of-war in British camps, particularly in Egypt and Cyprus, learned how to make small beaded objects to help pass the time and to sell to the British and Australian soldiers billeted nearby as war souvenirs, in exchange for food, cigarettes, and other items. Beadwork snakes were particularly popular with the British soldiers, who took them home as gifts for their children (Fig. 5.8).

Inmates in Turkish prisons today continue the beadwork tradition of World War I, making coin purses (Fig. 5.6), amulets to hang from automobile rearview mirrors (Fig. 5.9), and other small items. "Mostly produced by convicts who have received heavy sentences, who are away from their families, and who have limited means . . . [the] objects are generally prepared in the colors of football teams." (Celik 2007: 09.1).

In American Indian country, "North American multiple genders emerge as roles with great historical depth and continuity, with parallels in societies worldwide." (Roscoe 1998: 5). The most common of these multiple genders is that of the "two-spirit," or a Native biological male assuming the alternative gender of female. According to Roscoe (1998: 7), male two-spirits are documented in over 155 Native American tribes. Most of these tribes have their own linguistic terms for this transgender role, such as *winkte* in Lakota, which translates as "would be a woman." (DeMallie 1983: 243). Lakota winktes held institutionalized status and were identifiable by a common set of behaviors. Boys' change in gender often came to them in a dream or vision. Dreaming also endowed them with spiritual power. They dressed and behaved as women, taking on the tasks of women. Winktes were known to be exceptional quill- and beadworkers, achieving this excellence because of the power residing within them. Today, the Lakota winkte institution continues among traditional people, despite the repression by missionaries and government officials in the twentieth century. (Williams 1986: 191–200).

As a part of the lessening of the strict gender division of labor since the 1960s, throughout American Indian country, grandmothers are now teaching their male relatives to bead, if they express an interest. Marcus Dewey, Northern Arapaho, says that he beads in the traditional way as he was taught by his grandmother and mother. Dewey learned by observing his grandmother making moccasins when he was about ten years old. She wanted him to first learn to make moccasins, the hardest thing to produce. Then all other beaded items to follow would come easier. He had to make and remake the moccasins until he got them right. (Dewey 1995). Dewey now serves as a master beadworker for the Wyoming Arts Council, where apprentices work with him to learn traditional Arapaho beadwork. He beads eight to ten hours every day to fill orders for powwows and to keep the traditions alive (Fig. 5.10, Photo 5.3).

**FIG. 5.6
COIN PURSES,
1960S–70S**

Made by inmates in Turkish prisons, Central Anatolia region, Turkey

Cloth, glass beads, metal zippers, cotton thread

Various dimensions

Museum of International Folk Art, IFAF Collection, FA.2004.11.1; FA.2005.32.7, 8–11

FIG. 5.6

FIG. 5.7, *Left*
KINGS' (*OBA*) CROWNS, TWENTIETH CENTURY

Yoruba peoples, Nigeria

Cotton, glass beads

Various dimensions

Museum of International Folk Art, IFAF Collection, Gift of Diane and Sandy Besser,

FA.2003.37.41, FA.2002.49.32x, FA.2002.49.33x, FA.2006.77.19, FA. 2002.49.34

FIG. 5.8
SNAKE, 1957–70S

Made by an inmate in a Turkish prison, Central Anatolia region, Turkey

Cotton string, stuffing, glass beads

29$\frac{1}{2}$ x 1$\frac{3}{16}$ in. (75 x 3 cm)

Museum of International Folk Art, IFAF Collection, FA.2005.32.1

While made by a Turkish prisoner, this snake dates much later than the World War I examples.

FIG. 5.9
REARVIEW MIRROR AMULETS, 1960S–70S

Made by inmates in Turkish prisons, Central Anatolia region, Turkey

Cotton string, stuffing, glass beads, plastic beads, sequins

Left: 10$\frac{1}{4}$ x 5$\frac{1}{8}$ in. (26 x 13 cm); right: 6$\frac{1}{2}$ x 2$\frac{3}{4}$ in. (16.5 x 7 cm)

Museum of International Folk Art, IFAF Collection, FA.2005.32.5–6

Used as protective amulets to hang from car rearview mirrors, the inscription *mashallah* translates to "may Allah protect."

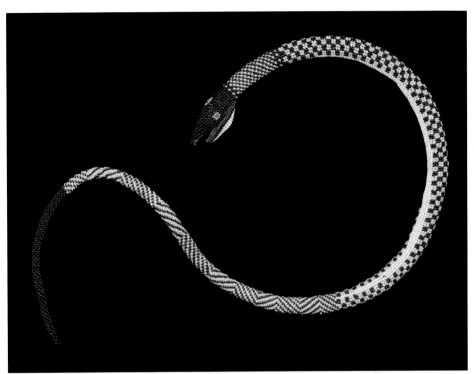

FIG. 5.8

FIG. 5.9

PHOTO 5.3

FIG. 5.11, *Opposite*
STORAGE BAGS, PAIR, EARLY TWENTY-FIRST CENTURY

Maker: Emil Her Many Horses (b. 1955) Oglala Lakota, Pine Ridge Reservation, South Dakota, USA

Elk hide, tanned deer hide, glass beads, metal sequins

Plains Indian Museum, Buffalo Bill Center of the West, Acquisitions Fund purchase, NA.106.997-998

Photograph courtesy of the artist

Working within the traditional tipi storage container form, or *parfleche*, Emil Her Many Horses has beaded a bird-and-floral design on a pair of bags. These bags were traditionally made in pairs from a single raw buffalo hide, painted with matching geometric designs. When commercial buckets and boxes became available, *parfleches* became important giveaway items at ceremonies. As a teenager, Emil Her Many Horses, currently an Associate Curator at the Smithsonian's National Museum of the American Indian, sought out an accomplished Lakota beadworker, Alice Fish, on Rosebud Reservation, asking her to teach him how to do the art form that he so admired.

PHOTO 5.3
AMY GOOD BEAR WEARING WAR SHIRT MADE BY MARCUS DEWEY, 1996

Maker: Marcus Dewey (b. 1956), Northern Arapaho peoples, Wyoming

War shirt is in the permanent collection of the Carnegie Museum of Natural History, Pittsburgh, Pennsylvania, USA

Photograph by Marsha Bol

FIG. 5.10
SADDLE, 1997

Maker: Marcus Dewey (b. 1956) Northern Arapaho, St. Stephen's, Wyoming

Wool cloth, deer hide, glass beads, metal, brass tacks

31 x 19.5 x 13.5 in. (78.4 x 14.9 x 34.3 cm)

Plains Indian Museum, Buffalo Bill Center of the West, Cody, Wyoming, USA, Museum purchase with funds provided by the Pilot Foundation, NA.403.203

Marcus Dewey uses an actual vintage McClellan saddle as the base, which he fully covers in bead embroidery. This type of saddle was used by the U.S. cavalry during the Plains Indian wars, from the end of the Civil War (1865) through the Battle of Little Big Horn (1876) until World War I. In his beadwork, Dewey depicts a mother buffalo and her calf.

FIG. 5.10

FIG. 5.11

FIG. 5.12

FIG. 5.12
NECKLACES, 2014

Maker: Rafael Cilaunime Candelario Valadez (b. 1988), Wíxaríka (Huichol)/Euro-American, Nayarit state, Mexico

Glass beads, thread

Left: 18 x 5⁷/₈ in. (45.7 x 14.9 cm); right: 16¹/₂ x 5⁵/₈ in. (41.9 x 14.3 cm)

Collection of the artist

Artist Cilau Valadez calls his necklace on the left, Grandfather Fire. He says that he based it on historic Huichol designs. On the right is his Eagle Spirit necklace. "All are reflections of our traditional arts and ceremonies," says Valadez.

PHOTO 5.4
CILAU VALADEZ WEARING HIS BEADED NECKLACE, 2013

Wíxaríka (Huichol)/Euro-American, Sayulita town, Nayarit state, Mexico

Photograph by Bob Smith, courtesy of the International Folk Art Alliance

---

Cilau Valadez excels in the traditional Huichol arts including beadwork, although he is known primarily for his yarn painting, which he learned from his master artist father, Mariano Valadez. Cilau straddles both the traditional Huichol world of the Sierra Madre Mountains in western Mexico and the outside world. With his ability to speak multiple languages and his leadership skills, he serves as an ambassador for his culture when he is abroad, sharing his heritage through his arts.

PHOTO 5.4

EMBLEMS OF SOCIAL STATUS, PRESTIGE, AND WEALTH

HOLDING A POSITION OF STATUS OR PRESTIGE WITHIN a society is generally accompanied by emblems, particularly personal regalia, which identify and legitimize such rank to other societal members. Visual elements can demarcate success in an occupation, achievement in a graded association, or prestige garnered through wealth or generosity in those societies that hold generosity as an important virtue.

As Ortner and Whitehead (1981: 18–19) point out, in the majority of traditional societies, status and prestige are gender based. "The 'public domain' or the 'sphere of wider social coordinations' is dominated by men, and it is in this domain that larger prestige structures take their shape. Simply put, the . . . prestige hierarchies of most societies are, by and large, male games. . . . Men compete for 'big man' status, and are differentiated accordingly, whereas women remain a relatively homogeneous social mass—at least from the official cultural point of view. . . . For even though both sexes participate in a designated social rank and follow behavioral codes appropriate to that rank, the feminine version of this code overwhelmingly emphasizes the woman's position" relationally, as mother, wife, or sister.

LAKOTA PRESTIGE

"In many of the societies of native North America, gender was partially fused with occupational specialization, the latter being an important arena of prestige." (Ortner and Whitehead 1981: 17).

FIG. 6.1 AND DETAIL
PIPE BAG, C. 1890

Lakota peoples, North or South Dakota, USA

Native-tanned hide, glass beads, porcupine quills, pigment

40 x 6½ in. (101.6 x 16.5 cm)

Hirschfield Family Collection, courtesy of Fighting Bear Antiques

Photograph by Garth Dowling

Both sides of the pipe bag depict a Lakota warrior with a trailing feather bonnet. On one side he carries a rifle and on the other side a sword. Above, the warrior holds his pipe and pipe bag.

FIG. 6.1 DETAIL

FIG. 6.1

Prestige was the principal goal of Lakota males during the glorious years, achievable through brave deeds, prior to social disruption by the U.S. government and military during the last quarter of the nineteenth century. As Bad Bear recalled at the turn of the twentieth century, "Every able-bodied [Lakota] boy was taught that he should become a warrior, not only in order to defend himself and his people against hostile persons, but to get honor by doing something against an enemy which required cunning and bravery. . . . Every boy was also taught that he should become a good hunter, not only in order to provide well for those depending on him, but because of the honor attached to the ability to hunt well." (Walker 1982: 27–28).

There was unlimited opportunity for a young Lakota man to advance his social position, since Lakota society had no tradition of transferring high positions through inheritance. As a result Lakota men were preoccupied with establishing their reputations among their peers. According to Iron Tail, "The ambition of an Indian is principally to be high among his fellow men, to be superior to them in killing enemies, stealing horses, owning a fast horse . . ." (Walker 1982: 34).

Once a Lakota man's reputation was established, there was no guarantee that it would last without continued good deeds plus verbal and visual reminders of his warrior/hunter successes. A warrior had the right to publicly recount his exploits in battle, wear warbonnets (Figs. 6.4 and 6.5) and other insignia that represented his achievements, and paint visual records documenting his heroic deeds upon his clothing and tipi. Painted scenes of historic hunting and war events in a pictorial style displayed men and their horses engaged in a narrative of action scenes scattered over the ground of the hide. These served as institutionalized forms of publicity that were always before the public eye, constantly reinforcing the reputation of the owner.

At the end of the Plains Indian wars, culminating in the Battle of Little Big Horn in 1876, the U.S. government outlawed activities providing cultural-affirming status and prestige. Even though there were no longer buffalo or other game to hunt, nor war parties venturing out, the Lakota people found other ways to sustain their tribal values of male prestige and status. Lakota women supported the male tradition of prestige, assuming the tradition of depicting hunting and warfare scenes on their male relatives' clothing and pipe bags in the female medium of beads in the late nineteenth and early twentieth centuries. (Figs. 6.3 and 6.1).

FIG. 6.2

FIG. 6.2
LANCE CASE, C. 1890

Crow peoples, Montana, USA

Native-tanned hide, rawhide, wool, glass beads

47 x 26 in. (119.4 x 66 cm)

Hirschfield Family Collection, courtesy of Fighting Bear Antiques

Photograph by Garth Dowling

Crow women beaded handsome lance cases for their warrior relatives in the typical Crow beadwork colors and design.

FIG. 6.3A

FIG. 6.3B

**FIGS. 6.3A (FRONT) AND B (BACK)
SCOUT COAT, C. 1900**

Lakota peoples, North or South Dakota, USA

Native-tanned hide, glass beads, pigment

30 x 23 in. (76.2 x 58.4 cm)

Hirschfield Family Collection, courtesy of Fighting Bear Antiques

Photograph by Garth Dowling

The beadworker depicted various exploits of the wearer on the jacket, including (on the front) two Lakota warriors on horseback wearing feather headdresses and wielding lances, a bullet hole with blood dripping, two Crow warriors (identifiable by their hairstyle) with rifles, and (on the back) two mounted Lakota warriors wearing buffalo horn headdresses and bearing lances, two Crow warriors with a bow and a pistol, and a buffalo.

FIG. 6.5

FIG. 6.4

FIG. 6.4
HORNED HEADDRESS WITH FEATHER TRAILER,
LATE NINETEENTH CENTURY

Lakota peoples, North or South Dakota, USA

Native-tanned hide, wool, cotton, horsehair, silk, ermine skin, eagle feathers, owl? feathers, buffalo horn, glass beads

62½ x 18 x 10 in. (158.75 x 45.72 x 25.4 cm)

Museum of International Folk Art, Gift of Florence Dibell Bartlett, A.1955.1.899 AW

FIG. 6.5
FEATHER BONNET, LATE NINETEENTH CENTURY

Cheyenne peoples, Wyoming, USA

Native-tanned hide, wool, horsehair, ermine skin, eagle feathers, glass beads

39 x 19 x 28 in. (99 x 48 x 71 cm)

Museum of International Folk Art, Gift of Florence Dibell Bartlett, A.1955.1.187 AW

Oglala Lakota elders told Dr. Walker in 1912: "Only braves of renown were permitted to wear the warbonnet, the [eagle feather] pendant indicating greater renown. . . . Only those who have accomplished much are entitled to wear the buffalo horns; . . . only those who are very cunning are entitled to wear the weasel [ermine] skins." (Walker 1980: 223, 276).

FIG. 6.6A

MARKERS OF STATUS ELSEWHERE

FIGS. 6.6A (SHIRT), B (LEGGINGS), AND C (DETAIL)
WEASEL-TAIL SHIRT AND LEGGINGS, C. 1890

Blackfeet peoples, Montana, USA, or Alberta, Canada

Native-tanned hide, ermine, wool, glass beads, pigment,
feathers

Shirt: 37 x 65⅜ in. (94 x 166 cm); leggings: 34 x 12 in.
(86.5 x 30.5 cm)

Museum of International Folk Art, Gift of Florence Dibell
Bartlett, A.1955.1.936 a–b

FIG. 6.6B

FIG. 6.6C

This special shirt and leggings made for a Blackfeet man of high
status is trimmed in a beaded disc and bands with tails and pelts
of black-tipped ermine (winter coat of a weasel). The shirt and
leggings have painted designs, which may be either bullets flying
or tadpoles, generally symbolizing the power of the tadpole to
transform itself into a frog. A fine outfit like this one was often made
as a result of instructions received by a Blackfeet warrior in a dream.
It was considered the owner's personal medicine, which imparted
supernatural power to him on the battlefield. (Ewers 1958: 118). The
beaded strips on the leggings may have been replaced at a later date.

FIG. 6.7 DETAIL

FIG. 6.7

**FIG. 6.7 AND DETAIL
WARRIOR'S TUNIC (*LUKUS
RUMOAN*), PRE-1895**

Atayal peoples, northern
Taiwan

Hemp, ramie, giant clamshell
(*Tridacna*) beads

39 3/8 x 17 11/16 in. (100 x
45 cm)

Museum of International Folk
Art, IFAF Collection, Gift
of Julia Meech and Andrew
Pekarik in honor of Nucy
Meech, FA.1986.539.86

Photographs by Addison
Doty

**FIGS. 6.8A (FRONT) AND B (BACK)
WARRIOR'S TUNIC (*LUKUS RUMOAN*), 1850–1875**

Atayal peoples, northern Taiwan

Raveled wool, cotton, hemp, giant clamshell
(*Tridacna*) beads

38 1/2 x 18 in. (98 x 46 cm)

Museum of International Folk Art, Gift of Lloyd
E. Cotsen and the Neutrogena Corporation,
A.1995.93.714

Photographs by Pat Pollard

Only an accomplished Atayal warrior/headhunter
had the right to wear this tunic during the
welcoming-of-the-heads ceremony. Its conspicuous
display of thousands of shell beads, traded in from
the coast, demonstrated the warrior's status and
prestige. Made from cloth woven on a backstrap
loom by an Atayal weaver, both headhunting
and weaving were banned during the Japanese
occupation of Taiwan from 1895 to 1945. (Sumberg
2010: 145).

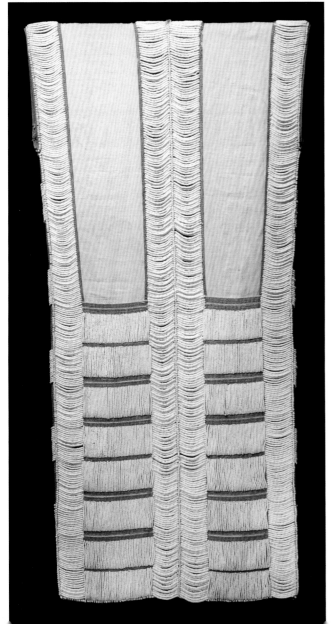

FIG. 6.8A

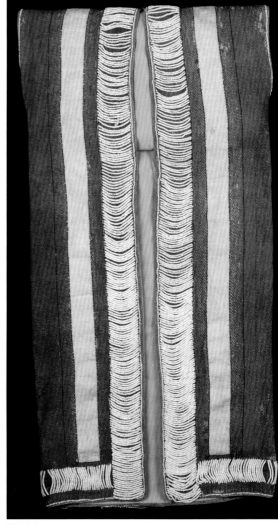

FIG. 6.8B

133

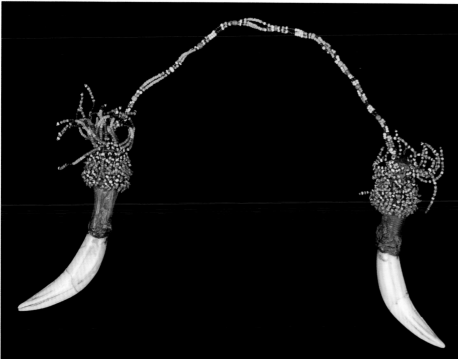

FIG. 6.9

FIG. 6.9
MAN'S EAR ORNAMENTS, TWENTIETH CENTURY

Kelabit peoples, Bario highlands, Sarawak state, Borneo island, Malaysia

Wood, fiber, leopards' teeth, glass beads

17 in. (40.3 cm)

David McLanahan Collection

In the past, as a sign of their status and hunting prowess, middle-aged Kelabit men perforated the upper lobe of their ears to wear a pair of leopard teeth attached by a string of beads worn behind their head.

FIG. 6.10
BELT DANGLE, TWENTIETH CENTURY

Iban peoples, Sarawak state, Borneo island, Malaysia

Cotton, fiber, glass beads

James Barker Collection

This dangle was used as a counterweight worn on the right side of a headhunter's belt to balance his knife on the left side of his belt. Headhunting was a practice of intertribal warfare until the early twentieth century. "The young [Iban] men's need for spectacular achievement contributed to the proliferation of feuds and intertribal warfare. They were known as Borneo's most inveterate headhunters." (Munan 2005: 19).

FIG. 6.11
WARRIOR'S CEREMONIAL SEAT MAT, EARLY TWENTIETH CENTURY

Maloh peoples, West Kalimantan province, Borneo island, Indonesia

Rattan, cotton, glass beads, buttons, orangutan hair, metal

Museum of International Folk Art, IFAF Collection, Gift of Sandy and Diane Besser, FA.2003.37.55

The seat mat hangs down behind the loincloth, ready to protect its wearer if he has to sit on damp or uncomfortable ground.

FIG. 6.12, *Opposite*
WAR DANCE CAP, TWENTIETH CENTURY

Kayan peoples, Orang Ulu group, Kalimantan region, Borneo island, Indonesia

Wood, glass beads, goat hair, hornbill and other feathers

14 x 29 in. (35.6 x 73.7 cm)

David McLanahan Collection

This hat continues to be called a "war" cap even though warfare ceased in the early twentieth century. Today the cap, with its tufts of goat hair and monumental feathers, is worn in festivals and weddings by both men and women.

FIG. 6.10

FIG. 6.11

FIG. 6.12

FIG. 6.13
CEREMONIAL SWORD
DANGLE, N.D.

Iban peoples, Sarawak state,
Borneo island, Malaysia

Hornbill beaks, glass beads,
organic, metal beads and bells

40 x 9 x 3½ in. (101.6 x 22.9 x
8.9 cm)

David McLanahan Collection

The magnificent warrior's
ceremonial sword ornament
is meant to dangle from the
carved handle of a sword. This
exceptionally elaborate example
has two hornbill casques creating
the infrastructure, the top casque
ornamented with fringes of
beads and bells, which cover the
lower one.

FIG. 6.13

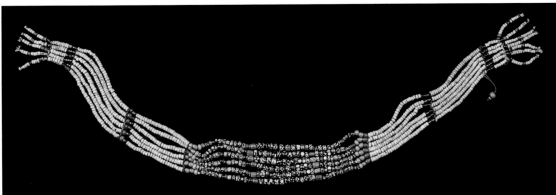

FIG. 6.14 AND DETAIL
CHIEF'S BELT, NINETEENTH
CENTURY OR EARLIER

Orang Ulu peoples, Kalimantan
region, Borneo island, Indonesia

Glass beads, organic

41 x 3 in. (104.1 x 7.6 cm)

David McLanahan Collection

Orang Ulu peoples, who were once highly stratified societies,
continue to value their heirloom beads. These beads are indicators
of wealth and confer status. Possession of fine old beads, such as
the multiple strands in the chief's belt, indicates high status. The
"yellow doughnut," or lavang, beads on the left and right sides of
the belt, have important ritual value. (Munan 2005:74).

Women carefully protect their beads, taking them with them
wherever they go, highly conscious of their family history and age.
On occasion they will take out their beads to display for visitors.

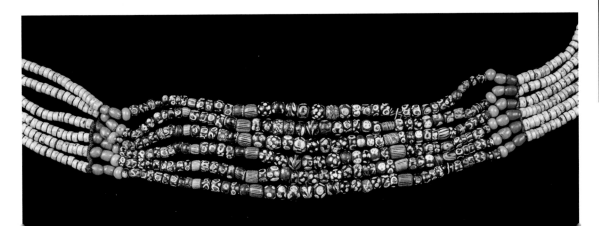

FIG. 6.15

PHOTO 6.1
WARRIOR WEARING
HIS PRIZED EARRINGS
(*BATLING*), C. 1912

Ilongot peoples, northern
Luzon, Philippines

National Geographic
magazine, 1912, volume
23, number 9

Only Ilongot men who
had taken heads in
headhunting had the right
to wear these prestigious
earrings from their upper
earlobes. In wearing these
earrings, they proclaimed
their hunting prowess.
No eligible unmarried
girl would consider
marrying a young man
who didn't have a pair
of these earrings.

PHOTO 6.1

FIG. 6.15
BIRD JACKET (*BAJU MANEK*),
EARLY TWENTIETH CENTURY

Iban peoples, Sarawak state, Borneo island, Malaysia

Cotton, wool, metal, glass beads

25½ x 17¼ in. (64.8 x 43.8 cm)

David McLanahan Collection

This highly decorated jacket was worn by men of
status—chiefs and shamans.

FIG. 6.16
WARRIOR'S EARRINGS
(*BATLING*), EARLY
TWENTIETH CENTURY

Ilongot peoples, northern
Luzon, Philippines

Red hornbill beak, brass,
mother-of-pearl shell

9 in. (23 cm)

Shari and Earl Kessler
Collection

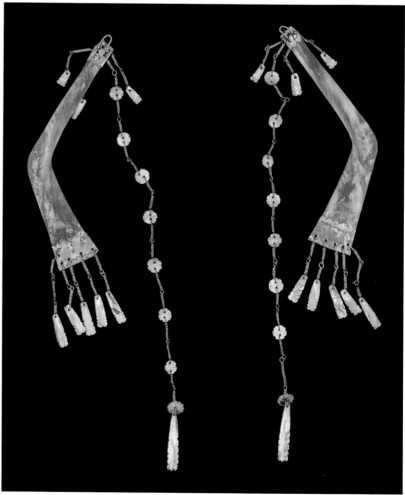

FIG. 6.16

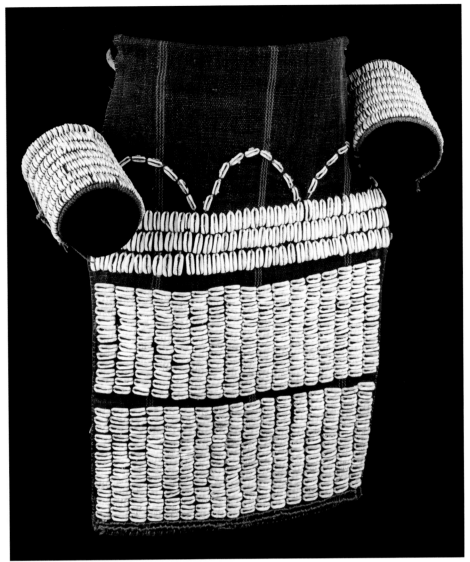

FIG. 6.17
HEADHUNTER'S NECKLACES, PRE-1940

Konyak Naga peoples, Nagaland, northeast India

Brass, glass beads, goat hair, conch shell

Brass heads: 11$^{1}/_{2}$ x 4$^{1}/_{2}$ in. (29 x 11.5 cm); blue beads: 22$^{6}/_{8}$ in. (58 cm); red beads: 10$^{1}/_{2}$ in. (26.5 cm)

Harry and Tiala M. Neufeld Collection

"Nagas are one of the most complexly ornamented tribes of the world. . . . The autocratic Konyaks readily pile ornaments one of top of the other," as one researcher says. (Kanungo 2007: 14.19). Even so, most ornaments may only be worn by those who have earned that right. Still into the 1950s, every Naga male held the ambition to take a head of an enemy, even though it had long been illegal to headhunt. A brass head, or multiple heads, worn on the chest indicated that the wearer was a successful headhunter, which brought him glory and status as a great warrior and prosperity to his village. Adding a fringe of red-dyed goat's hair (here tied to the end of the blue beads) to his ornaments also attested to his status as a headhunter. With human headhunting no longer an option, Nagas substituted the taking of tigers' heads in lieu of human heads as an option entitling a hunter to wear the same ornaments.

FIG. 6.18
MAN'S APRON AND PAIR OF WRISTLETS, PRE-1940

Ao Naga peoples, Nagaland, northeast India

Cotton, cowrie shells, plant fiber, cane

Apron: 17$^{1}/_{5}$ x 12$^{2}/_{5}$ in. (43.7 x 31.5 cm); wristlets: 3.9 x 2.4 in. (10 x 6 cm)

Harry and Tiala M. Neufeld Collection

In the past among Naga people, a man might elect to host a Feast of Merit to increase his prestige in his community. "The Feast converts material wealth (the cattle and rice for rice-beer) into social rank." (Jacobs 2012: 77). To achieve the highest rank, a Naga man must give multiple feasts of ever-increasing scale and cost, with completion of each stage carrying the rights to wear distinguishing personal adornment.

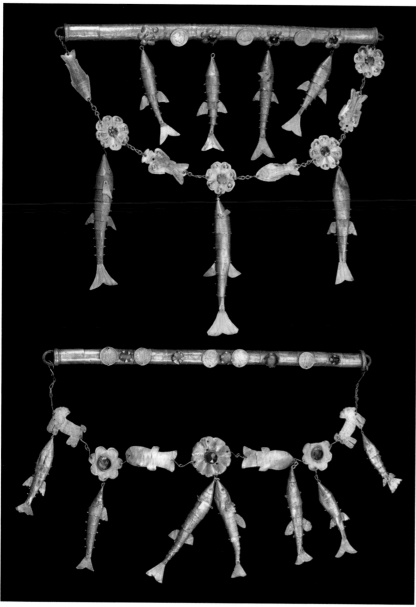

FIG. 6.19

FIG. 6.20A

FIG. 6.20B

FIG. 6.19
DANCE STAFFS, MID-TWENTIETH CENTURY

La Paz department, Bolivia

Silver, glass beads

Top: 16 1/2 x 18 in. (42 x 45.7 cm); bottom: 15 5/8 x 7 in. (39.7 x 17.8 cm)

Museum of International Folk Art, top: Gift of the Girard Foundation Collection, A.1980.2.179; bottom: Gift of David R. Thornburg, A.1977.5.1

Throughout Latin America, religious feast days are sponsored by couples elected annually from among the community. Sponsorship conveys status to the couple but entails a great deal of time, effort, and expense on their part. The sponsors are supported in their responsibilities with contributions of work and funds by their extended family. These dance staffs identify festival sponsors, who carry them, in the Lake Titicaca area. The articulated fish refer to the importance of fish in the lake.

FIGS. 6.20A (FRONT) AND B (BACK)
WOMAN'S HEADDRESS, N.D.

Chahar peoples, Inner Mongolia Autonomous Region, People's Republic of China

Cotton, silver, stone, coral beads, turquoise beads

22 3/16 x 7 1/16 x 6 5/16 in. (58 x 18 x 16 cm)

Museum of International Folk Art, Gift of Sharon Sharpe, A.2016.64.1

Worn by a Chahar woman on special occasions, this elaborate coral headdress is emblematic of her status and wealth in her society.

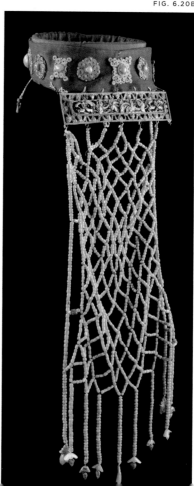

FIG. 6.21
MAN'S SOCIETY HAT (*MUKUBA WA BIFUNGO*), 1950S

Lega peoples, Democratic Republic of the Congo

Raffia fiber, elephant tail hair, buttons

6$^{11}/_{16}$ x 7 in. (17 x 18 cm)

Sara and David Lieberman Collection

Photograph by Craig Smith

Among the Lega people, this hat identifies its wearer as having been initiated into the highest grade level, called *kindi*, in the ranked *bwami* society. Very few Lega men ever attain this great achievement. "The elephant tail on the hat is its single most important part: it symbolically associates the *kindi* initiate with the calm power but potentially explosive fierceness of the elephant." (Biebuyck and Van den Abbeele 1984: 35).

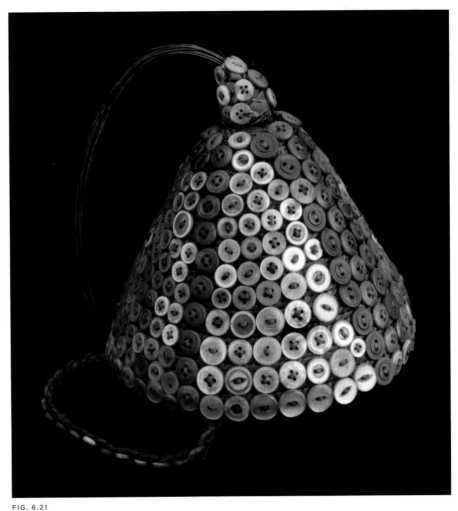

FIG. 6.21

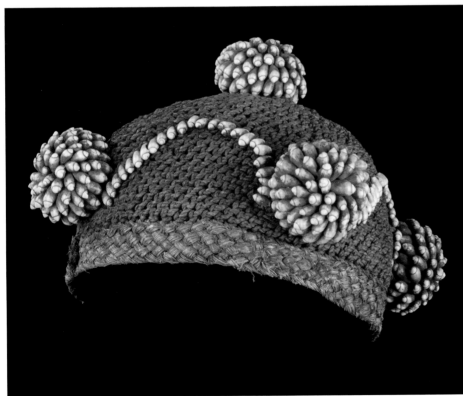

FIG. 6.22

FIG. 6.22
CHIEF'S HAT (*MPU A NZIM*), TWENTIETH CENTURY

Mbala peoples, southwest Democratic Republic of the Congo

Raffia, cowrie shells

6 x 9$^{1}/_{2}$ in. (15.2 x 24.1 cm)

Museum of International Folk Art, Gift of Lloyd E. Cotsen and the Neutrogena Corporation, A.1995.93.254

Cowrie shells are ornaments of status and prestige on this traditional hat worn by a Mbala chief or headman of a landowning group.

FIG. 6.23

FIG. 6.24

PHOTO 6.2
TWO MEN DRESSED IN PAIRS OF
BANDOLIER BAGS, C. 1900

Anishinabe (Chippewa) peoples, Mille
Lacs, Minnesota

State Historical Society of Wisconsin,
WHS-124296

FIG. 6.23
BANDOLIER BAG, C. 1900

Anishinabe (Chippewa) peoples, Minnesota or
Wisconsin, USA

Cotton, wool, glass beads

40 x 14 in. (101.6 x 35.6 cm)

Museum of Indian Arts and Culture/Laboratory of
Anthropology, 1638/12

FIG. 6.24
BANDOLIER BAG, C. 1900

Anishinabe (Chippewa) peoples, Minnesota or
Wisconsin, USA

Cotton, wool, glass beads

45 x 17¹/₂ in. (114 x 44 cm)

Museum of Indian Arts and Culture/Laboratory of
Anthropology, Gift of I.W. Schormoyer, 26374/12

Anishinabe (Chippewa) men (and sometimes women) were unmistakable when wearing enormous bandolier bags, sometimes two or three at a time, around the turn of the twentieth century (Photo 6.2). Curiously, these "bags" often had no opening, hence they were not intended for functional use.

"Wealth garnered through success in the fur trade had value only to the extent that it could be transformed into outward signs of that success, signs that could be worn upon the body or by those associated with the successful. Fashion that incorporated trade materials [such as glass beads], therefore, represented the wealth and high standing of participants of the fur trade in the most direct and fundamental way." (Penney, Phillips, and Wooley 1990: 13). In addition to those exhibiting their success in the fur trade, wearers of these bags may have been recipients of a fine bag at a giveaway ceremony, thereby demonstrating the host's generosity and enhancing his prestige.

The Anishinabe women who embroidered these bags learned the floral designs in mission schools' embroidery classes, making the switch from their former rectilinear designs to organic designs derived from nature. The floral designs often included the four stages of the life cycle of plants—seed, leaf, bud, and fruit (Fig. 6.24). (Penney in Pohrt 1996: 8).

FIG. 6.25A

FIG. 6.25C

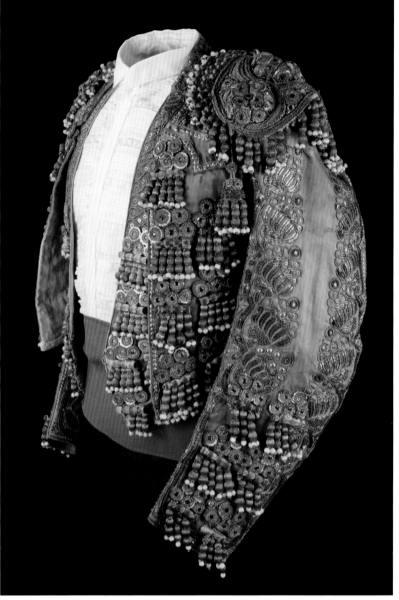

FIG. 6.25B

FIGS. 6.25A (FRONT), B (SIDE), AND C (BACK)
MATADOR'S COSTUME, C. 1888

Maker: Navarro Perpinan, Madrid, Spain

Silk, glass beads, sequins, gold and silver thread

Jacket: $25^{1}/_4$ x $27^{3}/_8$ x $13^{3}/_4$ in. (64 x 69 x 35 cm)

Museum of International Folk Art, IFAF Collection, FA.1962.22.1a–i

Some occupations, such as a matador in Spain, are considered heroes in their culture. A matador's ornate clothing flashes with sparkle, shine, and color to attract the bull.

SYMBOLS OF
LEADERSHIP

N HIERARCHICAL SOCIETIES, PARAMOUNT LEADERS, SUCH as kings, queens, and emperors, make themselves visible through lavish art objects, especially regalia, which uphold their supreme positions. Fraser and Cole (1972: 303–15) have identified some general principles of the arts associated with leadership:

1. **Visibility & Contrast:** "A basic function of these arts, then, is to set off in many ways (including aesthetically) the elite from common people . . . Personal regalia, elaborate . . . furnishings, and various objects used by leaders render them more conspicuous and thus enhance their superior status and power to control" (p. 309). This often entails elevating leaders above their subjects via a chair, stool, or litter.

2. **Elaboration:** The garments and other objects owned by leaders are quite elaborate, often with a profusion of detail, much more so than those owned by their subjects.

3. **Elite materials and iconography:** Leaders' art objects are made from relatively scarce materials, which the leaders often control, requiring specialized techniques of manufacture, and are imbued with iconography and symbols that are reserved for the leader.

4. **Embody the past:** Regal art objects often give tangible form to a culture's history, by connecting to origin stories, ancestors, and supernatural forces.

Glass beads, as trade items from Europe, are an example of elite materials that were under the complete control of the Zulu kings in South Africa. Dingiswayo, who formed the Zulu empire at the end of the eighteenth century and mentored young Shaka Zulu, established a monopoly over imported glass beads, and death was the punishment should any Zulu subject infringe upon his royal prerogative. Shaka Zulu followed suit by decreeing that only he and those chosen by him were permitted to wear glass beads. This monopoly continued through Shaka Zulu's successors until the 1850s.

Elsewhere in Africa, "beadwork of various sorts also seems to be an elite medium, particularly in the Cameroons, where it overlies many sorts of objects used by the nobility, and in Yorubaland, where beaded crowns are the most significant single emblem of divine kingship. Bead appliqués are found also on masks worn by dancers among the highly centralized Kuba peoples. Most of these masks function in court-associated roles." (Fraser and Cole 1972: 304). In all of these cases, the royal beaded objects are made by male professional beadworkers.

YORUBA KINGSHIP

All Yoruba people today accept that only direct descendants of Oduduwa, the first Yoruba king, are entitled to be crowned as kings or *obas*. Only they have the right

FIG. 7.1 AND DETAIL, *Opposite*
OBA'S GREAT CROWN (*ADENLA*), 1920S

Yoruba peoples, southwest Nigeria

Palm ribs armature (*pako*), cornstarch (*eko*), cotton, glass beads, thread

45 x 9 in. (114 x 22.9 cm)

Museum of International Folk Art, Museum of New Mexico Foundation Collections Purchase Fund, A.2014.49.1

Photograph courtesy of Douglas Dawson Gallery

This great crown has an unusual addition of three spires sprouting from the cone and topped by birds. This form is similar to examples found in the oba's collection in the town of Okuku, although which oba commissioned this crown is unknown.

FIG. 7.1

to wear the beaded regal dress and accompanying accoutrements. (Beier 1982:5). According to the generally accepted Yoruba origin myth, Olodumare (the supreme deity) sent Oduduwa down from the spirit world to create land. Oduduwa founded Ile-Ife, the first Yoruba town on land. There he had seven sons (some say sixteen) to whom he gave each a beaded crown with instructions to go out and found their own kingdoms. Today the Yoruba people are the third largest ethnic group in Nigeria, residing mainly in the southwestern region, where they are mostly urban dwellers.

According to the Yoruba belief system, the king's divine powers emanate from his head. Hence his crown is considered the most powerful object of his regalia. When the oba wears the crown, he embodies divinity. The conical-shaped beaded crown (*adenla*, translated as "big crown heavy with power") with its veil of beaded strands (Fig. 7.1) is the prime symbol of Yoruba divine kingship. The oba only rarely wears this crown, limiting its use to state occasions, such as his own coronation, ceremonial festivals, and conferment of titles and judgments. So powerful is the crown, imbued with the royal ancestral spirit, that it can serve as a material substitute for the king by being placed on the throne, where his subjects must observe the same protocols as if the king were present.

Traditional Yoruba beaded crowns must include three elements: 1) the veil, 2) frontal face/s in relief, and 3) one or more three-dimensional birds. The veil gives the crown its highest degree of efficacy. It shields the king's countenance from public view, thereby diminishing his individuality and linking him with his ancestors and all of their accompanying divine power. (Thompson 1970: 10, 16; Beier 1982: 24–26).

Many obas believe that the frontal face, or faces, represents the first Yoruba king, Oduduwa, thereby linking the king wearing the crown to his ancestors. The bird/s represents the royal bird, *okin*, a small bird with a white tail feather. On some crowns, actual okin tail feathers are attached to the pinnacle beaded bird (Photo 7.1). While there are many Yoruba stories about the symbolism of the birds, Thompson (1970: 78) suggests that: "the birds symbolize the . . . communication with the gods, with the spirits of departed kings, and with the king himself in full ancestral panoply."

When making a crown commissioned by the oba, the professional crown maker always works in the oba's palace. He must make sacrifices to the appropriate deities to insure that his work will succeed. A number of crowns were made of solidly beaded, coral tubular beads (Fig. 7.2), likely introduced by Portuguese traders. The coral comes from the Mediterranean Sea. All red coral beads belong to the oba, appearing mainly on his crowns and sometimes on his clothing.

When the king attends to daily secular matters and minor occasions, he wears an informal coronet (*orikogbofo*, which translates as "head must not be bare"). These coronets likely originated when obas began to have more contact with Europeans. Nigeria was officially a British colony from 1900 to 1960, although British control began much earlier. Indeed many of the coronets are modeled on

FIG. 7.1 DETAIL

PHOTO 7.1
OBA ADEMUWAGUN ADESIDA II, IN THE COURTYARD OF HIS PALACE, 1959

Akure, Nigeria

Eliot Elisofon Photographic Archives, National Museum of African Art, Smithsonian Institution, EEPA

Photograph by Eliot Elisofon, EECL 2071

the British crown (Figs. 7.4, 7.5, and 7.6) and other judicial (Fig. 7.8 and Photo 7.3) or ecclesiastic forms (Figs. 7.9 and 7.10), plus they incorporate European designs and motifs mixed with typical Yoruba designs. Although these coronets are not sacred, they are still made for the oba, who may own several different styles by professional crown makers.

When wearing the great crown, in his elevated state of power and separation from the mundane world, an oba's feet must not touch the ground. Beaded shoes and footstools, one for each foot, serve to prevent his feet from touching the earth (Photo 7.1 and Fig. 7.14). He is dressed in a magnificent robe and often holds his staff of office (Fig. 7.15) or his fly whisk (Figs. 7.16 and 7.17) in his right hand.

FIG. 7.2

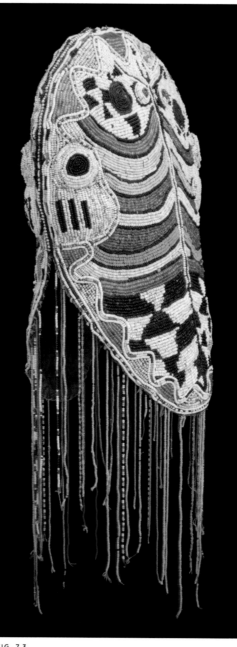

FIG. 7.3

FIG. 7.2
OBA'S CORAL CROWN, EARLY TWENTIETH CENTURY

Yoruba peoples, southwest Nigeria

Palm ribs armature, cornstarch cotton, coral beads, thread

15 3/8 x 7 1/2 in. (39 x 19 cm)

Sara and David Lieberman Collection

Photograph by Craig Smith

This crown bears a remarkable resemblance to an ancient coral crown that is depicted in Uli Beier's book, *Yoruba Beaded Crowns* (1982:29), although this crown no longer has its veil or pinnacle birds.

FIG. 7.3
OBA'S CROWN, MID-TWENTIETH CENTURY

Yoruba peoples, southwest Nigeria

Cotton, glass beads

22 3/8 x 9 7/8 x 5 1/2 in. (57 x 25 x 14 cm)

Sara and David Lieberman Collection

Photograph by Craig Smith

This unusual crown resembles a flattened conical great crown. With its veil, it too can be worn by the oba for ritual occasions.

FIG. 7.4

FIG. 7.6

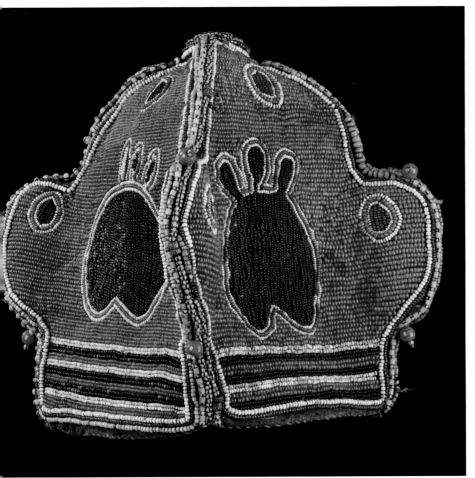

FIG. 7.5

FIG. 7.4
OBA'S BRITISH CROWN-STYLE CORONET, MID-TWENTIETH CENTURY

Yoruba peoples, Nigeria

Cotton, glass beads

Diameter: 6 in. (16 cm)

Museum of International Folk Art, IFAF Collection, Gift of Diane and Sandy Besser, FA.2002.49.35

Although this coronet takes the form of a British-style crown, it still has the typical Yoruba beaded birds, frontal faces, and fringe attachment.

FIG. 7.5
OBA'S BRITISH CROWN-STYLE CORONET, C. 1930

Yoruba peoples, southwest Nigeria

Cotton, glass beads

8^{11}/$_{16}$ x 5^{7}/$_{8}$ x 7^{7}/$_{8}$ in. (22 x 15 x 20 cm)

Museum of International Folk Art, IFAF Collection, Gift of Diane and Sandy Besser, FA.2006.77.6

FIG. 7.6
OBA'S BRITISH CROWN-STYLE CORONET, EARLY TWENTIETH CENTURY

Yoruba peoples, southwest Nigeria

Cotton, glass beads

7^{1}/$_{8}$ x 6^{7}/$_{8}$ in. (18 x 17.5 cm)

Sara and David Lieberman Collection

Photograph by Craig Smith

The coronet imitates the designs, jewels, and top projection of a British crown in glass beads.

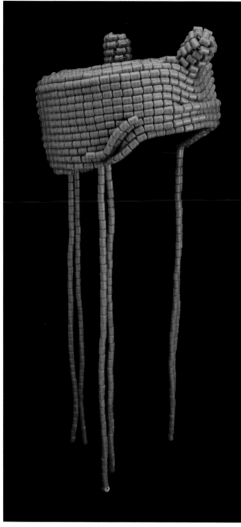

FIG. 7.7

PHOTO 7.2

PHOTO 7.3

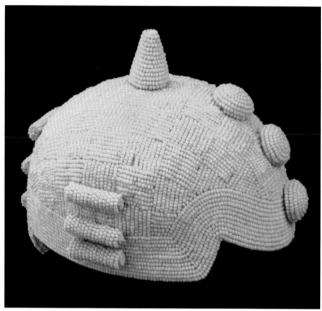

FIG. 7.8

FIG. 7.7
OBA'S CORAL CORONET,
TWENTIETH CENTURY

Yoruba peoples, southwest Nigeria

Cotton, coral beads

23$\frac{1}{4}$ x 9 x 9$\frac{7}{8}$ in. (59 x 23 x 25 cm)

Sara and David Lieberman Collection

Photograph by Craig Smith

PHOTO 7.2
SIR ADESOJI ADEREMI, OONI OF
IFE, 1959

Ife, Nigeria

Eliot Elisofon Photographic Archives,
National Museum of African Art,
Smithsonian Institution, EEPA

Photograph by Eliot Elisofon, EECL
02119

"Ooni" is the title for the oba in Ile-Ife,
the legendary cultural center of the
Yoruba people. He wears a coral
coronet and, as is traditional, he is
shaded by a large umbrella held by a
retainer. In the past, umbrellas were
associated only with royalty, who
prohibited their use by commoners.

PHOTO 7.3
DICKOLA OGUNDERE, CROWN COUNSEL AT THE
FEDERAL LEGAL DEPARTMENT, 1959

Lagos, Nigeria

Eliot Elisofon Photographic Archives, National
Museum of African Art, Smithsonian Institution,
EEPA

Photograph by Eliot Elisofon, EECL 01930

Crown counsel Ogundere, wearing a traditional
British barrister's wig, is a Yoruba from Ibadan and
has the traditional Yoruba facial scars.

FIG. 7.8
OBA'S "BARRISTER'S WIG" CORONET,
TWENTIETH CENTURY

Yoruba peoples, southwest Nigeria

Cotton, glass beads

8$\frac{1}{4}$ x 6$\frac{5}{8}$ x 5$\frac{7}{8}$ in. (21 x 17 x 15 cm)

Sara and David Lieberman Collection

Photograph by Craig Smith

The oba wears this look-alike barrister's wig
coronet, similar in all but the brilliant color, Yoruba
top projection, and three frontal disks, when he
performs opening ceremonies for local courts, or
attends other openings and social occasions.

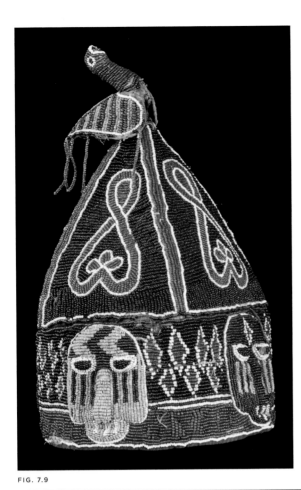

FIG. 7.9

FIG. 7.9
OBA'S MITER-TYPE
CORONET, EARLY
TWENTIETH CENTURY

Yoruba peoples,
southwest Nigeria

Cotton, glass beads

12³/₁₆ x 7¹/₁₆ in. (31 x
18 cm)

Museum of
International Folk Art,
Gift of Diane and Sandy
Besser, FA.2006.77.5

The miter, based on a
Catholic bishop's miter
model, is another prev-
alent coronet shape
fashioned by Yoruba
crown makers, who
also included frontal
faces and placed a bird
on its pinnacle.

FIG. 7.10
OBA'S MITER-TYPE CORONET, TWENTIETH
CENTURY

Yoruba peoples, southwest Nigeria

Cotton, glass beads

8¹/₄ x 7¹/₈ in. (21 x 18 cm)

Sara and David Lieberman Collection

Photography by Craig Smith

This miter-type coronet is decorated with an
interlace pattern that is often found on the great
crowns. Some Yorubas interpret this pattern as
two snakes intertwined, biting each other's tails,
to form an unbroken design. As Beier (1982: 31)
suggests: This design "most likely symbolize[s]
eternity: each end becomes another beginning.
Thus the interlace pattern can be understood as
the perfect image of royalty, each individual king
being only a part of the unending and eternal
royal beings . . . "

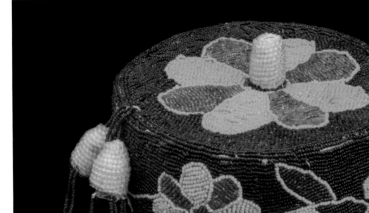

FIG. 7.11
OBA'S PILLBOX-TYPE CORONET,
TWENTIETH CENTURY

Yoruba peoples, southwest Nigeria

Cotton, glass beads

4¹/₄ x 7¹/₈ in. (11 x 18 cm)

Sara and David Lieberman
Collection

Photograph by Craig Smith

This coronet, like so many others, has
a projection from the top. Margaret
Drewal (1977: 44) has investigated
these projections, concluding that
"these projections from the head are
visualizations of the vital force that
resides inside." Even on the oba's daily
coronets, these projections appear,
indicating the divine power of the oba,
who is the link to the royal ancestors.

FIG. 7.12

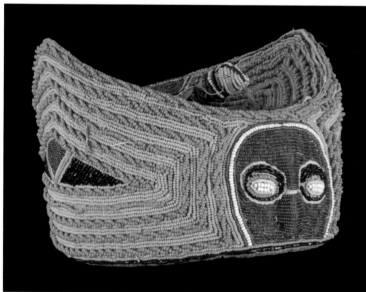

FIG. 7.13

FIG. 7.14

FIG. 7.12
OBA'S PILLBOX-TYPE CORONET, MID-TWENTIETH
CENTURY

Yoruba peoples, southwest Nigeria

Cotton, glass beads

8 x 9 in. (20.3 x 22.86 cm)

Museum of International Folk Art, IFAF Collection, Gift
of Diane and Sandy Besser, FA.2002.49.34

The birds on the top of this coronet are ingeniously
integrated into the design, accompanied by short bead
fringe and frontal faces.

FIG. 7.13
OBA'S CORONET, TWENTIETH CENTURY

Yoruba peoples, southwest Nigeria

Cotton, glass beads

5$\frac{1}{8}$ x 7$\frac{7}{8}$ in. (13 x 20 cm)

Museum of International Folk Art, IFAF Collection, Gift
of Diane and Sandy Besser, FA.2006.77.7

This European-style coronet in a vibrant color has
Yoruba frontal faces and a bird barely visible on top.

FIG. 7.14
OBA'S ROYAL FOOTSTOOL (*TIMUTIMU*), TWENTIETH
CENTURY

Yoruba peoples, southwest Nigeria

Cotton, fiber, glass beads

8$\frac{1}{2}$ x 17$\frac{1}{4}$ in. (21.6 x 43.8 cm)

The Field Museum, 271773

Photograph by Diane Alexander White

This royal footstool is embellished with the image of a
turtle or lizard and the zigzag, a design associated with
royal power, perhaps representing the power of the snake.

FIG. 7.15 AND DETAIL, *Opposite*
OBA'S ROYAL STAFF (*OPA*), MID-TWENTIETH
CENTURY

Yoruba peoples, southwest Nigeria

Wood, cotton, iron, glass beads

61$\frac{13}{16}$ x 7$\frac{1}{4}$ in. (157 x 18.4 cm)

Museum of International Folk Art, IFAF Collection, Gift
of Diane and Sandy Besser, FA.2006.77.18

The oba's staff, which he holds on occasion when in
state, can serve as his surrogate when he is not present,
much like his great crown. The staff must remain upright
at all times until the oba dies, when it may be laid on the
ground. Surmounted by a horse, the top of the staff has
a small veil reminiscent of the great crown.

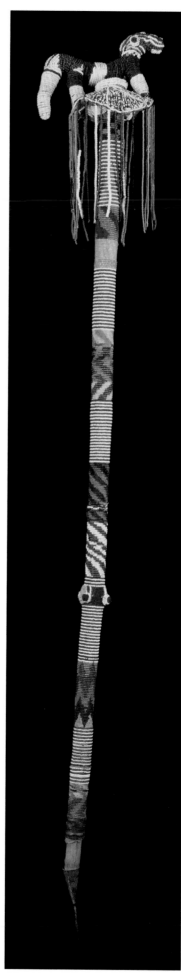

FIG. 7.15

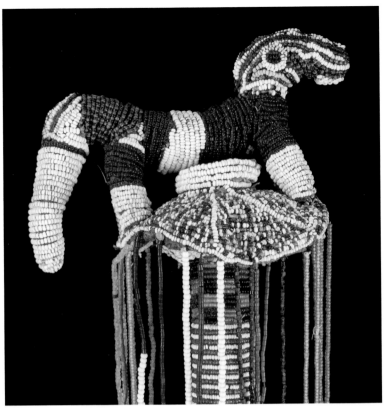

FIG. 7.15 DETAIL

FIG. 7.17

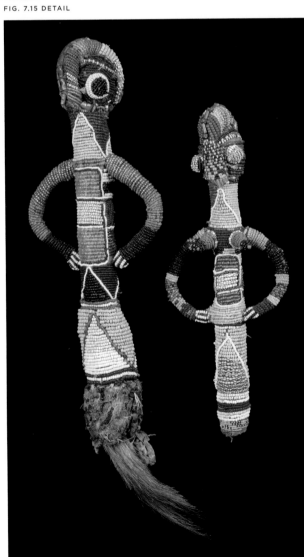

FIG. 7.16

FIG. 7.16
**OBA'S FLY WHISKS (*IRUKERE*),
EARLY TWENTIETH CENTURY**

Yoruba peoples, southwest Nigeria

Cotton, horse? tail, glass beads

Left: 17 11/16 x 5 1/8 in. (45 x 13 cm)

Museum of International Folk Art,
IFAF Collection, Gift of Diane and
Sandy Besser, FA.2006.77.20

FIG. 7.17
**OBA'S FLY WHISKS (*IRUKERE*),
MID-TWENTIETH CENTURY**

Yoruba peoples, southwest Nigeria

Cotton, animal tail or fur, glass
beads

Left: 22 1/16 in. (56 cm)

Museum of International Folk Art,
IFAF Collection, Gift of Diane and
Sandy Besser, FA.2003.37.58 & 59

The royal fly whisk serves as
the oba's speech when he
acknowledges his followers while
sitting in state. He waves his fly
whisk in response or brushes it on
the heads and shoulders of those
who approach, thus maintaining
his social distance. He frequently
holds it in front of his mouth to
shield his mouth, which holds the
power of his utterances.

The whisk is made from an
animal tail. Certain animals' tails,
such as the elephant's or the
horse's tail, are considered to
contain the animal's potency and
power, thus animating the fly
whisk's authority.

FIG. 7.18A

FIG. 7.18B

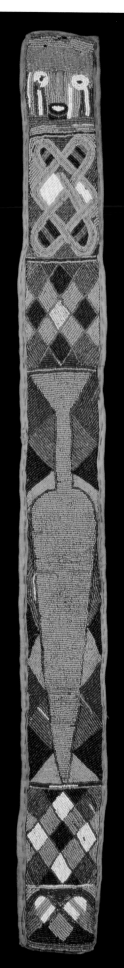

FIG. 7.19

FIGS. 7.18A (FRONT) AND B (BACK) PRIESTLY TUNIC, C. 1940

Yoruba peoples, Nigeria

Cotton, glass beads, cowry shells

20 x 20¼ in. (50.8 x 51.4 cm)

Museum of International Folk Art, Gift of Diane and Sandy Besser, A.1998.44.2

Although owning a wide assortment of solidly beaded regalia is a prerogative reserved for the obas, a few others who communicate with the deities are permitted to wear specialized beaded objects. This tunic, solidly beaded on both its front and back, may have belonged to a priest, perhaps devoted to Ogun, the deity of iron and war, identified by the snakes on the tunic. (Fagg 1980: 81). Other motifs include abstracted faces with facial marks and lizards.

FIG. 7.19 STAFF SHEATH (*EWU*), MID-TWENTIETH CENTURY

Yoruba peoples, southwest Nigeria

Cotton, glass beads

45¹¹⁄₁₆ x 4¾ in. (116 x 12.1 cm)

Museum of International Folk Art, IFAF Collection, Gift of Diane and Sandy Besser, FA.2002.49.20

The beaded sheath covers the shaft of the metal staff when not in use in rituals that pay homage to Orisha Oko, the deity of the farm. The staff in its sheath is housed in a household shrine to Oko and is cared for by a priestess who is a daughter of the household. The red and white vertical stripes on the face at the top are the identifying marks worn on ritual occasions by a priestess of the Orisha Oko. The green spear shape on the body of the sheath refers to the staff it is meant to enclose. The sheath also bears the interlace pattern found on many ritual objects.

CAMEROON ROYALTY

The Grasslands region of the Republic of Cameroon, although home to many different languages, is a generally homogeneous culture area, characterized by political centralization headed by a king, or *fon*, resulting in social stratification, and supported by men's secret societies and a high-ranking regulatory society. A tradition of elaborate beaded royal paraphernalia visually validates and reinforces the authority of the fons in the various kingdoms, most notably the Bamileke and Bamum peoples. Each fon is both the political leader and the chief religious leader of his kingdom. As such, he has various prerogatives, such as a monopoly on the large game animals—leopard, elephant, and buffalo—and the right to use their pelts, ivory, teeth, horns, as well as luxury trade goods for his royal regalia. "Since the trade and use of beads was a royal monopoly, one of the striking features of Bamum [and Bamileke] art was the use of beads in the allover decoration of wood sculpture. As William Fagg (1980: 24) has observed, no other African group has attempted to emulate this." (Pemberton 2008: 14).

Synonymous with the fon's royal office is the beaded stool, likened to a throne, which he sits upon to receive visiting dignitaries, hold audiences with his subjects, and when attending ceremonies (Fig. 7.20). In the Bamileke throne (Fig. 7.21), the stool is fused with a sitting royal ancestor figure as its back, thus according it "throne" status. According to Northern (1984:21): "This fusion of royal ancestor figure and stool is the most concentrated symbol of kingship." Such figures are commemorative of the royal predecessor to the present fon, carved during either the current or previous fon's reign. The figure's royal status is verified by his accoutrements, such as his prestige cap, his loincloth, chevron bead necklace, and bracelets. To further communicate his power and prestige, the figure sits on a small leopard figure, while the stool itself is supported by a leopard caryatid. These kingly symbols are combined with a complete covering of glass beads.

Cameroon Grasslands royal art centers around three-dimensional human and animal representations. The leopard is first among the royal animals, a symbol of the fon's power and leadership, and is his spirit animal. In praise songs, the king is referred to as the "leopard," and he is believed to possess the ability to transform himself into a leopard and vice versa, taking on the special capabilities and attributes of this powerful animal of the wild. The wilderness outside the village is considered a dangerous place, as opposed to the orderly space within the village. Fons, in the guise of a leopard, have the ability to enter the wild realm and mediate between the two spaces on behalf of their subjects. Leopard pelts, as a reminder of the special relationship between this animal and the fon, are displayed at the foot of or behind the fon's throne and on his bed (Fig. 7.22).

The elephant also features prominently as an emblem of regal strength. Like the leopard, the elephant may be featured as the caryatid on the fon's stool (Fig. 7.20), where the prominent tusks are a reminder of the fon's monopoly over ivory,

FIG. 7.20
FON'S ROYAL STOOL, NINETEENTH CENTURY

Bamileke peoples, Grasslands, Cameroon

Wood, raffia cloth, glass beads

16 1/8 x 17 3/4 x 19 6/8 in. (41 x 45 x 50 cm)

The Field Museum, 175558

Photograph by John Weinstein

Large tubular glass beads, which cover this double-headed elephant stool, were the most valued of trade beads, in keeping with their use on this fon's stool and many other royal Cameroon objects made for the kings. Small seed beads cover the tusks and create the outlines of the stool and ears and eyes of the elephant heads. The stool was carved from a single piece of wood, covered in raffia cloth, with the beads stitched to the cloth.

which serves both as a valuable commodity and a symbol of his leadership. A striking beaded textile mask of the elephant is unique to the Cameroon Grasslands, predominantly among the royal houses of the Bamileke kingdoms (Figs. 7.24 and 7.26). Two high-ranking men's societies, whose membership included all of the royalty, wealthy title-holders, and warriors of status, wear the cloth mask with its big floppy ears and long trunk-like panels (front and back) as their principle ceremonial regalia (Figs. 7.24 and 7.26). Robert Brain (1971: 100 ff.), who witnessed a funeral for a fon in 1951, provides the only description of a typical elephant mask society performance: "The Elephant society appears to the accompaniment of a single drum and a gong. There is relative silence among the spectators, as the maskers lope in slow motion round the field. . . . They whistle mysteriously and tunelessly as they gyrate in front of the crowd. . . . Their beaded masks flap heavily round them. . . ." The imposing human facial features on these masks are the embodiment of the fon, imbued with all of the elephant's inherent power. (Pemberton 2008: 120).

FIG. 7.21

FIG. 7.22

FIG. 7.21
FON'S ROYAL THRONE,
NINETEENTH CENTURY

Bamileke peoples, Bansoa, Cameroon

Wood, glass beads, shells, fiber

71 x 26 1/2 x 26 in. (180 x 67 x 66 cm)

Nelson-Atkins Museum of Art, purchased by William Rockhill Nelson Trust through the George H. and Elizabeth O. Davis Fund, 03.24.09

FIG. 7.22
FON'S CEREMONIAL MAT,
NINETEENTH CENTURY

Bamileke peoples, Grasslands, Cameroon

Leopard pelt, woven wax-resist indigo-dyed cloth, glass beads, cowrie shells, camwood powder

72 x 43 3/4 in. (183 x 111 cm)

Fine Arts Museums of San Francisco, Gift of the Bruce Moore Family, 2013.85.1

This leopard pelt covered with indigo cloth stitched with glass beads is a rare treasure. Only a portion of the leopard's paws and tail are visible, with the rest of the pelt covered with cloth, glass beads, and cowrie shells. The beaded pattern suggests the leopard's body, especially the spine, joints, and head. The reddish-brown patina is likely the result of an application of camwood powder, widely used in ceremonial contexts. Beaded isosceles triangles and check patterns, found here and on many other Cameroon beaded objects for royal prestige display, are an abstracted referent to the leopard's spots.

FIG. 7.23

FIG. 7.24

FIG. 7.25

FIG. 7.23
FON'S CEREMONIAL CALABASH,
TWENTIETH CENTURY

Bamileke peoples, Grasslands, Cameroon

Cloth, calabash (bottle gourd), glass beads

25³/₄ x 9¹/₂ in. (65 x 24 cm)

Collection of Sara and David Lieberman

Photograph by Craig Smith

The calabash, shaped like a bottle and topped by a leopard stopper, was used as a display piece and a palm wine container for the fon. Highly decorated with glass beads, pairs of these containers are usually placed on either side of the fon's stool when he is sitting in state at ceremonies. The motifs on the globular section of the gourd are abstracted spiders, another royal symbol.

FIG. 7.24
ELEPHANT MASK (*MBAP MTENG*) (PART OF A SET WITH LEOPARD CREST), NINETEENTH CENTURY

Bamileke peoples, Grasslands, Cameroon

Raffia splints, cloth, glass beads

31¹/₈ x 22¹/₁₆ x 16¹/₁₆ in. (79.1 x 56 x 40.8 cm)

The Field Museum, 174145

Photograph by John Weinstein

FIG. 7.25
LEOPARD CREST (PART OF A SET WITH ELEPHANT MASK), NINETEENTH CENTURY

Bamileke peoples, Grasslands, Cameroon

Raffia splints, cloth, glass beads, dried banana leaves

13¹³/₁₆ x 9⁷/₈ x 29¹/₂ in. (35 x 25 x 74.9 cm)

The Field Museum, 174144

Photograph by John Weinstein

The elephant masquerader on occasion wore a cap with a leopard crest placed atop his mask. Curiously these two elements, although a set, did not necessarily have any design relationship. According to Northern (1984: fig. 95): "Elephant masks with leopard crests are among the most powerful and demonstrative examples of iconic symbiosis and transference of royal symbols."

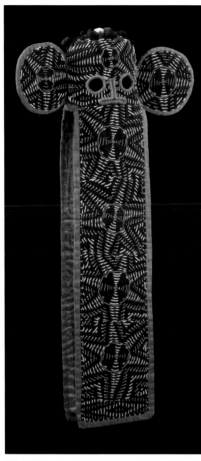

FIG. 7.26

FIG. 7.26 AND DETAIL ELEPHANT MASK (*MBAP MTENG*), TWENTIETH CENTURY

Bamileke peoples, Grasslands, Cameroon

Raffia splints, cotton, glass beads

45 x 20 x 4¹/₂ in. (114.3 x 50.8 x 11.4 cm)

Museum of International Folk Art, Gift of Lloyd E. Cotsen and the Neutrogena Corporation, A.1995.93.11

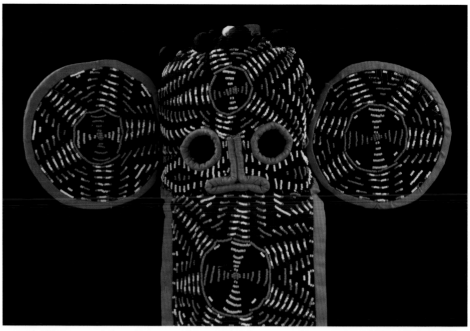

FIG. 7.26 DETAIL

FIG. 7.27

PHOTO 7.4

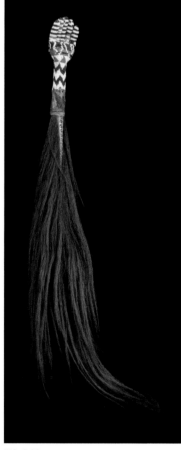

FIG. 7.28

PHOTO 7.4
KUOSI SOCIETY MEMBERS WEARING ELEPHANT MASKS, 1930

Bamileke peoples, Bandjoun, Cameroon

Musée du Quai Branly, Paris

Photograph by C. L. Christol

Kuosi society masqueraders pose for a photo in the marketplace of Bandjoun. In the center is the Fon Nkanga of Bandjoun, holding two fly whisks and wearing a leopard pelt on his back.

FIG. 7.27
LEOPARD HELMET MASK, C. 1900

Bamileke peoples, Grasslands, Cameroon

Raffia, indigo-dyed cotton and trade cotton, glass beads

20⁷/₈ x 31¹/₈ in. (53 x 79 cm)

Museum of International Folk Art, Gift of Rosina Lee Yue, A.1997.5.1

This helmet mask with a surmounted leopard— distinguished by his long tail, rounded ears, and the beaded lozenge-shaped designs representing stylized leopard spots—was likely used during the elephant masquerade. A similar helmet mask is depicted in a 1909 photograph. (Geary 1992: 252).

FIG. 7.28
ROYAL FLY WHISK, TWENTIETH CENTURY

Bamileke peoples, Grasslands, Cameroon

Horse tail, glass beads

45²/₃ in. (116 cm)

Sara and David Lieberman Collection

Photograph by Craig Smith

LEADERSHIP ELSEWHERE

PHOTO 7.5
KUBA KING (*NYIM*) KOT A-MBWEEKY III IN STATE DRESS, 1971

Kuba peoples, Mushenge, Democratic Republic of the Congo

Eliot Elisofon Photographic Archives, National Museum of African Art, Smithsonian Institution, EEPA

Photograph by Eliot Elisofon, EECL 02139

In 1988 photographer Daniel Lainé (2000: 138) traveled to Africa to photograph 70 African royal kings. Although Lainé did not

shoot this photo, he relates his experience photographing the next in-line Kuba king: "It took me three weeks to photograph the Nyimi (King) of the Kuba in his royal apparel, the *bwaantshy*. . . . The costume, made of material embroidered with beads and cowrie shells used as currency in parts of Africa, weighs almost 185 pounds. It takes more than two hours to dress the king and two days of rituals before he is sufficiently purified to put on the outfit. The bwaantshy is so heavy and warm that it cannot be worn for more than an hour. The previous king donned it only three times in his lifetime."

PHOTO 7.5

FIG. 7.29

FIG. 7.29
ROYAL BELT (*YET*), EARLY TWENTIETH CENTURY

Kuba peoples, Bushong subgroup, Democratic Republic of the Congo

Raffia palm, glass beads, cowrie shell, turban shell, tessellated helmet shell, scallop shell

6 x 31 in. (15.2 x 78.7 cm)

Fine Arts Museums of San Francisco, The Caroline and H. McCoy Jones Collection, Gift of Caroline McCoy-Jones, A335464_V1

The nyim (king) displays this special type of belt on the day he is enthroned. It may have as many as 20–30 pendants. This example has 30 pendants, including a variety of shells brought from the sea and beaded pendants in the likeness of various objects, such as rams' heads, which have royal significance, and royal bells. Pendants vary from one belt to another, implying that the artists may use their imaginations when deciding what pendants to make. All members of the royal family have the right to wear *yets* for ceremonial occasions.

FIG. 7.30 AND DETAIL
BELTS, LATE NINETEENTH–EARLY TWENTIETH CENTURIES

Kuba peoples, Democratic Republic of the Congo

Raffia palm, cowrie shells, glass beads

Right: 54 x 3⅛ in. (137.16 x 7.94 cm)

Museum of International Folk Art, Gift of Lloyd E. Cotsen and the Neutrogena Corporation, A.1995.93. 194 (top), 190 (upper middle), 193 (lower middle), 191 (bottom)

Photograph by Pat Pollard

The Kuba king wore one or more belts and bandoliers, highly decorated with cowrie shells and glass beads applied to woven raffia, on top of his many layers of beaded garments. He was literally covered from head to toe in beads. Both glass beads, traded from Europe, and cowrie shells, traded from the Indian Ocean, were emblems of power and wealth. Noble titleholders were also permitted to wear these belts.

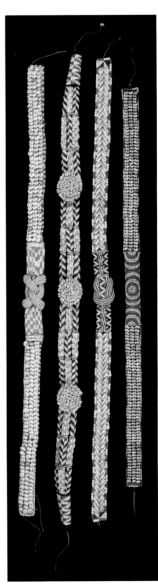

FIG. 7.30

FIG. 7.30 DETAIL

157

PHOTO 7.6
KUBA ROYAL TITLEHOLDERS
AT THE ROYAL COURT, 1971

Kuba peoples, Mushenge,
Democratic Republic of the
Congo

Eliot Elisofon Photographic
Archives, National Museum
of African Art, Smithsonian
Institution, EEPA

Photograph by Eliot Elisofon,
EECL 02184

Princes and high-ranking
noblemen (right) are also
permitted to wear lavish beaded
headdresses and garments with
cowrie shells and beads, similar
to those of the nyim.

FIGS. 7.31A (SIDE) AND B (BACK)
TITLEHOLDER'S HEADDRESS OR NYIM'S CROWN, LATE
NINETEENTH–EARLY TWENTIETH CENTURIES

Kuba peoples, Bushong subgroup, Democratic Republic of the Congo

Raffia palm, glass beads, seeds, fur, elephant hair, vine

17 11/16 x 8 1/4 in. (45 x 21 cm)

Museum of International Folk Art, IFAF Collection, Gift of Diane and
Sandy Besser, FA.2003.37.38

Among Kuba peoples, the wide variety of titleholders' headdresses
attest to "the intricate system of titleholding, the competition for
possessing a title, and the creativity of hatmakers. . . . Of particular
importance is the assortment of materials associated with a set of
symbols and titled positions, and their placement. . . . " (Arnoldi and
Kreamer 1995: 167). This particular headdress includes a wide variety
of materials from glass beads to animal fur. Such headdresses were
reserved for ceremonial or funeral contexts. However, because of
its chin strap and nose cover, this headdress, missing its feathers,
may have been a crown belonging to the nyim (king) rather than
a titleholder.

PHOTO 7.6

FIG. 7.31A

FIG. 7.31B

FIG. 7.32A

FIG. 7.32B

FIGS. 7.32A
(FRONT) AND B
(BACK)
MUKYEEM MASK,
PRE-1935

Kuba peoples,
Democratic Republic
of the Congo

Hide, wood, glass
beads, cowrie shells,
plant fiber

15 9/16 x 17 11/16 x
21 1/4 in. (39.5 x 44.9
x 54 cm)

The Field Museum,
175971

Photograph by John
Weinstein

The Mukyeem mask, found in the southern Kuba region, is a variant of one of the three royal masks identified with Kuba kingship. It has a top projection depicting the trunk of an elephant, a reference to the nyim's strength. When the wearer dances, a bundle of red parrot feathers dangles from the end of the trunk. The mask has a beard of cowries with its face made from either elephant or leopard skin. Facial features are indicated by beads, but there are no actual eyeholes. So when the dancer wears the mask, which entirely covers his face, he cannot see. On the mask's back, a beaded interlace design, found throughout all Kuba visual arts, predominates.

PHOTO 7.7
DANCE OF THE MUKYEEM MASK, 1972

Kuba peoples, Muentshi, Democratic Republic of the Congo

Eliot Elisofon Photographic Archives, National Museum of African Art, Smithsonian Institution, EEPA

Photograph by Eliot Elisofon, EECL 04099

The Mukyeem masquerader, an important member of the community, dances at the funerals for high-ranking persons. Since the mask covers his face giving him no visibility, the masquerader must move slowly.

PHOTO 7.7

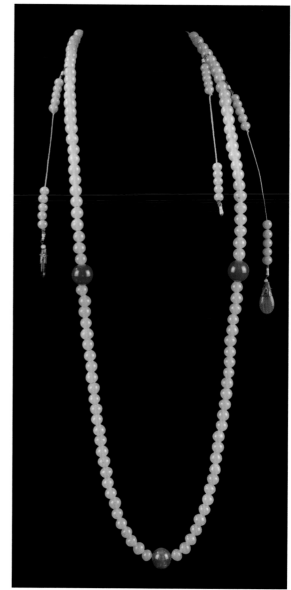

FIG. 7.33A

FIG. 7.33B

FIG. 7.34A

FIG. 7.34B

FIGS. 7.33A (FRONT) AND B (BACK) MANDARIN COURT NECKLACE, NINETEENTH CENTURY

People's Republic of China

Ivory, metal

47 in. (119.4 cm)

Museum of International Folk Art, Gift of Florence Dibell Bartlett, A.1955.1.803FE

FIGS. 7.34A (FRONT) AND B (BACK) MANDARIN COURT NECKLACE, NINETEENTH CENTURY

People's Republic of China

Fabric, glass beads

22⁴/₅ in. (58 cm)

Museum of International Folk Art, Gift of Florence Dibell Bartlett, FA.1956.34.32

During the Qing Dynasty (1644–1911), the rank of all members of the Emperor's court, his military, and their families could be identified by the court necklaces that they were required to wear. Although based on the Tibetan Buddhist rosary, they were first and foremost status symbols rather than aids for prayer. The pendant hanging down the back was used as a counterweight to the heavy necklace. The propitious 108 beads plus four spacers were made from semi-precious and glass beads, all of which were considered precious materials.

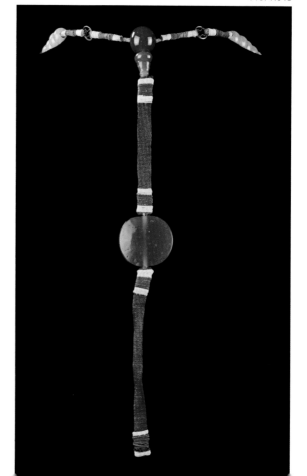

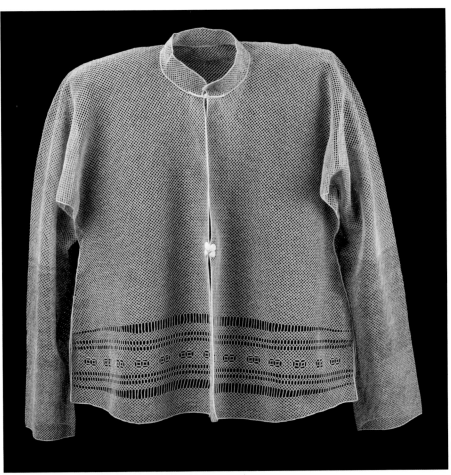

FIG. 7.35

FIG. 7.35
UNDERGARMENT, NINETEENTH
CENTURY

People's Republic of China

Cotton, bamboo beads

27½ x 66 in. (69.9 x 167.6 cm)

Museum of International Folk
Art, Gift of Lloyd E. Cotsen and
the Neutrogena Corporation,
A.1995.93.396

Photograph by Pat Pollard

Male members of the Chinese
emperor's court wore these
bamboo mesh undershirts
to create an absorbent layer
between the courtier's skin and
his many layers of silk under-
robes during long ceremonies,
especially during the heat of
the summer.

PHOTO 7.8
IROQUOIS CHIEFS WITH
WAMPUM BELTS, 1871

National Anthropological
Archives, Smithsonian
Institution, 86–58

Photograph by James N.
Edy

In this photograph, Iroquois chiefs of
the Six Nations are discussing their
sacred belts, significant symbols of
cultural patrimony belonging to the
various nations. Known as wampum
belts, these broad belts, constructed
in rows of thousands of white and
purple tubular beads hand-cut from
the quahog, or hardshell clam, are the
visual covenants of treaties between
the Iroquois Confederacy of the Six
Nations and other nations, both Indian
and European.

FIG. 7.36

FIG. 7.36
QUEEN ELIZABETH I,
C. 1588

Painted by unknown
English artist

Oil on panel

38½ x 28½ in. (97.8 x
72.4 cm)

National Portrait Gallery,
London, England, NPG 541

Pearls have a royal reputation
spanning the past to antiquity. Queen
Elizabeth I, who ruled Britain from
1558 to 1603, shared in the love of
pearls, having some 3,000 gowns
and 80 wigs embellished with them.
Known for her lavish costumes, she
is festooned in pearls, a symbol of
chastity, in her many portraits.

CONVERSING WITH

THE SPIRITS

COMMUNICATING WITH THE SPIRIT WORLD NECESSITATES a channel of mediation between the living and the gods and ancestors who award blessings to humans and ward off malevolent spirits. The intermediary can take many forms—a dance, a prayer, a song or chant, a sacred place, a ritual performed by a specialist, an object charged with power, or an ensemble of these and more. Here we focus on objects used in the process of conversing with spirits and the meanings ascribed to them by their communities.

YORUBA DIVINATION

Among the Yoruba people of southwest Nigeria, fully beaded regalia is the prerogative solely of kings and those few who communicate with the spirit world. Ifa diviners, chief among these ritual specialists, travel throughout Yorubaland to perform their rites, which include the knowledge of 256 divination verses, on behalf of devotees and communities. They wear beaded bags (apo) or necklaces (odigba) as a signifier of their special position. The bags hold the 16 palm nuts and other equipment that diviners use when mediating between the spiritual and the earthly worlds.

Devotees consult Ifa diviners not to learn their future, but to know their destiny, which they chose at the time of their creation before they entered the world. Pemberton (2008:103) explains: "Having touched the Tree of Forgetfulness before entering aiye, one must seek throughout life to know the destiny that one had chosen and learn how to know and address those spiritual powers, the orisa [gods] and the ancestors, that can aid in the realization of one's potential and also know those malevolent forces that can preclude the actualization of one's destiny. Hence, Ifa divination is a search for understanding."

FIG. 8.1

FIG. 8.2

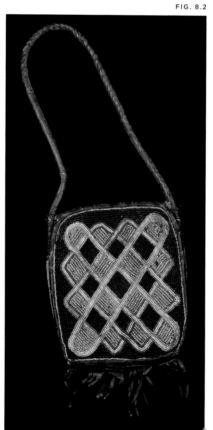

FIG. 8.1
DIVINER'S BAG (APO), C. 1900

Yoruba peoples, southwest Nigeria

Cotton, leather, glass beads

35 5/16 x 13 3/8 in. (82 x 34 cm)

Museum of International Folk Art, IFAF Collection, Gift of Diane and Sandy Besser, FA.2006.77.17

This Ifa diviner's bag has abstracted designs in many colors. Diviners commissioned their bags from the same professional beadworkers who made the regalia for the obas.

FIG. 8.2
DIVINER'S BAG (APO), LATE NINETEENTH CENTURY

Yoruba peoples, southwest Nigeria

Cotton, leather, glass beads

21 1/4 x 8 7/16 in. (54 x 21.4 cm)

Museum of International Folk Art, IFAF Collection, Gift of Diane and Sandy Besser,

FA.2002.49.23

This aged bag has the same interlace design that is also found on beaded objects belonging to the oba.

FIG. 8.3, Opposite
DIVINER'S NECKLACE (ODIGBA), EARLY TWENTIETH CENTURY

Yoruba peoples, southwest Nigeria

Cotton, leather, glass beads

2 3/4 x 15 3/4 in. (7 x 40 cm)

Museum of International Folk Art, IFAF Collection, Gift of Diane and Sandy Besser, FA.2006.77.4

Most Ifa diviners' necklaces have double bags containing substances for their protection, although some like this one have only one bag. The diviner wears it like a necklace. When there are two bags, one falls on his chest and one at the back of his neck to protect his most vulnerable places.

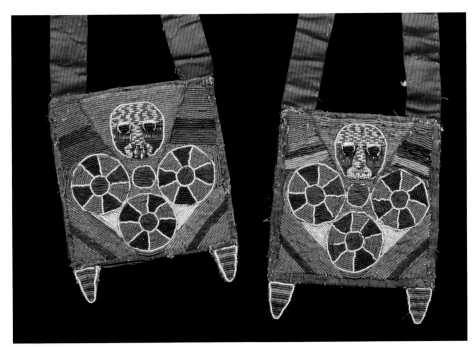

FIG. 8.4 DETAIL

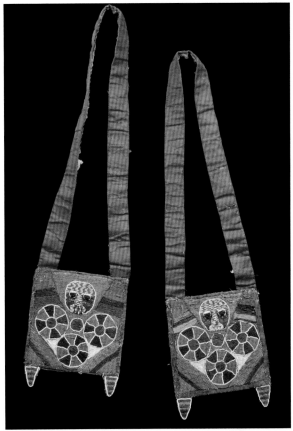

FIG. 8.4

**FIG. 8.4 AND DETAIL
DANCE PANELS (*YATA*), PAIR,
TWENTIETH CENTURY**

Yoruba peoples, southwest Nigeria

Cotton, leather, glass beads

27³/₁₆ x 7¹/₁₆ in. (69 x 18 cm)

Museum of International Folk Art,
IFAF Collection, Gift of Diane and
Sandy Besser, FA.2006.77.15 & 16

Worshippers of several Yoruba deities
(*orisa*) wear dance panels, usually in
pairs, at the annual festival for the
deity. The cloth straps crisscross over
the wearer's body, resting on the hips.

**FIG. 8.5
DANCE PANEL (*YATA*), EARLY-MID
TWENTIETH CENTURY**

Yoruba peoples, southwest Nigeria

Cotton, wood, glass beads

10¹/₂ x 10 in. (26.7 x 25.4 cm)

Museum of International Folk
Art, Gift of Lloyd E. Cotsen and
the Neutrogena Corporation,
A.1995.93.66

The face on this dance panel, one of
a pair, likely represents the spiritual
power of the devotee's inner head.
(Fagg 1980:42). Note the smiling
mouth with teeth indicated.

FIG. 8.5

FIG. 8.3

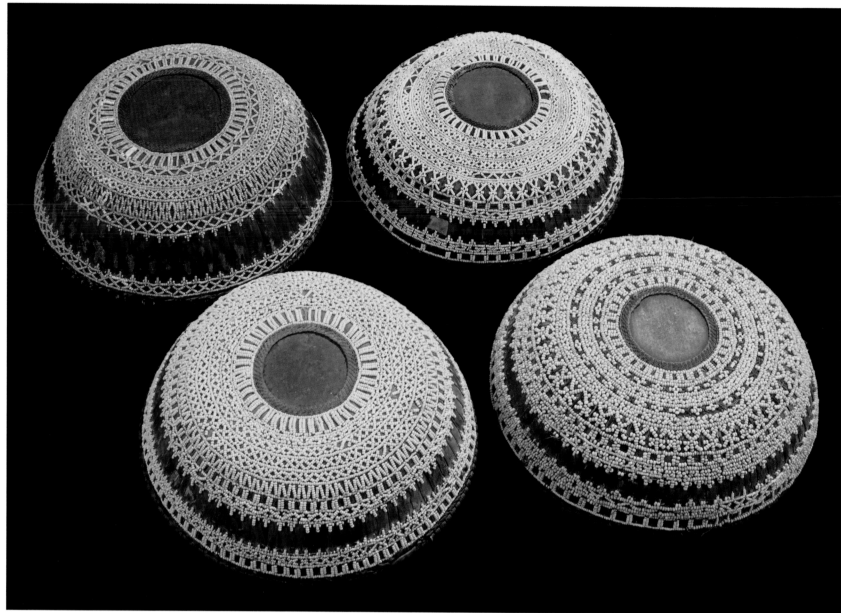

FIG. 8.6

RITUAL OBJECTS ELSEWHERE

FIG. 8.6
FOOD COVERS, C. 1900

Bali, Indonesia

Palm leaf, plant fiber, copper, glass beads

3¹⁵/₁₆ x 11⁷/₁₆ in. (10 x 29.1 cm)

Museum of International Folk Art, Gift of Ira Sachs, A.1987.484.5, 7, 8, and 10

These ornately beaded food covers are used to cover temple offerings.

FIG. 8.8
PRIESTESS' (*DAYUNG BARIS'*) HAT, MID-TWENTIETH CENTURY

Bidayah peoples, west Sarawak, Borneo, Malaysia

Rattan, palm leaf, glass beads

8¹/₂ x 10¹/₂ in. (21.6 x 26.7 cm)

David McLanahan Collection

Traditional female healers of the Bidayah peoples wear a tall hat composed of a framework of glass beads with a palm frond cap. Such a head covering with its eye-catching beads in symbolic colors of red, yellow, white, and black, which attract the spirits, gives protection to her head when she is communicating with the spirits during the healing ritual.

FIG. 8.8

FIG. 8.9
CHURCH CHASUBLE,
FIFTEENTH CENTURY

Probably Italy or Sicily

Silk, linen, gilt-metal, satin, coral beads, twill

44 5/8 x 26 1/4 in. (113.4 x 66.8 cm)

Art Institute of Chicago, 1601/75

A chasuble is the outermost sacred vestment worn by the clergy when celebrating the Eucharist, the sacrament of holy communion commemorating the Last Supper in Western Christian churches such as the Roman Catholic, Anglican, Lutheran, and the United Methodist churches. Before its first use, the vestment must be blessed by a priest who has the authority. A priest, whenever donning the chasuble, does so with a prayer, as this vestment is considered the "yoke of Christ."

Coral beads encrust this liturgical vestment down its center. The beads most likely came from the Bay of Naples and were made into beads in the town of Torre del Greco, the center of the Mediterranean coral industry for centuries. Some beads continue to be made there in spite of the over-fishing and inevitable decline of the coral industry in Italy. (Coles and Budwig 1997: 22–23).

FIG. 8.7
MAN'S
CEREMONIAL
BAG, C. 1925

Atoni peoples,
Timor island,
Indonesia

Cloth, glass beads

7 x 6 in. (17.8 x
15.2 cm)

Museum of
International
Folk Art, IFAF
Collection, Gift
of Diane and
Sandy Besser,
FA.2006.70.48

Atoni men
carried betel nut
paraphernalia and
medicinal items in
these bags.

FIGS. 8.10A, B, AND C (DETAIL)
PEYOTE FAN AND RATTLE

a—fan: Osage Nation, Oklahoma,
United States, twentieth century

Tanned hide, glass beads, macaw
and other feathers

18⅞ x 6⅛ x 2¹¹⁄₁₆ in. (48 x 15.5 x
6.8 cm)

Museum of International Folk
Art, Gift of the Girard Foundation
Collection, A.1980.8.773

b and c—rattle: Native American
peoples, United States, late 1970s

Gourd, tanned hide, glass beads

23 x 2.5 in. (58.4 x 6.4 cm)

Ralph T. Coe Center for the Arts

In the 1870s a new religion
based on the ritual consumption
of peyote, a small cactus with
hallucinogenic properties, was
founded in Indian Territory (now
present-day Oklahoma) and

later named the Native American
Church. This religion has spread to
hundreds of thousands of native
practitioners. Bird symbolism is at
its center, whereby birds are the
messengers that carry prayers to
the Creator and, in return, bring
back blessings to the supplicants.
The fan constructed of bird
feathers plays a significant role
in this ritual. Through the act of
fanning the peyote and the smoke,
the feathers transfer the blessings
to the worshippers. The leader
holds his fan in one hand and his
gourd rattle in the other.

These ritual instruments used in
the rites of the Native American
Church are beaded using tiny,
often faceted, beads sewn with a
specific stitch called the "peyote"
stitch. It requires an especially
skilled beadworker to make these
implements of mediation.

FIG. 8.7

FIG. 8.10 A

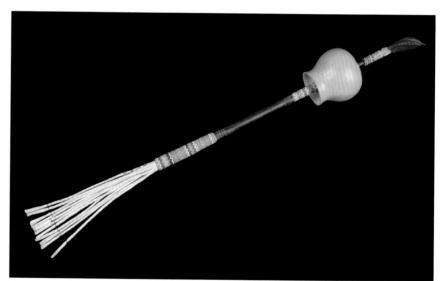

FIG. 8.10B

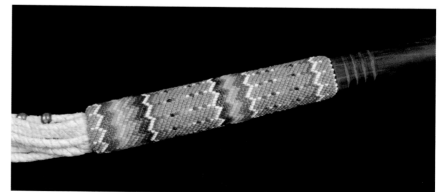

FIG. 8.10C DETAIL

FIG. 8.11

FIG. 8.11
VOTIVE BOWLS, C. 1934

Wíxaríka (Huichol) peoples, Tuxpan de Bolaños community, Jalisco state, México

Gourd (*lagenaria sisetaria*), glass beads, beeswax

Diameters: 27.4 to 55 in. (10.8 to 21.6 cm)

Museum of Indian Arts and Culture / Laboratory of Anthropology; 1593, 1595, 1215, 1447, 1445, 1456, 1590, 1451, 1175, 1591, 1448a

FIG. 8.12
VOTIVE BOWL, C. 1934

Wíxaríka (Huichol) peoples, Tuxpan de Bolaños community, Jalisco state, México

Gourd (*lagenaria sisetaria*), glass beads, beeswax

$8^{1}/3$ x $2^{4}/5$ in. (21.2 x 7.2 cm)

Museum of Indian Arts and Culture / Laboratory of Anthropology, 1542

Votive bowls, made from a split gourd embellished with beaded designs pressed into beeswax, serve as offerings to the Huichol deities (Fig. 8.11). The central design identifies the deity to whom the bowl is dedicated, which may be the sun deities, water deities, or the fire deity who maintains a delicate balance between the dry season and the wet season. The bowls are stored and cared for in the community temple, a household shrine, or deposited at sacred sites during pilgrimages. Each bowl is offered as a prayer for a favor from the gods or in gratitude for a request granted. The bowl (Fig. 8.12) with beaded deer, one of the three life sustainers—deer, corn, peyote—is a prayer to the Corn Goddess for successful crops or a gift in gratitude for the successful growing season. (Grady 2010: 38). Lacquered gourd bowls continue to be used today for Huichol votive purposes.

FIG. 8.12

HAITIAN VODOU FLAGS

Haitian hand beaded-and-sequined ritual flags, or *drapo*, function as liturgical implements in the Afro-Caribbean religion of Vodou. They are also made for sale to the international art market. Some of the Haitian flag artists are Vodou priests themselves or members of a priest's family, who advise the maker.

Mireille Delismé began making drapo in 1990 after she lost her job when the factory, where she sewed beads and sequins onto bridal gowns, closed in Port-au-Prince. Delismé had a dream around this same time, which she related to her father, a Vodou priest. He interpreted the dream for her, saying that the design in her dream was a Vodou spirit, or *lwa*. Lwa, the deities who assist Vodou initiates in coping with life's daily struggles, deliver their messages through the dreams of Vodou practitioners. She continued to have these dreams and pursued the art of making drapo. Her sister, who inherited the tradition of the Vodou priesthood, uses Mireille's flags when conducting Vodou rituals and continues to help her interpret her dreams. "Drapo are important within Vodou primarily because they are powerful liturgical objects. When utilized in rituals, they exemplify . . . the strength and power of the deities' active presence within the *ounfò* [temple]. Because of this, flags are among the most sacred and expensive ritual implements in the temple, and their presence is essential in most Vodou rites." (Polk 1997: 15).

On January 12, 2010, Delismé's hometown was at the epicenter of a massive earthquake, which killed some 30,000 Haitians. Although she was safe, she lost family members in the earthquake. Delismé responded by making a special drapo, *Catastrophe du 12 Janvier 2010*, which depicts the buildings in rubble and bodies of the dead, including a pregnant woman (Fig. 8.13). Another

gifted Haitian drapo artist, Evelyn Alcide, was also moved to depict the earthquake. In her version, *Le Jour du Seisme* (Fig. 8.14), winged lwas, who have arrived to comfort the injured and bereaved, hover overhead.

Mireille Delismé employs eight seamstresses in her workshop. Their earnings support them and their families. As she says, "My art has become a very large and important part of my life. With the earnings that I can make by selling my art, I support not only my daughters [affording them an education], mother, sisters, and brother but also my friends and community. . . . My artwork is crucial for their sustainability." (Delismé 2011: 7).

FIG. 8.13 AND DETAIL, *Opposite*
CATASTROPHE DU 12 JANVIER 2010, VODOU FLAG (*DRAPO*), 2010

Maker: Mireille Delismé, Port-au-Prince, Haiti

Polyester satin, glass beads, plastic beads

42 x 54 in. (106.7 x 137.1 cm)

Museum of International Folk Art, Gift of Mireille Delismé, A.2012.78.1

FIG. 8.14, *Opposite*
LE JOUR DU SEISME, VODOU FLAG (*DRAPO*), 2010

Maker: Evelyn Alcide, Port-au-Prince, Haiti

Polyester satin, glass beads, plastic sequins, cotton thread

38 x 50³⁄₁₆ in. (96.5 x 127.5 cm)

Museum of International Folk Art, IFAF collection, FA.2011.15.1

Three lwa, divine spirits, arrive to assist those devastated by the earthquake. On the left is Lasirèn, depicted as a mermaid, with her fish tail, long flowing hair, and likely holding a trumpet in her hand. On the right is Danbala, an especially popular spirit, here depicted in his serpent guise, dressed as St. Patrick, identifiable by his robe, bishop's miter, and staff.

FIG. 8.13

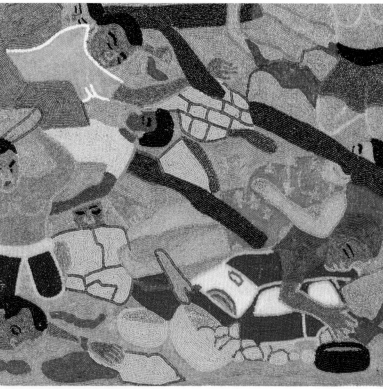

FIG. 8.13 DETAIL

FIG. 8.14

PROTECTIVE AMULETS IN HISTORIC PALESTINE

Believed to have supernatural powers, an amulet is an object whose purpose is to safeguard its owner from evil spirits and to provide good health and fortune. Found throughout much of the world, amulets are particularly prevalent in the Islamic world, where they are used to protect the precious and most vulnerable. Generally worn daily on the body as a prophylactic object embedded in jewelry or clothing, an amulet's protective power may be derived from its color, the material, the shape, or often a combination for multiple effect. Historic Palestine, with its mixed population of townspeople, villagers, and tribal Bedouins, provides a view into the multiple types and uses of amulets.

Glass beads, especially in the efficacious color blue (Fig. 8.15), are imbued with protective powers to ward off the Evil Eye associated with envy and jealousy. The Evil Eye can be cast by anyone who is envious of another person's good fortune, cast even without the conscious knowledge of its giver. Even a compliment given by an admirer to a beautiful bride or a new baby can place them in danger, resulting in misfortune, illness, or possibly death. Hence protection from the Evil Eye is necessary at all times and continues to be taken quite seriously. A Palestinian child is given an amulet to wear at birth and is expected to wear it throughout adulthood.

Blue eyes are an anomaly in a region of brown-eyed people. Both plain blue beads and the blue "eye" beads cause the Evil Eye to become confused when confronted by these blue beads (Fig. 8.16), drawing the evil attention away from the wearer. Blue glass eye beads are sold in markets in all varieties of sizes (Fig. 8.18) and are worn around the neck, pinned to clothing, hung above the doorways of homes and shops, and adorn donkeys, horses, camels, other livestock, and their barns. Rural women in southern Palestine began to wear a blue crocheted cap with blue and red-orange beads in the 1930s as a more modern and less cumbersome alternative to wearing dowry jewelry daily as a safeguard (Fig. 8.17).

Other colors and materials also possess the supranormal power to protect wearers from the malicious intent of the Evil Eye. Coral, or even glass beads in coral colors ranging from reds to oranges (Fig. 8.19, Fig. 3.32), can be equally effective in protecting against evil spirits, including the Evil Eye. Coral's "magical powers are drawn from both the vegetable and the mineral world. Its color is that of blood, the vehicle of life." (Paine 2004: 90). In addition to coral, amber and turquoise (revered for its blue coloration) also have prophylactic powers against the Evil Eye (Fig. 8.20). Amber in particular has long been revered by Bedouin tribes.

Cloves were also favored by Bedouin women in Palestine. With its strong odor, cloves are believed to have many healthful characteristics and are repellant to evil spirits. In these special clove necklaces (Figs. 8.21a and b), a combination of many protective elements, including blue and red glass beads, eye beads, and a block of beaded alum, safeguard the Bedouin bride, who traditionally wears this necklace at her wedding, a particularly vulnerable time in her life. The mineral alum,

FIG. 8.15
BLUE AMULETS, LATE NINETEENTH CENTURY TO 1900

Bedouin peoples, historic Palestine

Glass beads, coral, alum, fiber

$1^{3}/_{8}$–$2^{3}/_{8}$ in. (3.5–6 cm)

Museum of International Folk Art, IFAF Collection, FA.1981.48.110 (left), .16 (middle), .17 (right)

The amulet in the center is in the shape of a hand with five fingers, known as a *hamsa* in the Muslim world.

FIG. 8.16

characterized by its translucency, is cut into a pyramidal shape and covered in blue beads. The Evil Eye, while staring at the translucent chunk of alum, causes it to crack instead of harming its wearer.

Years ago, a young American couple noticed a long string of garlic, alum, and blue beads (Fig. 8.22) hanging over the doorway of a house they were going to lease in Palestinian Jerusalem. When they asked the landlord the meaning of this assemblage, he said, "Bin-Adam [son of Adam] is covetous. This house might strike the fancy of a passerby, who would covet it. Then certainly something [bad] would be sure to happen to the house. The blue beads are a protection against the eye of envy, the alum will take the shock, and the genie [*jinn*] do not like the smell of garlic, so they will keep at a safe distance." (Whiting 1981: 3).

In much of the world jewelry is more than just an adornment; it serves amuletic purposes. The metal silver is itself endowed with power. Additionally its shiny, bright appearance lures the Evil Eye away from the wearer (Fig. 8.23). Silver coins are frequently incorporated into jewelry and headpieces, not only for their monetary value but more importantly for their protective powers (Fig. 8.24, Fig. 8.25). When at her most vulnerable, a bride adorns herself in her silver dowry jewelry. Her waist, associated with her fertility, needs protection from evil spirits. Silver belts and dangling coins serve as her safeguard (Fig. 8.26). Often made in silver, the symbol of the hand, called the hand of Fatima or the *hamsa* ("five" in Arabic), is ubiquitous throughout the Islamic world. "Its fingers can pierce the evil eye." (Paine 2004: 164) (Fig. 8.27, Fig. 3.31).

Particular shapes also prohibit evil spirits from harming the wearer. Triangles, with their sharp points, are found everywhere in both silver and cloth and are sometimes embroidered onto clothing. Silver triangle cases hanging from women's necklaces (Fig. 8.28) often contain a piece of paper with a prayer, or *sura*, from the Quran tucked inside to give added protection. "Today highly decorated triangles are one of the most common forms of jewelry throughout the Muslim world." (Paine 2004: 152).

FIG. 8.17
CAP (*ṬAYYET ṢUNNĀRA*), C. 1935

Be'er Sheva region, southern historic Palestine

Cotton, glass beads

7⅞ x 11¹³/₁₆ in. (19 x 28 cm)

Museum of International Folk Art, IFAF Collection, FA.1972.25.3c

FIG. 8.16, *Opposite*
EYE BEAD AMULET, FIRST HALF TWENTIETH CENTURY

Turkey

Metal, glass beads

Museum of International Folk Art, Gift of Madame Isvan, A.1955.27.3

FIG. 8.18
DISPLAY CARD OF EYE BEADS (DETAIL), C. 1910

Hebron, southern West Bank, Palestinian territories

Glass beads

Various up to 1 in. (2.2 cm)

Museum of International Folk Art, IFAF Collection, FA.1981.48.33

FIG. 8.18

FIG. 8.19

FIG.8.20

FIG. 8.19
NECKLACE, 1910

Irbid, Jordan/northern historic Palestine

Silver, glass beads

13 in. (33cm)

Museum of International Folk Art, IFAF Collection, FA.1972.25.49

FIG. 8.20
AMBER NECKLACE, C. 1900

Bedouin peoples, historic Palestine

Amber beads, Roman glass beads

10¼ x 3½ in. (26 x 9 cm)

Museum of International Folk Art, IFAF Collection, FA.1972.25.31

FIGS. 8.21A AND B
A: CLOVE NECKLACE AND
B: ALUM PENDANTS, C. 1910

Syria and historic Palestine

Cloves, glass beads, alum

Necklace: 16 x 29½ in. (40.6 x 75 cm); pendants: (left): 4⅞ in. (12.4 cm); (right): 5½ in. (14 cm)

Museum of International Folk Art, Gift of Florence Dibell Bartlett, necklace: A.1955.86.636; pendants: IFAF Collection, FA.1981.48.147x

FIG. 8.22
HOUSE AMULET, C. 1910

Bedouin peoples, Hebron, southern West Bank, Palestinian territories

Paper, glass beads, alum, garlic, watercolor

Drawing: 11½ x 9 in. (29.2 x 22.9 cm)

Museum of International Folk Art, IFAF Collection, FA.1981.48.22

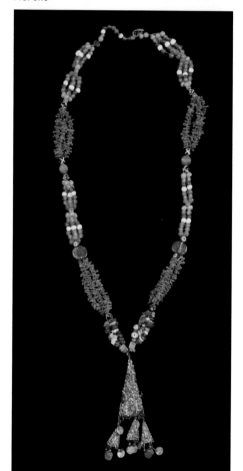

FIG.8.21A

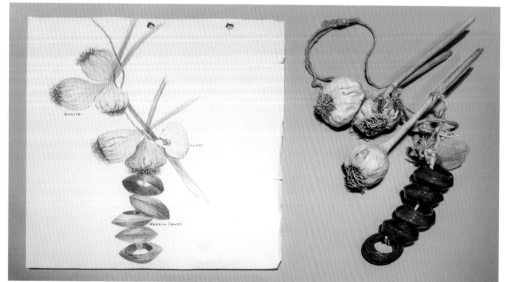

FIG. 8.22

FIG.8.21B

FIG. 8.23

FIG. 8.24

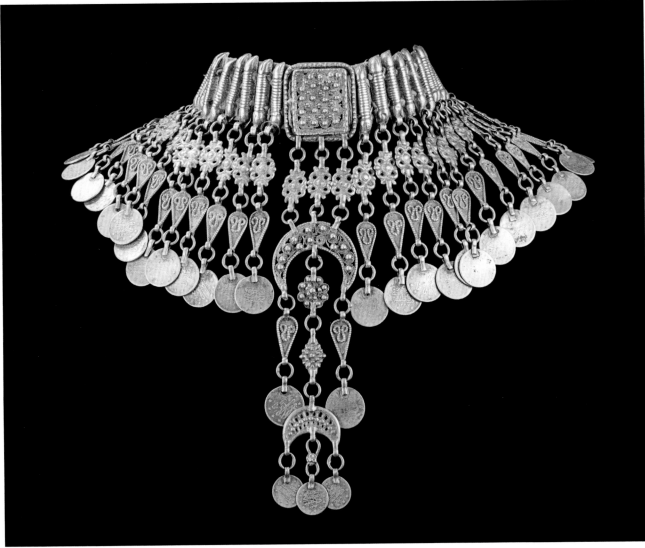

FIG. 8.25

FIG. 8.23
HEADBAND, C. 1910

Sudan

Silver

23 in. (58.4 cm)

Museum of International, Gift
of Florence Dibell Bartlett,
A.1955.86.689

FIG. 8.24
COIN HAT, C. 1840

Historic Palestine

Cotton, silver coins

6¼ in. (15.9 cm)

Museum of International Folk
Art, Gift of Florence Dibell
Bartlett, A.1955.86.918

FIG. 8.25
SILVER CHOKER (*KIRDAN*),
C. 1920

Southern historic Palestine

Silver, cotton

8 x 13 in. (20.5 x 33 cm)

Museum of International
Folk Art, IFAF Collection,
FA.1972.25.61

FIG. 8.26A

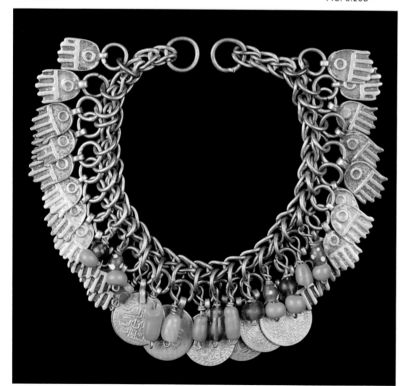

FIG. 8.27

FIG. 8.26B

FIG. 8.28

FIGS. 8.26A (FRONT) AND B (BACK) BRIDE'S ENSEMBLE, C. 1900

Prilepsko Pole, Macedonia

Cotton, wool, silver, glass beads, bast fiber

Dimensions: various

Museum of International Folk Art; the Ron Wixman/Stephen Glaser Collection, Gift of Bernard W. Ziobro, Gift of Mr. and Mrs. William F. Hennessey

Photographs by Addison Doty

When a Macedonian bride wears this elaborate bridal outfit, she is laden with silver ornaments with prophylactic powers. Presumably, her appearance is so changed that she avoids recognition by the evil spirits. The dominant red color of the embroidery and fringe also has magical functions.

FIG. 8.27 HEADDRESS ATTACHMENT, C. 1910

Historic Palestine

Silver, glass beads

15⅜ x 1¾ in. (39 x 4.5 cm)

Museum of International Folk Art, IFAF Collection, FA.1981.48.105

Blue beads add to the protective power of this chain of hamsa dangles and silver coins. This ornament was likely worn across a woman's forehead and attached to the sides of her headdress.

FIG. 8.28 SILVER NECKLACE WITH TRIANGLE, SECOND HALF OF NINETEENTH CENTURY

Tayāha Bedouin peoples, southern historic Palestine

Silver

23⅔ in. (60 cm)

Museum of International Folk Art, IFAF Collection, FA.1972.25.3j

FIG. 8.29

SAFEGUARDING THE BODY AND HOME ELSEWHERE

The same practices that hold true for Palestinian use of amuletic safeguards generally are found throughout central Asia, north Africa, the Arabian Peninsula, eastern Europe, and even into Latin America.

FIG. 8.29
CORAL AND SILVER NECKLACE, C. 1840

Christian Copt peoples, Egypt

Coral, silver

25 in. (63.5 cm)

Museum of International Folk Art, Gift of Florence Dibell Bartlett, A.1955.86.680

This amuletic necklace provides protection for its wearer with its crescent-shaped dangles and coral and silver beads.

FIG. 8.30
SILVER NECKLACE WITH CYLINDER CASE, C. 1940

Bedouin peoples, Abha, Asir province, Saudi Arabia

Silver, cotton

11⁴/₅ in. (30 cm)

Museum of International Folk Art, IFAF Collection, FA.1996.40.27

The cylinder case is meant to hold a small piece of paper with a prayer, or *sura*, from the Quran written on it, which serves to safeguard the wearer.

FIG. 8.31
WOMAN'S HEAD COVER (BACK), TWENTIETH CENTURY

San'a, Yemen

Cotton, silver, glass beads

10¹/₂ x 5¹/₄ in. (27 x 13 cm)

Museum of International Folk Art, IFAF Collection, FA.2002.11.7

The coral-colored glass beads, silver coins, silver medallions, and silver prayer cases cover the back of the woman's head and frame her face. Because a woman's long plaits of hair attract the Evil Eye, hair must be covered with protective elements to ward off evil spirits.

FIG. 8.30

FIG. 8.31

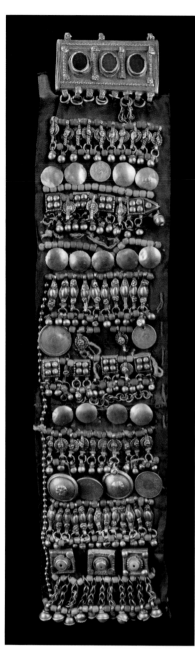

FIG. 8.32

FIG. 8.32
WOMAN'S PLAIT COVER, 1940S

Taiz, south Yemen

Cotton, silver, coral beads

19 x 4 in. (48 x 10 cm)

Museum of International Folk Art, IFAF Collection, FA.1994.56.1

FIG. 8.33
WOMAN'S FACE VEIL (*CHECHVAN*), EARLY TWENTIETH CENTURY

Samarkand, Uzbekistan

Cotton, horsehair, glass beads

50 x 26⁹/₁₆ in. (127 x 67.5 cm)

Museum of International Folk Art, A.2012.62.1

This Uzbek woman's face veil is made of black horsehair. Small, shiny, clear glass beads are woven into the horsehair to attract the evil spirits into the horsehair, where they are trapped in the mesh. For this reason, no woman will wear another's veil. (Paine 2004: 123). "A protest movement by women in the 1920s, the *khudjum*, ended the wearing of these veils, but in fundamentalist areas they can be seen again." (Paine 2004: 150).

FIG. 8.34
YURT DECORATIONS, PAIR, TWENTIETH CENTURY

Northern Afghanistan

Cotton, glass beads

20¼ in. (51.4 cm)

Anne and Bill Frej Collection

In addition to protection of the self from evil spirits, the safeguarding of the home is vital. For homes, the entrances and gables are the most vulnerable places. Residents of yurts protect their home with beaded tassels and hangings at the entrance and the top of the tent.

PHOTO 8.1
SILK WORKSHOP WITH BUNCH OF DRIED PLANTS, 2012

Fergana Valley, Uzbekistan

Photograph by Marsha Bol

In Central Asia a strong-smelling plant (locally known as *isrik* or *chirak*) repellent to evil spirits is dried and hung in bunches outside homes and businesses for its amuletic power. The Fergana Valley was an important route on the North Silk Road.

PHOTO 8.2
YURT CAMP, 2012

Son Köl Lake, Kyrgyzstan

Photograph by Pam Najdowski

FIG. 8.33

FIG. 8.34

PHOTO 8.1

PHOTO 8.2

FIG. 8.35

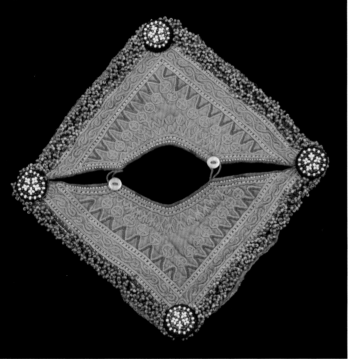

FIG. 8.36

FIG. 8.38 DETAIL

FIG. 8.35
TRIANGLE AMULET, TWENTIETH CENTURY

Northern Afghanistan

Cotton, glass beads

9¼ x 10 in. (23.5 x 25.4 cm)

Anne and Bill Frej Collection

FIG. 8.36
CHILD'S COLLAR, TWENTIETH CENTURY

Pashtun nomadic peoples, northern Afghanistan

Cotton, glass beads

11 x 11 in. (27.9 x 27.9 cm)

Anne and Bill Frej Collection

When this collar is placed on the child, it hangs to form a triangle on both the front and back. The triangle plus the blue beads safeguard the child's most vulnerable places from evil spirits.

FIG. 8.37
CAMEL TRAPPING, TWENTIETH CENTURY

Northern Afghanistan

Cotton, glass beads

27¾ in. (70.5 cm)

Anne and Bill Frej Collection

Domestic animals, such as camels, donkeys, horses, and oxen are considered to be among the precious and vulnerable susceptible to the Evil Eye. Draped in ornaments of blue and red cotton tassels with glass beads, the animals have the necessary protection against the evil spirits.

FIG. 8.38 AND DETAIL
WOMAN'S WEDDING DRESS, PRE-1973

Pashtun nomadic peoples, Afghanistan

Silk?, glass beads

49 x 65¾ in. (124.5 x 167 cm)

Museum of International Folk Art, IFAF Collection, Gift of John L. Goodwin, FA.1973.29.1

The beaded disks on the bodice are termed "dress flowers" (*qul-i-peron*). With their blue and red glass beads, buttons, and metal disks, these dress flowers are emblems of good fortune for the bride and are meant to deflect the Evil Eye. The blue beaded band at the waist serves the same purpose. Dress flowers have a deep history, having been found in burials dated before 400 B.C. (Harvey 1997: n.p.).

FIG. 8.37

FIG. 8.38

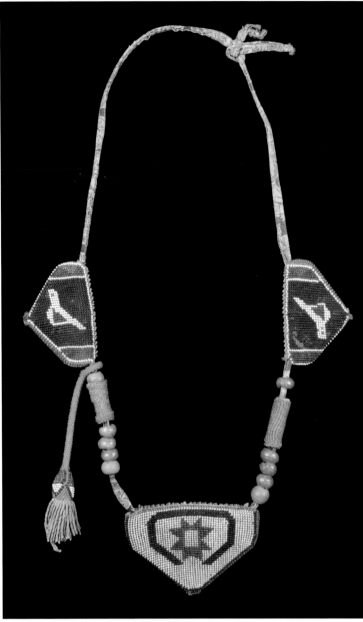

FIG. 8.39

FIG. 8.39 DETAIL

FIG. 8.39 AND DETAIL ANIMAL AMULET, EARLY TWENTIETH CENTURY

Kutahya city, Turkey

Fiber, glass beads

4⁷/₁₆ in. (11.3 cm)

Museum of International Folk Art, IFAF Collection, FA.1986.491.136

Made by Turkish men while in prison, this amulet can be identified by its blue beads and triangular pendants. It was meant to protect a horse or work animal from the Evil Eye.

FIG. 8.40 NECKLACE WITH AMULET HOLDER (*TUMAR*), C. 1900

Yomut Turkmen peoples, Central Asia or Iran

Silver, gilt, carnelian

29⁵/₈ x 7¹⁵/₁₆ in. (75.2 x 20.2 cm)

Museum of International Folk Art, long-term loan from Monir Farmanfarmaian, IL.1999.582.66

While Bedouin peoples prefer amber for its amuletic powers, Turkmen peoples have a preference for carnelian inset in silver as protection.

FIG. 8.41 CHEST ORNAMENT WITH AMULET HOLDER (*TUMAR*), C. 1900

Teke Turkmen peoples, Central Asia or Iran

Silver, gilt, carnelian

14¹/₂ x 14 in. (36.8 x 35.6 cm)

Museum of International Folk Art, long-term loan from Monir Farmanfarmaian, IL.1999.582.55

This enormous triangular chest ornament certainly provides a distraction for the evil spirits with its size, shape, silver and gold metal, and carnelian insets.

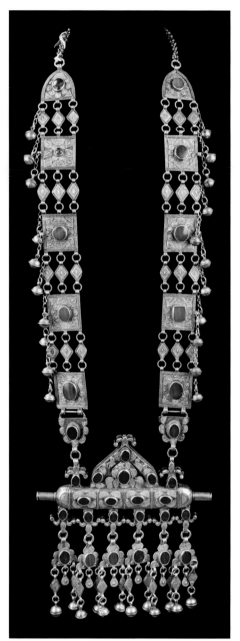

FIG. 8.40

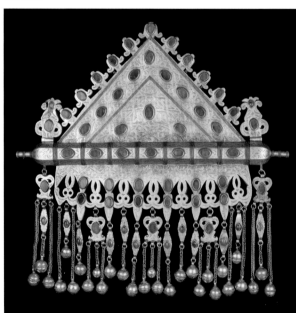

FIG. 8.41

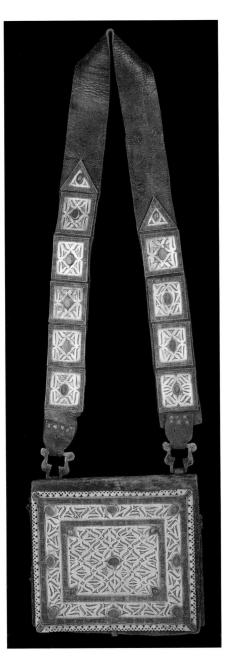

FIG. 8.42

FIG. 8.43
AMULET BOX (*GA'U*), NINETEENTH CENTURY

Tibet

Silver, brass, turquoise

2⁴/₅ x 2⁴/₅ in. (7 x 7 cm)

Museum of International Folk Art, A.1960.12.1

Traditionally Tibetans were never without their amulet box, containing a written prayer or small relics, worn around their neck. Women's daily dress included boxes inlaid with turquoise, their preferred stone for warding off evil and preventing misfortune or illness. After the Chinese invasion of Tibet in 1950, most Tibetan refugees had to sell their traditional treasures.

FIG. 8.44
AMULET WITH BAG, TWENTIETH CENTURY

Lower or Middle Sepik River region, Papua, New Guinea

Plant fiber, cowry shells, dog teeth, wood, mother-of-pearl shell

Bag: 15¹/₂ x 1¹⁵/₁₆ in. (39.4 x 5 cm); amulet: 3³/₄ x 1 x 1 in. (9.5 x 2.5 x 2.5 cm)

Museum of International Folk Art, Gift of Arlen Westbrook Clinard, A.2010.28.1ab

FIG. 8.42
AMULET BAG (*HAIKAL*), EARLY TWENTIETH CENTURY

Teke Turkmen peoples, Central Asia or Iran

Leather, silver, gilt, carnelian

6¹/₂ x 7¹/₁₆ in. (16.5 x 18 cm)

Museum of International Folk Art, long-term loan from Monir Farmanfarmaian, IL.1999.582.49

Flat leather bags with highly decorated front flaps and straps housed amulets or prayer scrolls.

FIG. 8.45
AMULET (*KARA UT*), C. 1950

Abelam peoples, Maprik district, East Sepik province, Papua, New Guinea

Plant fiber, shells, teeth, boars' tusks

22¹³/₁₆ x 4¹/₂ in. (58 x 11.5 cm)

Museum of International Folk Art, Gift of Bernie and Herb Beenhouwer, A.2009.55.3

This amulet gives strength to an Abelam warrior. He holds it in his teeth during ritual preparations for war or in dance. With the boars' tusks projecting from his mouth, the amulet provides courage and protection for the warrior and strikes fear in his foe.

FIG. 8.43

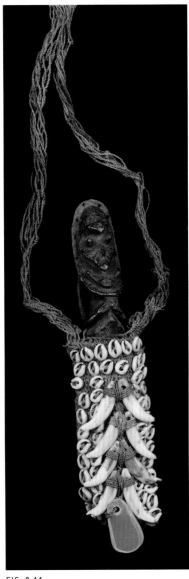

FIG. 8.44

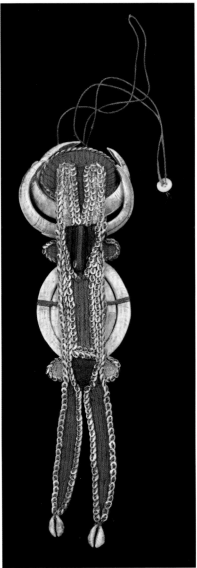

FIG. 8.45

FIG. 8.46

182

FIG. 8.46, *Opposite*
THREE CROSS NECKLACES

Left: Zapotec peoples, Sierra Juarez, Talea de Castro, Oaxaca state, México, date unknown

Silver, glass beads

16 in. (40.8 cm)

Center: Zapotec peoples, Talea de Castro, Oaxaca state, México, date unknown

Silver, glass beads

16$^1/_3$ in. (41.3 cm)

Right: Zapotec peoples, Oaxaca state, México, post-1810

Silver, glass beads, claws (possibly jaguar)

17$^2/_5$ in. (44.2 cm)

Museum of International Folk Art, IFAF Collection, FA.1975.1.207, 208, 204

Crosses on necklaces can serve both protective and religious purposes, depending upon the wearer's beliefs. The crosses on the left and the right are etched with the implements of Christ's Passion.

FIG. 8.48

FIG. 8.47

FIG. 8.47
PENCA DE BALANGANDÃS **(BUNCH OF CHARMS), C. 2004**

Salvador city, Bahia state, Brazil

Metal, wood

15$^1/_8$ x 6$^5/_8$ in. (38 x 16.5 cm)

Museum of International Folk Art, Gift of Dr. James Bert Smith and Dr. Beej Nierengarten-Smith Collection, A.2012.66.1

Brought to Brazil by African slaves beginning in the mid-sixteenth century, the *penca* was a series of charms, or amulets, hanging from a metal brooch, which protected its wearer from evil and brought much needed blessings to the slaves in their new home. Eventually the slaves began making pencas for themselves, especially in Bahia, one of the primary states where they were relocated. Afro-Bahian women fastened the smaller pencas to their waist, hung larger ones on walls in their homes, or placed them on the dining table. Each charm, or *balangandã*, has its own specific meaning, symbolized by its form. The *figa* (clenched-fist amulet) drives away illness and envy, and the pomegranate brings fertility.

FIG. 8.48
LLAMA ORNAMENT, MID-TWENTIETH CENTURY

Cuzco region, Peru

Wool, brass

21 x 15 in. (53.3 x 38.1 cm)

Museum of International Folk Art, IFAF Collection, FA.2007.41.4

The bells on the lead llama of the herd not only aid the herder in keeping track of his animals but they also protect the animals by frightening off any lurking evil spirits.

DRESSING
FOR FESTIVE
OCCASIONS

EVERYWHERE IN THE WORLD, HUMAN SOCIETIES SET aside their everyday routines to hold festivals and ceremonies. "During celebrations people think and feel more deeply than in everyday life. They express the meanings and values of their societies in special, often vivid ways. Among these is the creation of beautiful or striking objects, which exist only because humankind celebrates its own existence." (Turner 1982: 15).

Preparation for festivals requires cooking, home and ritual space decoration, dance and music rehearsals, making or freshening special dress for humans and even animals. Usually festivals require a change of clothes from everyday wear since many twenty-first century cultures no longer wear their traditional clothing on a daily basis. At festival time, revelers often choose to dress in traditional finery from the past, whether newly made or passed down through the generations, which expresses their identification with their heritage.

FINE DRESSING ON THE PLAINS

Traditional clothing is often used as a metaphor for physical boundary. It is a means of protecting and maintaining personal identity and showing social solidarity. In response to contact with new peoples and threatening situations, ethnic groups throughout the world have frequently donned their traditional dress.

As the Lakota and other central Plains Indian people were forced onto reservations in the fourth quarter of the nineteenth century, they chose to wear their tradition clothing that served as both a personal and a group identifier. The U.S. government placed a great deal of pressure on Plains people to change to Western-style dress as a ploy for moving forward the government's goal of assimilation into Euro-American society. Additionally, the buffalo and other animals were hunted out, eliminating the availability of materials for making hide clothing other than with cowhide. But Plains traditional clothing, a great source of pride and connection to ancestral knowledge, prevailed if only to be worn on occasion. The women's knowledge about making traditional dress continued to be transmitted from generation to generation. Each generation passed their finest clothing on to the next to store for safekeeping and to be taken out only for special occasions and ceremonies.

FIGS. 9.1A, B (DETAIL), AND C (DETAIL)
BOX-AND-BORDER WOMAN'S ROBE, 1870S

Lakota nation, North or South Dakota, USA

Native-tanned buffalo hide, glass beads, sinew

64 x 72 in. (162.5 x 188.9 cm)

Linda Marcus Collection

PHOTO 9.1
LAKOTA WOMAN CARRIES HER BABY, 1898–1905

Rosebud Reservation, South Dakota, USA

South Dakota State Historical Archives, 77.27.187

Photograph by Arthur McFatridge

Throughout their history and into the nineteenth century, Lakota people wrapped themselves in buffalo robes. A woman's hide robe could be distinguished by the geometric painting on the non-hair side of the robe, whereas a man's robe often bore painted autobiographical narratives. The box-and-border painted robe was considered a woman's robe, which they wore until woolen blankets became readily available as trade items. In photo 9.1, the Lakota woman carries her child wrapped in her painted buffalo robe long after buffalo herds had ceased to exist in Lakota territory; perhaps she wore her heirloom robe in pride when going to the military fort for provisions. A box-and-border robe was very rarely decorated in beads (Fig. 9.1) rather than paint, and such a robe would be highly prized.

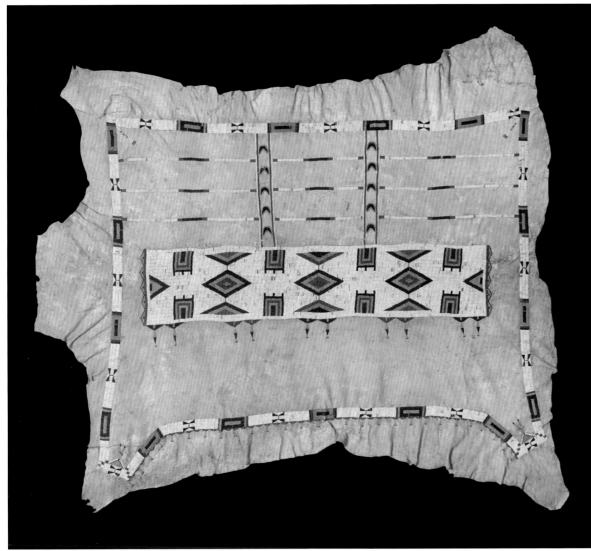

FIG. 9.1A

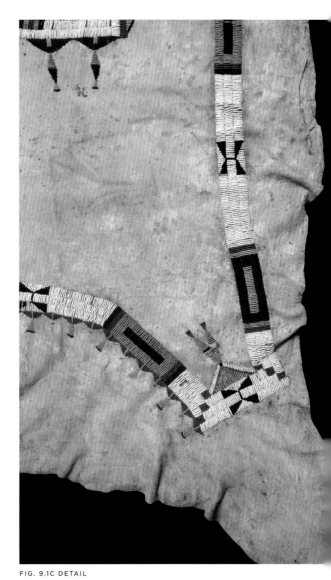

FIG. 9.1C DETAIL

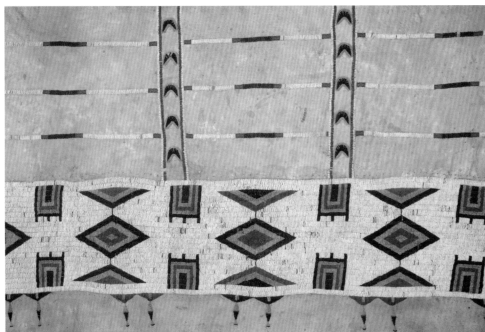

FIG. 9.1B DETAIL

PHOTO 9.1

FIG. 9.2

FIG. 9.2 DETAIL

FIG. 9.2 AND DETAIL
WOMAN'S DRESS, C. 1880

Lakota nation, North or South Dakota, USA

Native-tanned hide, glass beads

Roswell Museum and Art Center, New Mexico

Photograph by José Rivera

FIG. 9.3, *Opposite*
WOMAN'S LEGGINGS, 1890S

Lakota nation, North or South Dakota, USA

Native-tanned hide, glass beads

Museum of Indian Arts and Culture / Laboratory
of Anthropology, 42901 a & b

PHOTO 9.2, *Opposite*
UNITED TRIBES POWWOW, SEPTEMBER 1992

Bismarck, North Dakota

Photograph by Marsha Bol

Fully beaded dress yokes, usually covered in light blue
beads, became the signature of Lakota women beginning
in the 1860s (Fig. 9.2). Underneath their dresses they wore
heavily beaded leggings (Fig. 9.3) for modesty and warmth.
Lakota women continued to make hide dresses with
completely beaded yokes into the 1930s, even though they
were rarely worn. Today skilled Lakota beadworkers will
occasionally undertake the exacting task of making a hide
dress with a fully beaded yoke for a special family member,
anticipating that it will be cherished and passed down for
many generations to come.

Plains Indian powwows provide the opportunity today
for traditional dress to be paraded and danced. Women of
all ages wear their heirloom or newly created beaded hide
dresses (Photo 9.2) to perform the Women's Traditional
Dance, moving in a modest and dignified style appropriate
to this dance category.

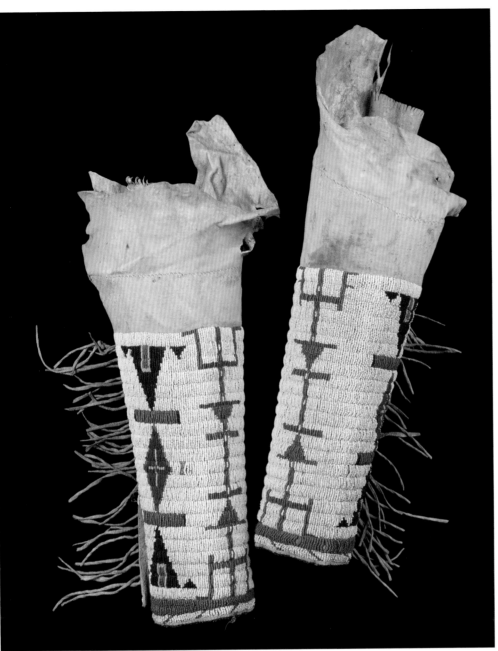

FIG. 9.3

PHOTO 9.2

FIG. 9.4

FIG. 9.4
MEN'S PIPE BAGS, C. 1890

Southern Cheyenne nation, Oklahoma, USA

Native-tanned hide, glass beads, pigment, dyed horsehair, metal

Left: 31 x 6⁵/₁₆ in. (78.7 x 16 cm); right: 31¹/₃ x 6¹¹/₁₆ in. (79.5 x 17 cm)

Museum of Indian Arts and Culture / Laboratory of Anthropology, 11868/12a&b

Central Plains men never appeared at special occasions without their pipe bag, whether it be at a Fourth of July procession or a trip to meet with officials in Washington. As anthropologist Clark Wissler noted regarding the Lakota-made pipe bags in 1904: "All things considered, these [pipe]bags are the culmination of Dakota decorative design. They are used solely by men, but made by women, and both regard them as works of art. Their practical value is nil. For ordinary use the men carry plain pouches of the same general form, reserving the highly decorated ones for formal social functions and ceremonies." (1904: 237–38).

PHOTO 9.3

FIG. 9.6

FIG. 9.5

PHOTO 9.3
CROW [*APSÁALOOKE*] GIRL READY FOR A
PARADE, C. 1904

Crow Indian Reservation, Montana, USA

University of Nebraska-Lincoln, O'Connor
Foundation Collection, GPN-05-044

Photograph by Fred E. Miller

FIG. 9.5
HORSE TRAPPINGS (BRIDLE, FOREHEAD
ORNAMENT, MARTINGALE), C. 1900–1930

Crow Indian Reservation, Montana, USA

Native hide, glass beads

Martingale: 36³/4 x 15¹/2 in. (93.3 x 39.4 cm)

Roswell Museum and Art Center, New Mexico

Photograph by José Rivera

FIG. 9.6
SADDLE, SADDLE BAGS, AND SADDLE
BLANKET, 1890–1920

Lakota nation, North or South Dakota, USA

Native-tanned hide, glass beads, brass bells,
wool cloth, commercial saddle

Bob and Lora Sandroni collection

With the acquisition of horses in the eighteenth century, the lifestyle of Plains Indian people changed radically. Once mounted on horseback, from this advantageous position they became much more successful hunters and warriors. This animal became so intrinsic to Plains culture that they were, and continue to be, honored with fine beaded horse trappings (Figs. 9.5 and 9.6).

Beginning in 1904 at Crow Agency, Crow people have continued to hold the annual Crow Fair (Photo 9.3). Horse owners display their horse's finery, both heritage and newly made pieces, during the fair parades. As Joe Medicine Crow (1992: 123) said: "in a more serious way the Crow *Um-basax-bilua* [Crow Fair] is a time of cultural renewal, a time to display the Crow culture in action. This annual event is the time to tell the world that Crow Indians of Montana have a strong cultural persistence. . . ."

FIG. 9.7

SPECIAL OCCASION DRESS
ELSEWHERE

FIG. 9.7
DANCE SKIRT SECTION, LATE NINETEENTH CENTURY

Hupa peoples, Klamath River region, California, USA

Squaw grass, hide, pine nuts, glass beads

27 x 20 in. (68.6 x 50.8 cm)

Museum of International Folk Art, Gift of Lloyd E. Cotsen and the Neutrogena Corporation, A.1995.93.1053

Photograph by Pat Pollard

FIG. 9.8
BREASTPLATE NECKLACE, LATE NINETEENTH CENTURY

Pomo peoples, northern California, USA

Plant fiber, cut clam shell beads, abalone

7³/₄ x 12¹/₂ in. (19.7 x 32.4 cm)

Ralph T. Coe Center for the Arts

FIG. 9.9
BELT, PRE-1931

Unknown tribe, California, USA

Rawhide, olivella shell, glass beads

Museum of Indian Arts and Culture / Laboratory of Anthropology, 40883/12

There were over 100 federally recognized tribes in California, with at least 80 distinct languages. They lived in isolated mountain valleys, and wore minimal clothing given the mild climate. They fashioned their skirts, necklaces, and belts from the abundant plant and sea life surrounding them, adding shells, seeds, nuts, and glass beads as adornment, especially on their dance clothing.

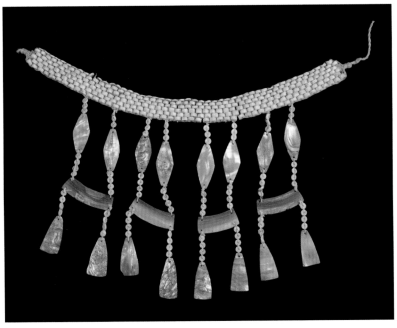

FIG. 9.8

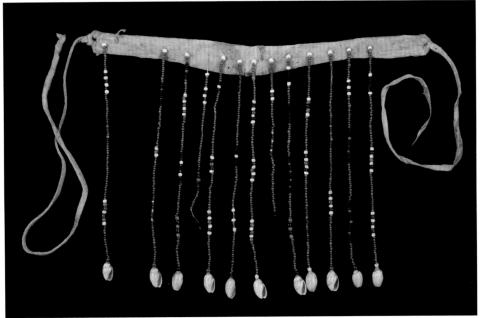

FIG. 9.9

191

FIG. 9.10A

FIG. 9.11

FIG. 9.10B

FIGS. 9.10 A (FRONT) AND B (BACK) WOMAN'S VEST, DATE UNKNOWN

Krakow, Poland

Velvet, glass beads, metal sequins

Museum of International Folk Art, Gift of Florence Dibell Bartlett, A.1955.1.352

FIG. 9.11 AND DETAIL WOMAN'S BODICE, TWENTIETH CENTURY

Chad, Bohemia, Czech Republic

Silk, cotton, glass beads, metal sequins, metallic thread

$29^{5}/_{8}$ in. (75.3 cm)

Museum of International Folk Art, A.1991.74.1

FIG. 9.11 DETAIL

FIG. 9.12

FIG. 9.12
WOMAN'S SHIFT, NINETEENTH CENTURY

Romania

Cotton, glass beads, metal sequins

55 x 44 in. (139.7 x 111.8 cm)

Museum of International Folk Art, Gift of Florence Dibell Bartlett, A.1955.1.141

FIG. 9.13 AND DETAIL
MAN'S BELT, 1881–1921

Romania

Leather, cotton, glass beads, metal

$34^{13}/_{16}$ x $3^{15}/_{16}$ in. (88.5 x 10 cm)

Museum of International Folk Art, Gift of the Hendershott Family, A.2009.64.2

Although eastern European traditional folk dress is renowned for its exquisite embroidered adornment, beadwork is often embedded into the embroidery. Glass beads were easily available from nearby Bohemia, now the Czech Republic. Today these objects from the past are worn only for special occasions.

FIG. 9.13

FIG. 9.13 DETAIL

FIG. 9.14
CHINA POBLANA SKIRT
WITH BLOUSE, LATE 1920S

México

Skirt: Cotton, metal sequins, glass beads; 39 3/4 in. (101 cm)

Blouse: Cotton, glass beads; 26 3/4 x 27 3/16 in. (68 x 69.1 cm)

Museum of International Folk Art, A.1993.113.7 & A.1996.17.1

FIG. 9.15 AND DETAIL
CHINA POBLANA BLOUSE,
C. 1935

Puebla city and state, México

Cotton, glass beads

24 1/2 x 21 1/16 in. (62.25 x 53.5 cm)

Museum of International Folk Art, Gift of Florence Dibell Bartlett, A.1955.1.135

The *china poblana* outfit, worn by women for fiestas and fancy dress occasions, gained great popularity in both urban México and the United States during the 1930s. With its origins shrouded in legend, this style can only be traced back to the nineteenth century.

FIG. 9.16, *Opposite*
NECKLACES WITH TRIPLE
CROSSES, 1950–1975

Zapotec peoples, Sierra Juárez region, Oaxaca state, México

Silver, glass beads, silver beads

Left: Choapan cross, 15 1/3 in. (39 cm); right: Yalalag cross, 21 1/4 in. (54 cm)

Museum of International Folk Art, IFAF Collection, FA.1973.39.17 & FA.1975.1.197

FIG. 9.15

FIG. 9.15 DETAIL

FIG. 9.14

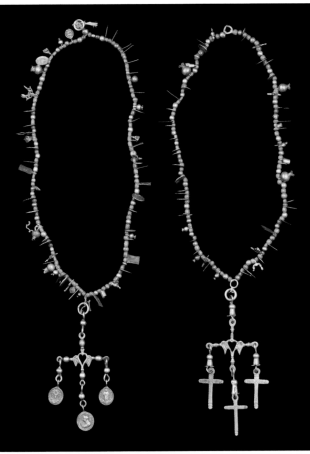

FIG. 9.16

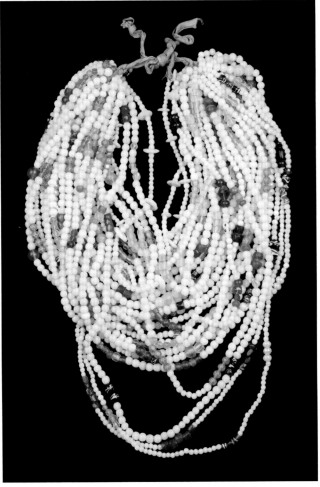

FIG. 9.18

FIG. 9.17
NECKLACE OF TRADE BEADS, DATE UNKNOWN

Zapotec peoples, San Pedro Quiatoni, Oaxaca state, México

Museum of International Folk Art, Gift of Stafford and John Thomas from the Davis and Pack Collection of Mexican jewelry, A.2015.19.25

FIG. 9.18
28-STRAND NECKLACE, DATE UNKNOWN

Mixe peoples, Mixistlán or Yacochi villages, Oaxaca state, México

Cotton, ceramic, glass beads

20½ in. (52 cm)

Museum of International Folk Art, IFAF Collection, FA.1975.1.242

PHOTO 9.4
ZAPOTEC GIRL FROM SANTIAGO CHOAPAN, OAXACA, WEARING VERY OLD JEWELRY, 1941

Arizona State Museum, Tucson

Photograph by Donald Cordry

PHOTO 9.5
SAN PEDRO QUIATONI, OAXACA, GIRL, WEARING A NECKLACE OF OLD TRADE BEADS, 1964

Arizona State Museum, Tucson

Photograph by Donald Cordry

Oaxaca is the most ethnically complex of México's states because of its high percentage of indigenous peoples. These peoples, who have a lengthy history in this region, account for 53 percent of México's total indigenous population. Indian women from the state of Oaxaca have historically put great effort and expense into dressing their finest. Each village or locale developed its own distinctive and identifiable dress, which included splendid beaded necklaces, composed of locally made silver beads and pendants plus imported glass beads. Many have continued to retain their own community dress, brought out for religious fiestas and other special occasions.

FIG. 9.17

PHOTO 9.4

PHOTO 9.5

FIG. 9.19

FIG. 9.19
WRAPPINGS FOR WOMEN'S FOREARMS AND ANKLES, TWENTIETH CENTURY

Kuna peoples, San Blas Islands, Panama

Cotton, glass beads

Wrapped beadwork: 5½ in. (14 cm)

Museum of International Folk Art, Gift of J.M. Thorington, FA.1976.131.50

Kuna women wrap strings of beads, exactingly threaded to create a pattern, on their forearms and ankles. When not in use, they are wrapped onto a roll of cloth for storage.

FIG.9.20

FIG.9.20
PECTORALS, LATE NINETEENTH–EARLY TWENTIETH CENTURY

Mapuche (Araucanian) peoples, La Frontera region, Chile

Silver

Average length: 10 in. (25.4 cm)

Museum of International Folk Art, A.1974.19.3; Gift of General and Mrs. Barksdale Hamlett, A.1975.9.1, 8, 12; Gift of Mr. and Mrs. Thomas Pearce, A.1965.10.1

FIG. 9.21
HEADBANDS, EARLY TWENTIETH CENTURY

Mapuche (Araucanian) peoples, La Frontera region, Chile

Silver

Top: 19 x 2½ in. (48.3 x 6.4 cm); bottom: 23¼ x 2⅜ in. (59 x 6 cm)

Museum of International Folk Art, top: Gift of General and Mrs. Barksdale Hamlett, A.1975.9.4; bottom: IFAF Collection, Gift of Sallie Wagner, FA.1976.38.3

In the late nineteenth century, Mapuche Indian silversmiths developed a women's jewelry form not found elsewhere in Latin America. These distinctive pectorals with their unusual linked chains (Fig. 9.20) can easily be recognized as typical Mapuche wear, although today women only wear these heirlooms for communal ceremonies or a shopping trip to town. "The creativity of the Mapuche silversmiths reached its peak in the designing of these pectorals. The wealth of their forms is notable." (Schindler 1985: 36).

Typical Mapuche jewelry also included a woman's lavish headband (Fig. 9.21) consisting of a linked chain with suspended dangles. On occasion the wearer might wear the headband attached to the front of her clothing below the shoulders, hanging rather like a necklace.

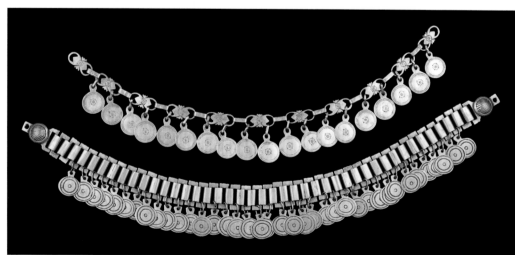

FIG. 9.21

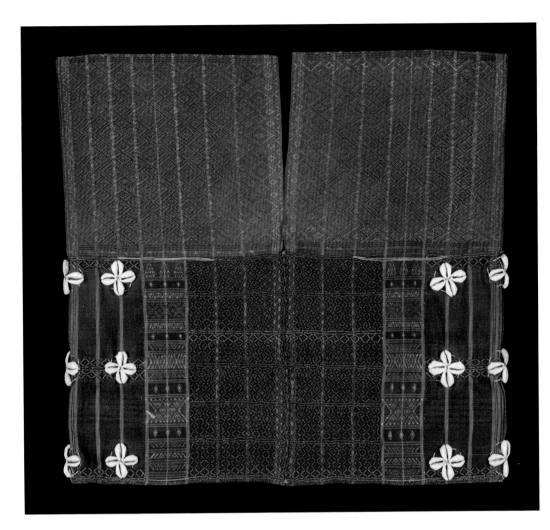

FIG. 9.22 AND DETAIL
WOMAN'S BLOUSE, MID-
TWENTIETH CENTURY

Chin peoples, Burma

Cotton, glass beads, cowrie shells

16 15/16 x 17 5/16 in. (43 x 44 cm)

Museum of International Folk Art,
IFAF Collection, Gift of Diane and
Sandy Besser, FA.2002.49.10

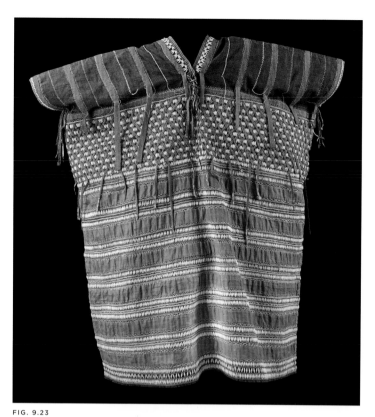

FIG. 9.23

FIG. 9.23 DETAIL

**FIG. 9.23 AND DETAIL
MARRIED WOMAN'S
BLOUSE, 1850–1900**

Sgaw Karen (Pg'a Kanyaw
Sg'aw) peoples, Burma

Wool, cotton, grass, Job's
tears seeds

32 x 29 in. (81.3 x 73.7 cm)

Museum of International
Folk Art, Gift of Lloyd E.
Cotsen and the Neutrogena
Corporation, A.1995.93.343

Photograph by Pat Pollard

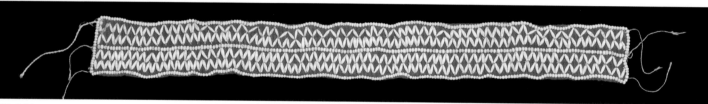

FIG. 9.24

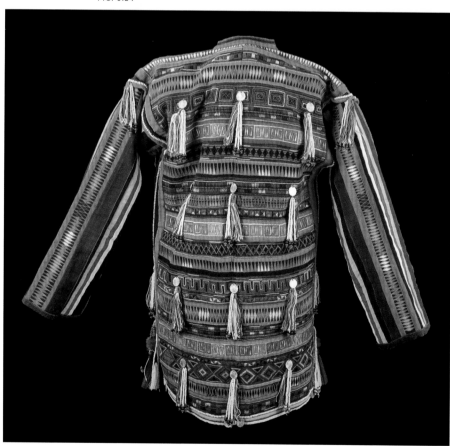

FIG. 9.25

**FIG. 9.24
WOMAN'S BELT, C. 1955**

Loimi Akha peoples, Burma

Cotton, Job's tears seeds

26¹⁵/₁₆ x 2³/₄ in. (68.5 x 7 cm)

Museum of International Folk Art, Gift of Dr. Nathaniel Tarn,
A.2000.19.97

**FIG. 9.25
WOMAN'S JACKET, C. 1980**

Loimi Akha peoples, Shan state, Thailand

Cotton, glass beads, Job's tears seeds, metal coins

55¹/₈ in. (140 cm)

Museum of International Folk Art, A.1990.25.1

Tribal women in Burma and Thailand look to nature for
decorative material to adorn their lavishly stitched dress. Hard
seeds, known as Job's tears, produced by a tropical grass
(*Coix lacryma-jobi*), furnish a decorative element used much
like glass beads. The seeds when immature are long and thin,
becoming round as they mature. Thus they furnish a variety of
shapes for inclusion on women's blouses, belts, and jackets.
Heating the seeds in the embers of a fire turns their natural
grey color to white. (Crabtree & Stallebrass 2009: 9, 131).

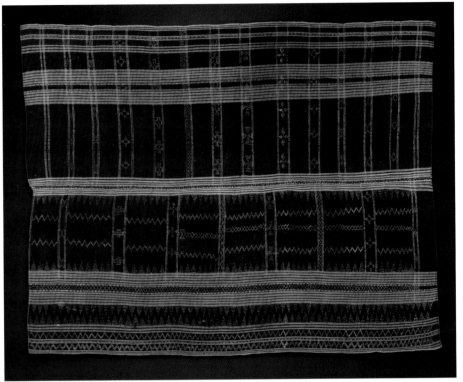

FIG. 9.26

FIG. 9.26 DETAIL

FIG. 9.26 AND DETAIL
SARONG, EARLY TO MID-TWENTIETH CENTURY

Ta Oi peoples, Vietnam or Laos

Cotton, metal beads

45 11/16 x 60 1/4 in. (116 x 153 cm)

Museum of International Folk Art, Gift of Janis and
William Wetsman, A.2011.36.2

The subtle white designs in this textile are made by
white metal beads woven into the fabric.

FIG. 9.27
HIP ORNAMENT (*FIKUM*), TWENTIETH CENTURY

Bontoc peoples, Mountain Province, northern Luzon,
Philippines

Mother-of-pearl bivalve shell, cut coconut shell,
rattan cording

9 in. (23 cm)

Shari and Earl Kessler Collection

Bontoc men wore these highly prized giant mother-
of-pearl bivalve shell ornaments at their waists, either
in front or on their hip, only for ceremonial occasions.
The inside rim of the shell is etched with designs
drawn from tattoo and textile patterns and a piece of
coconut shell is mounted in the center.

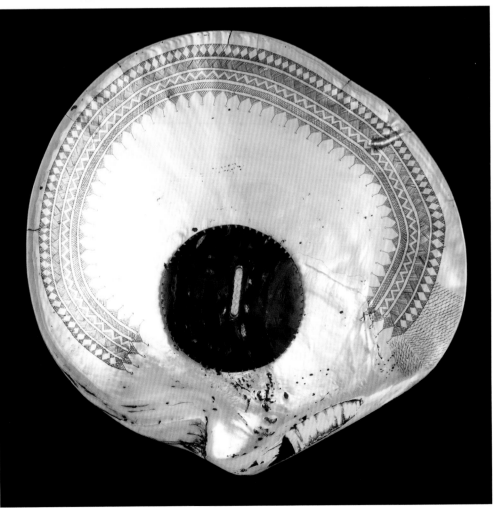

FIG. 9.27

FIG. 9.28

WOMAN'S VEST, 1930S–1950S

T'boli peoples, southern Cotabato province, southern
Mindanao island, Philippines

Glass beads

13³/₄ x 15¹/₃ in. (35 x 39 cm)

Shari and Earl Kessler Collection

FIG. 9.29
WOMEN'S BELTS, 1930S–1950S

T'boli peoples, southern Cotabato province, southern
Mindanao island, Philippines

Abacá (banana leaf stems fiber), brass, glass beads

18¹/₂ x 8¹/₄ in. (47 x 21 cm)

Shari and Earl Kessler Collection

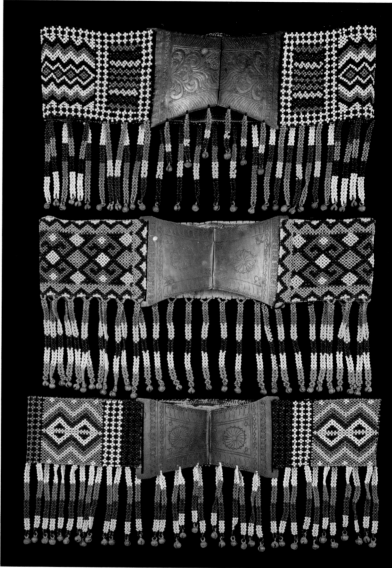

FIG. 9.29

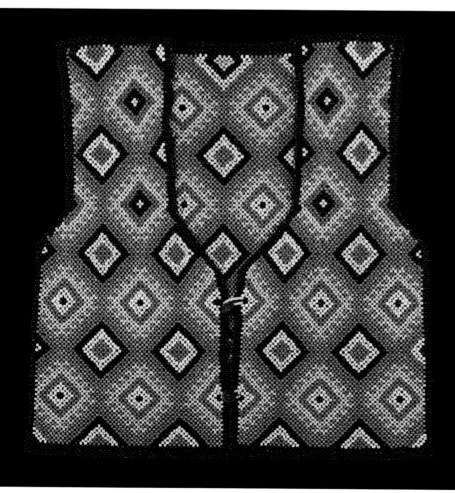

FIG. 9.28

FIGS. 9.30A (FRONT) AND B (BACK), *Opposite*
SHIRT/BLOUSE, 1920–40

B'laan peoples, southern Mindanao island, Philippines

Cotton, glass beads, shells

14³/₁₆ x 47 in. (36 x 119.4 cm)

Museum of International Folk Art, Gift of Lloyd E. Cotsen and
the Neutrogena Corporation, A.1995.93.1172

Photograph by Pat Pollard

The maker of this type of shirt, worn by both men and
women, created the decoration by sewing white glass beads
flat thereby achieving the same effect as with more labor
intensive hand-cut mother-of-pearl beads.

FIG. 9.30A

FIG. 9.31
WOMAN'S DANCE APRON (*SASSANG*), C. 1915

Sa'dan Toraja peoples, Sulawesi, Indonesia

Cotton, glass beads

25 x 19 in. (63.5 x 48.3 cm)

Museum of International Folk Art, IFAF Collection, Gift of Diane and Sandy Besser, FA.2008.74.385

"According to ritual speech of the Sa'dan Toraja peoples of south-central Sulawesi, ancestors descend to earth on stairs of beadwork and beadwork covers the door to the dwelling-place of the supreme God, Puang Matua." (Nooy-Palm 1979: 161, 171, in Hector 1995: 26). Thus beadwork, understandably, figures prominently in the rituals of these people. The red motifs (*sekong*), represent squatting ancestors. "Displaying *sekong* motifs during funeral rituals activates the benevolence of these ancestors whose favor the Toraja habitually seek so that their rice crops may flourish, and their family groups prosper and multiply." (Hector 1995: 27). Interestingly, these beaded aprons, worn by women, are made by Toraja male specialists, who make all Toraja beadwork.

FIG. 9.30B

FIG. 9.31

FIG. 9.32A

FIG. 9.32B

202

FIG. 9.33A

FIGS. 9.33A (FRONT), B (BACK), AND C (DETAIL)
VEST AND SKIRT, MID-LATE TWENTIETH CENTURY

Maloh peoples, west Kalimantan, Borneo island, Indonesia

Cotton, pineapple fiber, glass beads, metal, plastic buttons

Vest: 18$\frac{1}{8}$ x 15$\frac{3}{8}$ in. (46 x 39 cm); skirt: 20$\frac{1}{2}$ x 15$\frac{9}{16}$ in. (52 x 39.5 cm)

Museum of International Folk Art, IFAF Collection, Gift of Diane and Sandy Besser, FA.2008.74.377 & 378

Maloh beaded skirts and vests are worn only on festive occasions. Even if they are new, they are still considered treasures of the community, which has a long tradition of making entirely beaded skirts and tunics. (Munan 2005: 102). The vest prominently features repeating motifs of the squatting female, who holds potent magic to dispel evil spirits.

FIG. 9.33B

FIGS. 9.32A (FRONT), B (BACK), *Opposite*
VEST AND SKIRT, LATE NINETEENTH CENTURY

Orang Ulu peoples, Borneo island, Indonesia

Cotton, cowrie shells, glass beads, brass

Vest: 22 x 18 in. (55.9 x 45.7 cm); skirt: 19 x 17$\frac{1}{2}$ in. (48.3 x 43.2 cm)

David McLanahan Collection

Few of these jackets and skirts, elaborately embroidered with cowrie shells, remain. The cowrie shells on the jacket are likely arranged into dragon designs, offering great protection to its wearer.

FIG. 9.33C DETAIL

FIG. 9.34

PHOTO 9.6

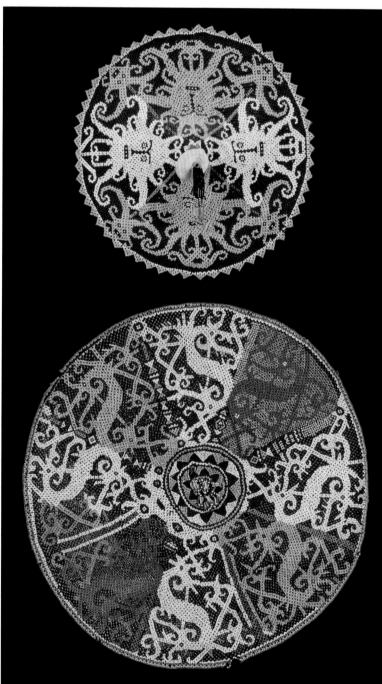

FIG. 9.35

FIG. 9.34
SUN HAT, TWENTIETH CENTURY

Kenyah peoples, Borneo island, Indonesia

Cotton and synthetic fiber, palm leaves, rattan, glass beads

8 x 31 in. (20.3 x 78.7 cm)

David McLanahan Collection

FIG. 9.35
SUN HAT TOPS, C. 1925

Kenyah peoples, Kalimantan province, Borneo island, Indonesia

Fiber, glass beads

Bottom: $21^{1}/_{4}$ x $33^{7}/_{8}$ in. (54 x 86 cm)

Museum of International Folk Art, IFAF Collection, Gift of Diane and Sandy Besser, FA.2006.70.43v

Kenyah broad-brimmed sun hats protect the wearer's head with both their structure and their beaded images. The dragons, hornbills, and the godly faces with dragons, depicted in beadwork on the beaded hat and the tops, provide protection in daily life.

PHOTO 9.6
IBAN MAIDENS WEARING BEADED YOKES FOR MIRING CEREMONY, UNKNOWN DATE

Iban peoples, Sarawak state, Borneo island, Malaysia

David McLanahan Collection

Iban people generally perform the Miring ceremony to appease the spirits and receive their blessings. "In the olden days, when all other real-life measures failed to solve a problem, people were compelled to perform the miring ceremony." (Dato Sri Edmund Langgu 2010). It is also performed as a welcome and blessing ritual to appease the spirits when important visitors come into the longhouse. (Ong 2016).

Two maidens wear beaded yokes (see also Fig. 3.26), while one woman is dressed in her wedding train (with "frog" bells) reversed as a necklace (see also Fig. 3.24). She has a right to wear her train in ceremonies after she has married.

FIG 9.36

FIG 9.36
WOMAN'S NECKLACES, PRE-1945

Ao Naga peoples, Nagaland, northeast India

Carnelian beads, shell, brass

15.7 in. (40 cm)

Harry and Tiala M. Neufeld Collection

FIG. 9.37
WOMAN'S NECKLACE, TWENTIETH CENTURY

Chakhesang (formerly Eastern Angami) Naga peoples, Nagaland, northeast India

Glass beads, carnelian beads, shell beads, conch shell

19.7 in. (50 cm)

Harry and Tiala M. Neufeld Collection

Indigenous Naga people are renowned for wearing an abundance of elaborate bead necklaces, such as these necklaces of carnelian beads and shells, especially for festive occasions.

FIG. 9.37

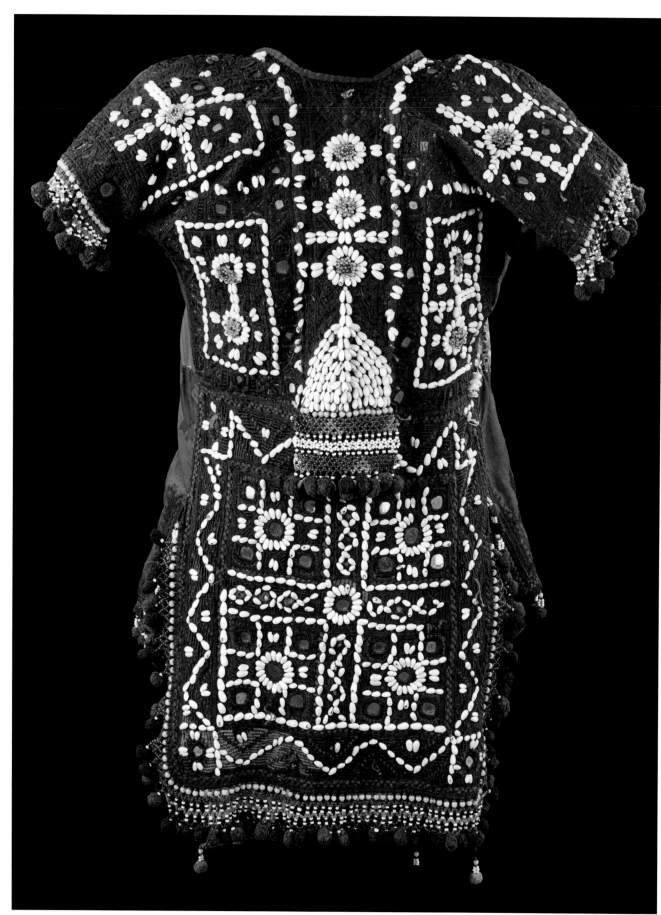

FIG. 9.38

FIG. 9.38
BLOUSE, C. 1960

Sindh, Pakistan

Cotton, shells, glass
beads

21¹⁄₄ in. (54 cm)

Museum of International
Folk Art, IFAF Collection,
FA.1986.458.7

FIG. 9.39 AND DETAIL,
Opposite
MEN'S HATS, 1930S

Pashtun nomadic
peoples, northern
Afghanistan

Cotton, glass beads

Approximately 3³⁄₄ x
7¹⁄₈ in. (9.5 x 18 cm)

Anne and Bill Frej
Collection

Muslim Pashtun men
wear these skull caps
underneath their long
wrapped turbans. The
various designs identify
the origin and status
of the wearer. (Harvey
1996: 205).

FIG. 9.39

FIG. 9.39 DETAIL

FIG. 9.40
WOMAN'S DANCE OUTFIT, 2012

Latuka (Otuho) peoples, Torit county, Equatoria state, South Sudan

Cotton, glass beads

Museum of International Folk Art, IFAF Collection, FA.2012.47.2

Latuka married women wear beaded outfits, consisting of a headpiece, waist beads, a short skirt, and a shawl, on special occasions such as ritual ceremonies, weddings, and funeral rites.

FIG. 9.40

HOUSE DECORATION

FIG. 9.41

PHOTO 9.7

Thresholds in many cultures separate the safe, protected space inside the home from the dangers of the outside. To protect those welcome to enter the safe zone and to prevent malevolent spirits from entering, doorways are adorned with ritual hangings, especially during auspicious times. A new beautifully decorated *toran* is hung over the doorway as part of wedding preparations (Photo 9.7).

Around the beginning of the twentieth century in Gujarat, a beadwork tradition emerged as a feminine craft revolving around making beaded objects for home decoration. Kathi women and girls from a wealthy land-owning class in Gujarat took up beadwork in place of embroidery, which by then was mainly produced professionally.

These beaded objects tend to include pictorial images drawn from both Hindu iconography and from secular sources, all worked together into a white beaded background. The images do not represent narratives; rather they are depicted individually solely as decoration. For example, the Hindu goddess, Mahalakshmi, appears with her two attendants, perhaps to bless the residents of the house with abundance and fertility (Fig. 9.42—on the third tab from the left, and Fig. 9.43d). A central depiction of two women churning butter, bracketed by lions and elephants (Fig. 9.41), shows an everyday woman's domestic activity. Animals generally associated with high status and wealth, such as these lions and elephants, peacocks (Fig. 9.42), horses (Fig. 9.43e) and horse-drawn carriages (Fig. 9.43b), plus flowers and plants, appear in abundance, perhaps displaying the family's prosperity.

FIG. 9.41
DOORWAY DECORATION (*SAKH TORAN*), C. 1930

Kathi peoples, Saurashtra region, Gujarat state, India

Cotton, glass beads

24 x 32¹¹⁄₆ in. (61 x 83 cm)

Museum of International Folk Art, Gift of Clara Farwell Allen, A.1952.15.2

PHOTO 9.7
JANI BHALASARA RESTS BENEATH A NEW *TORAN*, 1989

Ahir peoples, Paddar village, Kutch region, Gujarat state, India

Photograph by Nora Fisher

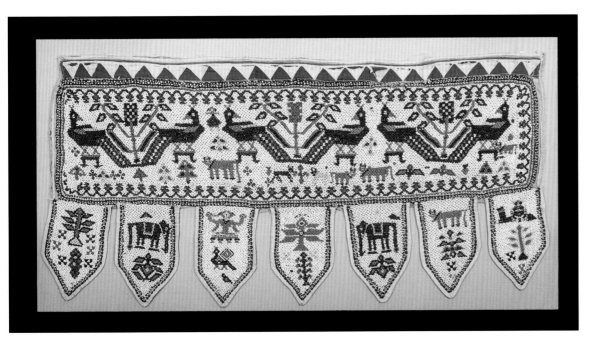

FIG. 9.42

FIG. 9.42
DOORWAY DECORATION (*SAKH TORAN*), C. 1890

Kathi peoples, Gujarat state, India

Cotton, glass beads

18 1/8 x 39 3/38 in. (46 x 100 cm)

Museum of International Folk Art, IFAF Collection, Gift of Diane and Sandy Besser, FA.2006.70.20

FIG. 9.43A

FIG. 9.43B

FIGS. 9.43A, B, C, D, E, AND F
FRIEZE (*PATTA*), C. 1945

Kathi peoples, Saurashtra region, Gujarat state, India

Burlap, glass beads

75 3/16 x 5 1/2 in. (191 x 14 cm)

Museum of International Folk Art, Gift of the Girard Foundation Collection, A.1980.1.733

FIG. 9.43C

FIG. 9.43D

FIG. 9.43E

FIG. 9.43F

FIG. 9.44

FIG. 9.44, *Opposite*
WALL HANGING (*CHAKLA*),
C. 1920

Kathi peoples, Saurashtra
region, Gujarat state, India

Cotton, glass beads

13³/₁₆ x 10⁷/₁₆ in. (33.5 x
26.5 cm)

Museum of International
Folk Art, Gift of Ronald H.
Goodman, A.1979.83.34

These panels were hung in
homes and, on occasion,
used as part of a family's
house shrine. The image
depicts Lord Krishna inside
a shrine. He appears as a
baby, crawling and holding a
vessel of butter with his right
hand. A candelabra sits in
front of the shrine, flanked by
elephants and two musicians
playing music for the deity.
The figures in the two upper
corners are also deities in
smaller shrines. (Sethi 2016).

FIG. 9.45
WALL HANGING (*CHAKLA*),
C. 1920

Kathi peoples, Saurashtra
region, Gujarat state, India

Cotton, glass beads

15³/₄ x 14¹⁵/₁₆ in. (49 x
37.9 cm)

Museum of International
Folk Art, Gift of Ronald H.
Goodman, A.2000.47.1

The center figure on a horse is
a deity or royalty, identifiable
by the umbrella over its head.
The figure of Krishna with his
blue-colored skin appears
multiple times with the Gopis
dancing the Garba or Dandiya
Raas folk dances. (Sethi 2016).

FIG. 9.45

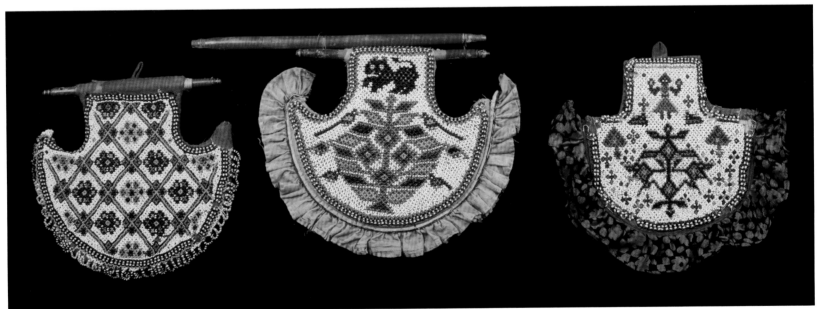

FIG. 9.46
FANS (*VINIJHANAS*), C. 1890

Kathi peoples, Saurashtra region, Gujarat
state, India

Wood, cotton, glass beads

Approximately 9¹/₂ x 10 in. (24.1 x
25.4 cm)

Museum of International Folk Art, IFAF
Collection, Gift of Diane and Sandy
Besser, FA.2006.70.17-19

Beaded fans serve to cool their owners
during the hottest part of the year when
temperatures can reach 115 degrees
Fahrenheit.

FIG. 9.47

PHOTO 9.8

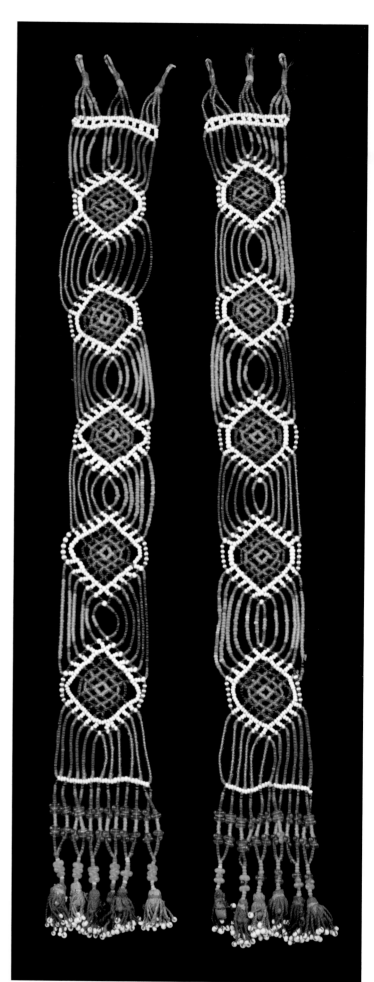

FIG. 9.48

FIG. 9.49

FIG. 9.50

FIG. 9.47, *Opposite*
DOILY, 1970S

Pashtun nomadic peoples, Hazarajat, Afghanistan

Cotton, silk, glass beads

9³/₄ x 9¹/₂ in. (24.8 x 24.1 cm)

Anne and Bill Frej Collection

PHOTO 9.8, *Opposite*
YURT INTERIOR, 2012

Russian mountain camp, Zhabagly, Kazakhstan

Photograph by Pam Najdowski

FIG. 9.48, *Opposite*
YURT HANGINGS, TWENTIETH CENTURY

Northern Afghanistan

Glass beads

20 x 8 in. (50.8 x 20.3 cm)

Anne and Bill Frej Collection

FIG. 9.49
YURT DECORATION, C. 1950–2000

Pashtun nomadic peoples, northern Afghanistan

Synthetic backing, glass beads

5 x 17¹/₂ in. (12.7 x 44.5 cm)

Anne and Bill Frej Collection

FIG. 9.50
PAIR OF YURT HANGINGS, TWENTIETH CENTURY

Northern Afghanistan

Cotton, glass beads, silver

14¹/₂ in. (36.8 cm)

Marsha Bol Collection

FIG. 9.51

FIG. 9.51 DETAIL

FIG. 9.51 AND DETAIL
HANGING, 1900–1940

Montagnard peoples, central highlands, Vietnam

Cotton, silk, glass beads, wool, mirror

11 x 38³/₈ in. (28 x 97.5 cm)

Museum of International Folk Art, Gift of Elizabeth Berry, A.1999.26.37

FIG. 9.52
WALL HANGING (*KALAGA*), LATE NINETEENTH CENTURY

Shan peoples, Burma

Cotton, metallic thread, glass beads, sequins

22⁷/₁₆ x 50 in. (57 x 127 cm)

Museum of International Folk Art, Gift of Mary Hunt Kahlenberg and Robert T. Coffland, A.1993.110.2

This type of wall hanging was originally hung in monasteries. Desired by tourists, they soon became a rare commodity. Beginning in the 1980s, a cottage industry developed to meet this demand. Families made smaller wall hangings suitable for home décor. Many of the figures depict stories from the Ten Lives of Buddha, the epic poem Ramayana, or local folk tales. (Stanislaw 1987).

FIG. 9.52

ANIMAL DECORATION

PHOTO 9.9
CAMEL IN FULL TRAPPINGS, 1983

Rabari peoples, Samakhiali, India

Photograph by Judy Frater

Even domestic animals, important to the lives of communities, are dressed in their finery for festival occasions. In particular horses (Figs. 9.5, 9.6, and 9.54), donkeys, camels (Figs. 9.53, 8.37, and Photo 9.9), and bullocks (Fig. 3.18) are adorned in their finest.

FIGS. 9.53A, B (DETAIL), AND C (DETAIL)
CAMEL TRAPPINGS, C. 1950

Rabari peoples, Jhangi, Gujarat state, India

Fiber, mirror, buttons

Museum of International Folk Art, FA.1990.16.96v

PHOTO 9.9

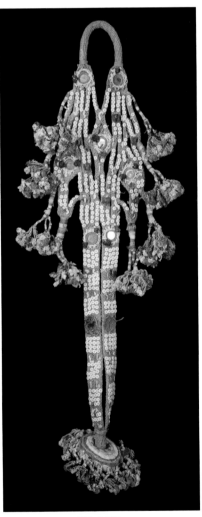

FIG. 9.53A

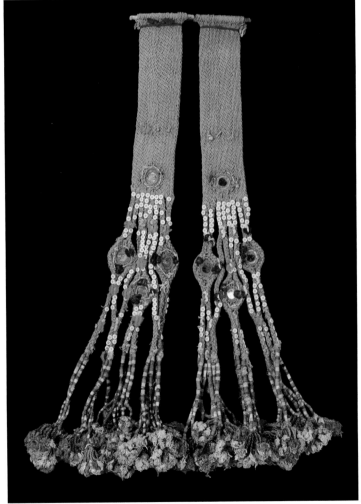

FIG. 9.53B

FIG. 9.53C

FIG. 9.54 AND DETAIL
HORSE NECK COVER, (*GHUGHI*),
C. 1930

Kathi peoples, Saurashtra region,
Gujarat state, India

Cotton, silk, glass beads, mirror,
metal

50½ x 64 in. (128.3 x 162.6 cm)

David McLanahan Collection

The horse's ears fit through the
holes. Multicolored beaded figures
include peacocks, parrots, lions,
dogs, cows, a horse and rider,
candelabras, and Krishna playing
a flute.

FIG. 9.55 AND DETAIL
BUMBA-MEU-BOI **BULL, 1968**

São Luís, Maranhão state, Brazil

Fabric, bull horns, sequins, glass beads

59 x 43³⁄₄ x 14¹⁄₄ in. (150 x 111.1 x 36.2 cm)

Museum of International Folk Art, Gift of Katarina
Real-Cate Collection, A.1986.511.6v

The Portuguese brought not only cattle but their
associated folk dramas when they colonized Brazil.
The *Bumba-Meu-Boi*, a very popular comic drama,
has been adapted to reflect typical northeast
Brazilian rural life. Originally the plot centered around
the death and resurrection of a prized bull. São
Luís, in the northern state of Maranhão, is especially
famous for its version of the bull drama, performed
for the feast of St. John in late June. Elsewhere in
Brazil, the drama continues to be performed during
the Christmas holidays, carnival, and other feast days.

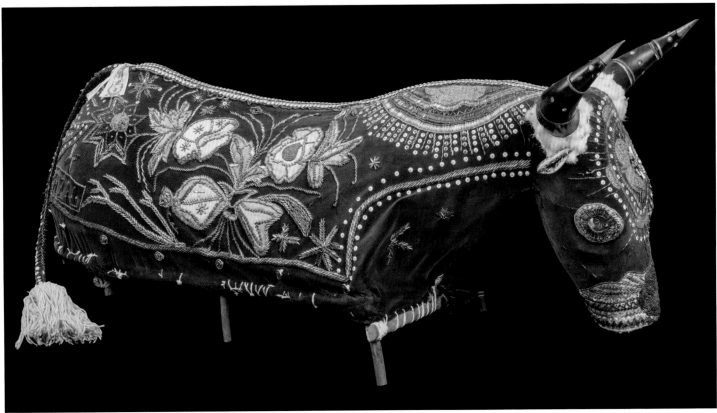

BEYOND
THE VILLAGE

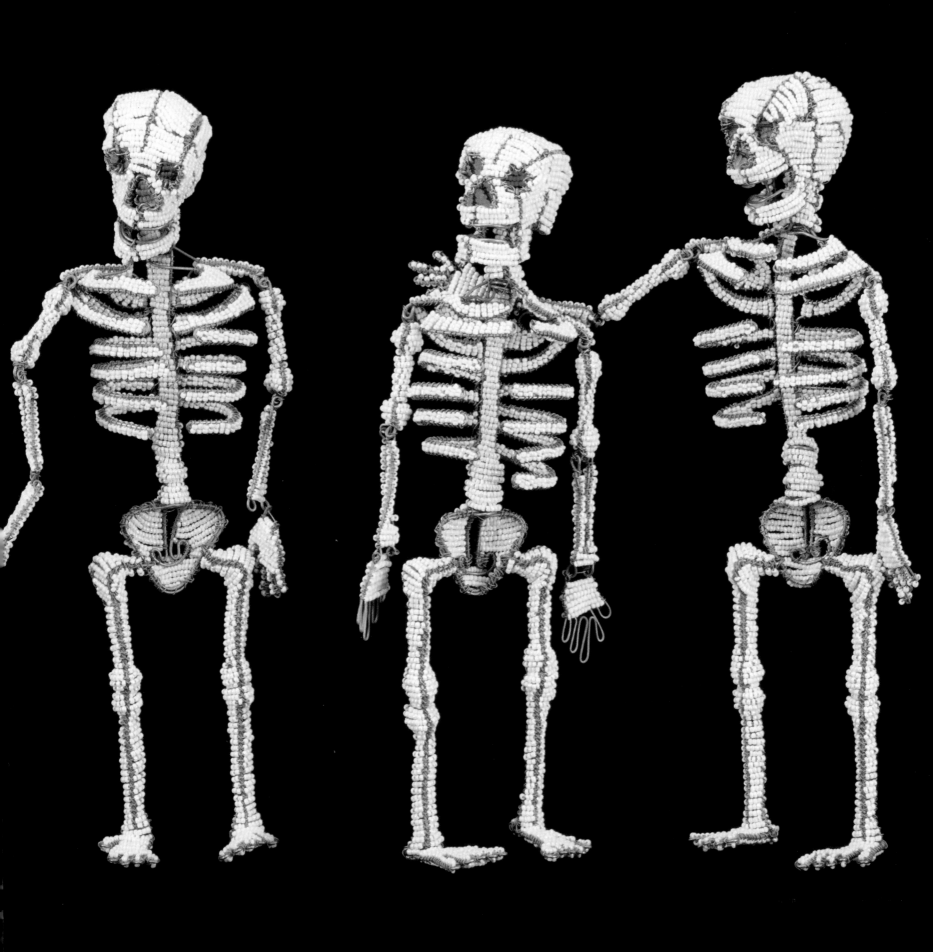

VERY FEW CULTURES HAVE EVER LIVED IN TOTAL ISOLATION FROM other peoples, even though popularly held belief tends to say otherwise. Tribes were aware of others outside their boundaries. Wide-reaching trade routes brought cultures into contact with their desire for exotic trade goods. Once explorers began to circumnavigate the world and conquerors to colonize other peoples, contact became unavoidable, often to the detriment of those on the receiving end. As a byproduct of contact, new markets opened up for locally produced products. New ideas were exchanged across boundaries, resulting in innovations for use both within the village and outside.

CHANGING CIRCUMSTANCES FOR THE LAKOTA PEOPLE

WILD WEST SHOWS

The image of the Lakota warrior represents the classic American Indian. Lakota warriors fought in the renowned Battle of Little Big Horn and the Battle of Wounded Knee. As a result of the Plains Indian Wars with the U.S. government and settlers encroaching into their territory, the Lakota people were confined to reservations, thus ending any opportunity for them to continue their nomadic hunting life.

These war veterans found a place to reenact their traditional lifestyle with the advent of Wild West shows. Buffalo Bill Cody toured his "Wild West" show from 1883 to 1913, including several tours to Europe. Buffalo Bill's Wild West was one of the most popular forms of entertainment in the world; in all, some 50 million people saw his show in 30 years. He employed mainly Oglala Lakotas from the Pine Ridge Reservation, often enlisting them to play the roles of other Indian nations as well. The Lakotas' reputation as renowned warriors made them a huge draw for the show where they appeared in mock battles on horseback dressed in their traditional garb.

Those selected to perform in the Wild West shows were chosen largely based on their finery of "buckskins, feathers, and beads." (Moses 1996: 24–25). The recruitment for the shows surely stimulated the production of beaded clothing for the large numbers of applicants and performers. Lakota women spent a great deal of time making the attractive outfits.

In addition to producing costumes for the performers, relatives at home on the reservations helped to meet the demands of the eager non-Native audiences, who flocked to the Wild West's Indian tipi encampment to purchase a souvenir from the Lakota performers and their families. One store owner near the Rosebud and Pine Ridge reservations wrote to the Miller Brothers' 101 Ranch Wild West in 1907, saying: "The Indians here are making a good deal of beadwork to send to their relatives in your show. . . ." (Barton 1907).

Wives traveled with their husbands as members of the troupe, appearing in the opening entry parade and in the encampments where they likely spent much time producing traditional goods to sell to the multitudes that thronged the camp. The Lakota family of John Y. Nelson traveled with Buffalo Bill's Wild West show for more than ten years beginning in 1883. His wife Jenny Nelson, an Oglala woman, produced a distinctive body of beadwork for her family and, likely, to sell. She and her children appeared in numerous photos wearing her showy beadwork, most notably a fully beaded adult-size dress (Photo 10.1—the names are reversed on the image). On many of Nelson's beadwork productions, including boys' fully beaded shirts and girls' beaded dress yokes, she embroidered beaded vertical bands of alternating rectangular units of color, echoing the bands on her fully beaded adult dress skirt (Fig.10.1).

Just as Lakotas were eagerly competing for the opportunity to join one of the Wild West troupes, the Bureau of Indian Affairs commissioners in Washington were actively engaged in preventing Indian participation in these shows. The U.S. government was intently legislating the assimilation of Indian people through a series of mandated programs aimed at "civilization," such as schooling for children, breaking up reservations into land allotments, and vocational training in farming, dairying, etc. All the while, the Wild West shows perpetuated the converse image of the American Indian as the Plains equestrian warrior. As the controversy waged throughout the tenure of Wild West shows, Lakotas found a format for empowerment in the shows, where they could peaceably, yet actively, resist U.S. government restraints on their traditional lifestyle and confinement to the reservations. At the same time the Lakotas were building an international image of themselves as The American Indian, which was to have far-reaching effects over time and space.

JULIE & JENNY NELSON, MOTHER & DAUGHTER.
Buffalo Bill's Wild West.
ELLIOTT & FRY   Copyright   55, BAKER St., LONDON.W.

PHOTO 10.1
"JENNY AND JULIE NELSON, MOTHER AND DAUGHTER, BUFFALO BILL'S WILD WEST", C. 1892

Produced by Elliot & Fry, London

Buffalo Bill Center of the West, Cody, Wyoming, USA, P.69.1579

FIG. 10.1
BOY'S SHIRT, C. 1883-93

Lakota nation, South Dakota, USA

Native-tanned hide, glass beads

16 x 23 in. (40.6 x 58.4 cm)

Hirschfield Family Collection, courtesy of Fighting Bear Antiques

Photograph by Garth Dowling

FIG. 10.1

NEW USES FOR BEADS

Most closely approximating the hunter-warrior occupation, the work of the cowboy was the most appealing of the activities available to Lakota men on the reservation, far more preferable than farming. Herding cattle on the open range from horseback, dressed in a cowboy outfit with fine trappings for their horses, all contributed to the transition of the Lakota from buffalo hunter to cowboy. Here was a potential source to garner honor and prestige. And, so, cowboy clothing, such as gauntlets (Fig. 10.3), wrist cuffs (Photo 10.2; Fig. 10.2), waistcoats (Fig. 10.4), and even an occasional necktie (Photo 10.4), entered into the Lakota bead-workers' repertoire.

Ironically, the Fourth of July became the major Lakota annual celebration, which continues as an important event to this day. Although July 4th may seem an incongruous holiday for the Lakota people to adopt, the national independence day of their oppressors, the Lakotas found in the Fourth of July, which was within the allowable guidelines of the U.S. government, a substitute for the banned Sun Dance. The holiday provided the format for a large intratribal gathering during the summer, much like the Sun Dance. It was an opportunity to express Lakota nationalism and to accomplish many of the ritual activities which had formerly been conducted during the Sun Dance.

FIG. 10.2
PAIR OF WRIST CUFFS, C. 1890

Lakota nation, North or South Dakota, USA

Native-tanned and raw cowhide, glass beads

3¹/₂ diam. x 5¹/₈ in. (8.9 x 13 cm)

Museum of Indian Arts and Culture / Laboratory of Anthropology, 37118/12ab

PHOTO 10.2
PATRICIO CALABAZA, SANTO DOMINGO PUEBLO, NEW MEXICO, C. 1927

Photo by T. Harmon Parkhurst, Courtesy of Palace of the Governors Photo Archives (NMHM/DCA), 46763

Plains Indian beadwork was a coveted trade item between the Plains Indians and the Pueblo Indians of New Mexico. This Pueblo man wears a pair of Plains beaded cuffs.

FIG. 10.2

PHOTO 10.2

Splendid parades gave an opportunity to display elaborate outfits and finely adorned horses. Some horses wore beaded head covers and even an occasional set of beaded moccasins (Fig. 10.6). Lakota men dressed in their traditional warrior attire or cowboy outfits. The U.S. flag motif was beaded on a variety of fine objects, such as tipi bags (Fig. 10.7) and waistcoats (Fig. 10.8). There are many theories speculating about the use of the American flag in Lakota beadwork. No one theory can totally account for its significance, given the variety of meanings offered by native accounts, leading one to recognize that motifs often carry multiple meanings.

Reservation life brought with it access to an abundance of manufactured objects to serve as models or actual foundations for decoration. It seems that anything within sight was a potential for decoration by Lakota women. A solidly beaded violin case (Fig. 10.9), a pictorial beaded valise (Fig. 10.10), and even beaded umbrellas give testimony to the virtuosity of these beadworkers. Such curiosities as a doctor's stethoscope are still beaded occasionally even today (Fig. 10.11). Local ranchers and members of the Masonic Temple would sometimes commission beaded pieces from Lakota women to adorn their ranches or their temples (Photo 10.3).

Most of these objects were made as gifts to be given to specific family members or distributed at giveaways. Dates, names, and occasions were often integrated into the beadwork. Too often the names of these accomplished beadworkers are forgotten, but one beadworker from Standing Rock reservation, Nellie Gates, is still remembered by her family. She worked in the pictorial style of beadwork that began to appear in the late nineteenth century, when a male family member would do the drawing for a woman to bead. Her valise (Fig. 10.9), which Nellie Gates made for her daughter Josephine, depicts Josephine's grandfather, Two Bears, offering his two sons, his brother, and himself as hostages during the Battle of Whitestone Hill in 1863. (Hirschfield 2012: 60).

PHOTO 10.3
SARAH BLUE EYES HOLDING A
BEADED PILLOW DECORATED
WITH A MASONIC DESIGN, C. 1900

Nebraska State Historical Society,
RG2095-0056

FIG. 10.3

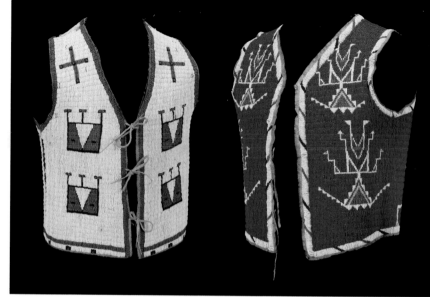

FIG. 10.4

PHOTO 10.4

FIG. 10.3
COWBOY GAUNTLETS, C. 1920

Shoshone-Bannock? Nation, Idaho, USA

Tanned hide, glass beads

Bob and Lora Sandroni Collection

This pair of gauntlets, a form borrowed from traditional cowboy wear, also depicts in beads a Native cowboy dressed in fine clothing.

FIG. 10.4
WAISTCOATS, LATE NINETEENTH– EARLY TWENTIETH CENTURIES

Lakota nation, North and South Dakota, USA

Native-tanned hide, cotton, glass beads

Left: 15 x 19¼ in. (38 x 49 cm); right length: 19 in. (48 cm)

Museum of Indian Arts and Culture / Laboratory of Anthropology, L: 11877/12, R: 46547/12

PHOTO 10.4
LAKOTA MAN DRESSED IN A BEADED WAISTCOAT AND QUILLED NECKTIE, C. 1904

Rosebud Reservation, South Dakota, USA

National Anthropological Archives, Smithsonian Institution, T-15322

FIG. 10.6
SET OF HORSE MOCCASINS, LATE NINETEENTH CENTURY

Lakota nation, North and South Dakota, USA

Native-tanned hide, glass beads

Wyoming State Museum, Department of State Parks and Cultural Resources

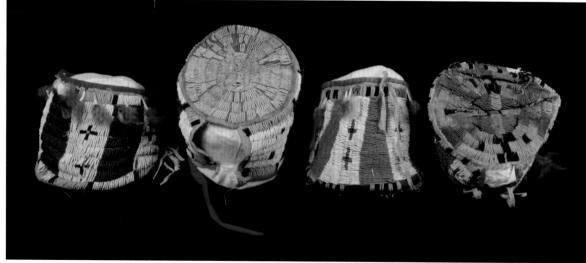

FIG. 10.6

FIG. 10.7

FIG. 10.7 DETAIL

FIG. 10.7 AND DETAIL
TIPI BAG, LATE NINETEENTH–EARLY
TWENTIETH CENTURIES

Lakota nation, North and South Dakota, USA

Native-tanned hide, dyed horsehair, glass
beads

Roswell Museum and Art Center, New Mexico

Photographer: José Rivera

Tipi bags were usually
made in pairs, since two
bags could be cut from a
single hide. This bag is one
of a pair.

FIGS. 10.8A (FRONT) AND B (BACK)
BOY'S WAISTCOAT, LATE NINETEENTH–
EARLY TWENTIETH CENTURIES

Lakota nation, North and South Dakota, USA

Cowhide, glass and metal beads

15½ in. (39.4 cm)

Museum of Indian Arts and Culture /
Laboratory of Anthropology, 51257/12

FIG. 10.8A

FIG. 10.8B

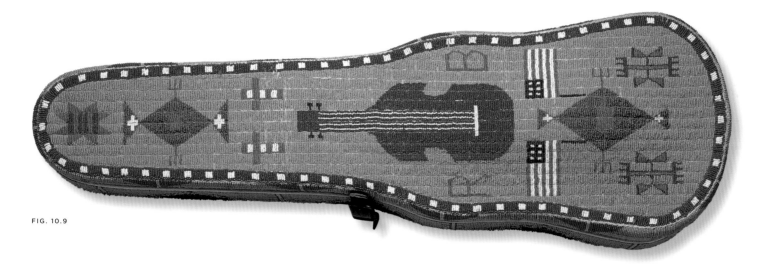

FIG. 10.9

FIG. 10.9
VIOLIN CASE, 1891

Brulé Lakota, Rosebud Reservation, South Dakota, USA

Commercial wood case, Native-tanned hide, metal trim, glass beads

32 x 10 x 4.5 in. (81.3 x 25.4 x 11.4 cm)

Stars and Stripes Foundation, San Francisco, California, USA

This violin case has an inscription: "Rubin Bass, Elk Falls, Feb 1, 1891" on its back side. A very similar violin case with an inscription dating "1899" was likely made by the same beadworker.

FIG. 10.10
PICTORIAL VALISE, 1903

Maker: Nellie Two Bears Gates (b. 1854)

Yanktonai (Sioux), Standing Rock Reservation, North and South Dakota, USA

Commercial and Native-tanned hide, glass beads, metal

9 1/2 x 15 in. (24.1 x 38.1 cm)

Hirschfield Family Collection, courtesy of Fighting Bear Antiques

Photograph by Garth Dowling

FIG. 10.10

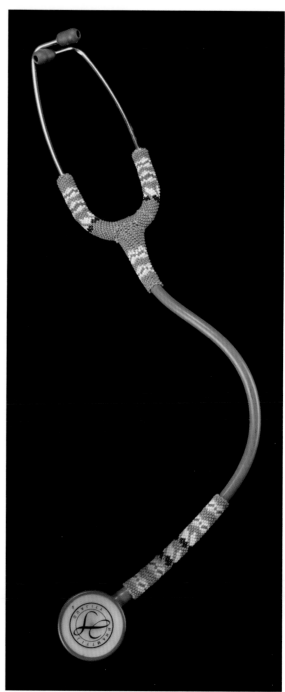

FIG. 10.11
STETHOSCOPE, 1993

Lakota nation, Pine Ridge Reservation, South Dakota, USA

Commercial stethoscope, glass beads

22 3/4 in. (9 cm)

Michael S. Katz, M.D., Collection

FIG. 10.11

SURVIVING CREATIVELY

On the eastern side of the American continent, the Six Nations of the Iroquois Confederacy, who call themselves the Haudenosaunee (the People of the Longhouse), searched for alternative sources of income. A diminishing land base and the depletion of game and fur-bearing animals left them with very few opportunities for earning a living in the nineteenth century. Iroquois women began producing beadwork made especially for non-Native audiences. They sold their products at resorts and tourist attractions to the ever-increasing numbers of visitors.

Niagara Falls was the first and foremost American tourist attraction. European and American tourists of all ages, particularly honeymooners, flocked to see the spectacle of the falls. After the War of 1812, Tuscarora women were granted the exclusive right to sell their beadwork at Niagara Falls by the family who owned the land on the American side (Photo 10.5). For well over 100 years, tourists to the falls and area resorts purchased souvenirs from Iroquois women to take home as gifts and memories of their trips. By the mid-nineteenth century the arts had become an important economic activity. Iroquois women's earnings played a major role in their families' survival.

The Victorian tastes of the tourists determined the types of items the artists made. Many of the novelties, or "whimsies," as they came to be termed, were destined for "cozy corners" in Victorian homes. With ingenuity, Native women produced objects that delighted female tourists interested in purchasing clothing accessories (Fig. 10.12), sewing sets (Figs. 10.13 and 10.14), and household decorations suited to the Victorian lifestyle. Many of these demonstrate the cycle of exchange from Euro-American prototypes to Native arts and back to the Euro-Americans as artistic products (Fig. 10.15).

Today the Iroquois people look upon these art forms as a part of their artistic legacy. What may once have been considered art for a white market is now regarded as an expression of Native identity and a source of pride.

PHOTO 10.5
TUSCARORA WOMEN SELLING THEIR ARTS ON LUNA ISLAND, NIAGARA FALLS, 1865–75

George Eastman Museum, #1981.6374.0001

Photograph by George Barker

FIG. 10.12
PURSES, 1850–1875

Iroquois Confederacy, New York, USA

Commercial cotton and silk, glass beads, metal sequins

Right: $5^7/_8$ x $5^7/_8$ in. (15 x 15 cm)

Sara and David Lieberman Collection

Iroquois small purses, produced in innumerable variations on the same theme, sold in the greatest numbers. Their makers incorporated an assortment of materials—beads, sequins, ribbon—to make the bags eye-catching to both tourists and Native people, who also used them.

FIG. 10.12

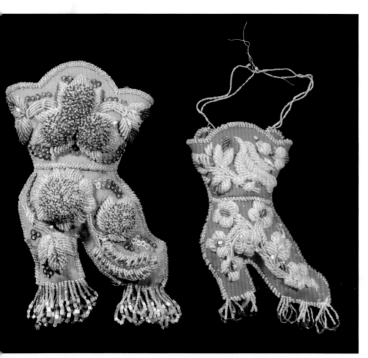

FIG. 10.13

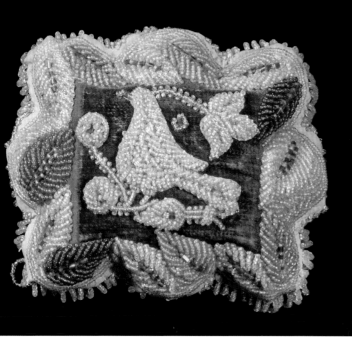

FIG. 10.14

FIG. 10.15

FIG. 10.13
BOOT PINCUSHIONS, LAST QUARTER OF THE NINETEENTH CENTURY

Mohawk? Nation, New York, USA

Wool, glass beads, metal sequins

Left: 11 x 6^{11}/$_{16}$ in. (28 x 17 cm); right: 9^{1}/$_{16}$ x 5^{1}/$_{8}$ in. (23 x 13 cm)

Museum of International Folk Art, Gift of the Girard Foundation Collection, A.1980.9.39 & 40

Pincushions made in the shape of a Victorian woman's boot proved to be a very popular sales item. The Iroquois style of beadwork for Victorian pincushions is unmistakable. Large translucent glass beads are clustered together to form ornate, raised patterns, usually of flowers, leaves, or birds, on contrasting colored wool or velvet.

FIG. 10.14
BIRD PINCUSHION, 1890S

Tuscarora? Nation, New York, USA

Cotton, glass beads

11 x 9^{4}/$_{5}$ in. (28 x 25 cm)

Museum of International Folk Art, Gift of the Girard Foundation Collection, A.1980.8.994

Some of the pillow-shaped pincushions were meant to hold Victorian women's long hatpins, which they kept on their dressing tables. (Phillips 1998: 228–230).

FIG. 10.15
GLENGARRY CAP, C. 1875

Tuscarora? Nation, New York, USA

Cotton, silk, glass beads

3^{15}/$_{16}$ x 4^{15}/$_{16}$ x 10^{7}/$_{16}$ in. (10 x 12.5 x 26.5 cm)

Museum of International Folk Art, Gift of Ronald and Vicki Sullivan, T.2015.90.8

The Scottish Glengarry-style beaded cap proved a popular tourist item made by Iroquois beadworkers. One wonders how Iroquois women thought to reproduce this style of cap. Perhaps they witnessed the Glengarry cap being worn by British regiments serving in Canada or among fur traders in the Great Lakes region, where the cap was popular. These or other encounters may have served as sources of inspiration.

In response to the Victorian craving for travel gear, Iroquois made and offered for sale these "gentlemen's traveling caps." "The conditions of travel during the second half of the nineteenth century provided the occasion for a whole subcategory of novelties connected with the needs of travelers." (Phillips 1998: 245–246).

NEW FORMS ELSEWHERE

FIG. 10.16
CENTERPIECE MAT, 1950S

Inuit peoples, Greenland, Denmark

Glass beads, thread

16 x 16 in. (40.6 x 40.6 cm)

Museum of International Folk Art, Gift of Karen Beall, A.2015.65.15

FIG. 10.17
BICYCLE SEAT COVERS, TWENTIETH CENTURY

Northern Afghanistan

Cotton, glass beads

14 x 10 in. (35.6 x 25.4 cm)

Anne and Bill Frej Collection

PHOTO 10.6
GIRLS IN SOUTH GREENLAND DRESS, 1926

Hand-tinted glass lantern slide

The Peary-MacMillan Arctic Museum, Bowdoin College, #3000.32.1418

Photograph by Donald Baxter MacMillan

A traditional form, such as the beaded yokes worn by the three young Inuit women in the photo, has been cleverly reworked into a table mat, a form which has aesthetic and practical appeal to non-Native buyers. Today the women continue to make their beaded yokes for themselves to wear on special occasions.

FIG. 10.16

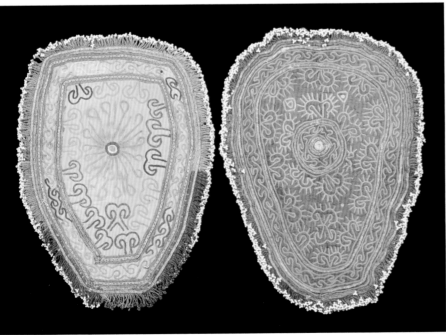

FIG. 10.17

PHOTO 10.6

FIG. 10.18

FIG. 10.18
PISTOL HOLSTER,
TWENTIETH CENTURY

Northern Afghanistan

Cotton, glass beads

20³/₈ x 5¹/₄ in. (50.8 x 6 x
13.3 cm)

Anne and Bill Frej Collection

FIG. 10.19
GOURD BOWLS,
1960S–70S

Wíxaríka (Huichol) peoples,
Nayarit state, México

Gourd, glass beads, beeswax

Top: c. 1975, 3¹/₁₆ x 8¹/₄ in.
(7.8 x 21 cm); bottom left:
c. 1960, 2⁵/₁₆ x 7⁷/₁₆ in. (5.9
x 18.9 cm); bottom right:
c. 1960, 2⁹/₁₆ x 7¹/₁₆ in. (6.5
x 18 cm)

Museum of International
Folk Art, top: IFAF
Collection, Gift of Diane
and Sandy Besser, FA,
2002.49.52; bottom left
and right: Gift of Girard
Foundation Collection,
A.1979.5.506 & 509

FIG. 10.20
DEER AND LIZARD,
C. 1975

Wíxaríka (Huichol) peoples,
Nayarit state, México

Wood, glass beads, beeswax

Deer: 8¹/₄ x 7¹¹/₁₆ x 3¹/₈ in.
(21 x 19.54 x 8 cm); lizard:
2¹/₂ x 2¹/₂ in. (6.4 x 6.4 cm)

Museum of International
Folk Art, IFAF Collection,
Gift of Diane and Sandy
Besser, FA.2002.49.54 & 55

FIG. 10.21
SNAKES, 1990

Makers: Upper left: Nicolasa
Bautista Carillo; lower right:
Pablita Bautista (b. 1973)

Wíxaríka (Huichol) peoples,
San Andrés, Coamiata,
Jalisco state, México

Wood, glass beads, beeswax

Center: 1⁵/₁₆ x 2³/₈ in. (3.3 x
6 cm)

Museum of International
Folk Art, IFAF Collection,
FA.1990.23.15, 16, and 34

FIG. 10.19

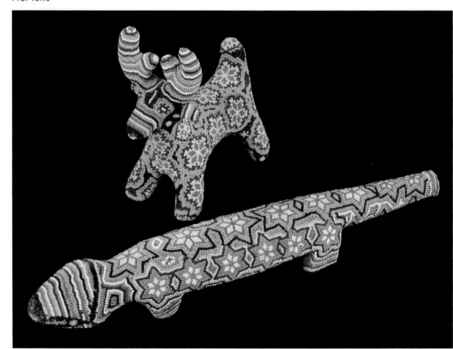

FIG. 10.20

FIG. 10.21

FIG. 10.22

FIG. 10.22
COMANCHE DOLLS, C. 1960

Maker: Winifred Caweyoke?

Zuni Pueblo, New Mexico, USA

Cloth armature, glass beads

Male: 10¼ in. (5.7 cm)

Museum of International Folk Art,
Gift of Girard Foundation Collection,
A.1980.8.822, 824

At Zuni Pueblo, "Comanche" is the
term used to identify all Plains Indian
tribes. The Comanche Dance is a
popular social dance at Zuni and most
other Pueblos. The dancers wear
Plains-style dress and perform to
Plains music.

FIG. 10.23

FIG. 10.23
DOLLS, 1970S

Ndzundza Ndebele peoples, Transvaal
region, South Africa

Glass beads, metal

Tallest: 11⁷⁄₁₆ in. (29.5 cm)

Museum of International Folk Art,
Gift of Girard Foundation Collection,
A.1981.42.73–75, 86, 96, 98–99

As tourists began to visit the Ndebele
villages to view their brightly
painted house murals, encouraged
by marketing from the South African
government, Ndebele women found
an opportunity to sell dolls and other
novelties at roadside tables outside
their front doors.

FIG. 10.24

FIG. 10.25

FIG. 10.24
MASKS, 1980–1990

Makers: Left: Jesús Jiménez; right: Ascención Carrillo, San Andrés

Wíxaríka (Huichol) peoples, Nayarit state, México

Wood, glass beads, beeswax

Left: 13 1/2 x 6 1/2 in. (34.3 x 16.5 cm); right: 14 3/16 x 5 1/2 in.
(36 x 14 cm)

Museum of International Folk Art, Left: Gift of Lloyd E. Cotsen and the
Neutrogena Corporation, A.1995.93.2039; Right: A.1996.4.11

Since the last decades of the twentieth century, Huichol (the name these people are known as in the outside world) art made for sale has gained the attention of the international art market. Huichol artists produce beaded objects using the same media, designs, and techniques, yet create different products than those they make for their own sacred use. The gourd bowls (Fig. 10.19) are covered completely in beads unlike the votive gourd bowls (Figs. 8.11 and 8.12) used for offerings. Beaded animals (Figs. 10.20 and 10.21) and especially fully-beaded masks (Fig. 10.24) attract buyers but serve no purpose for the people themselves.

As Huichol scholar C. Jill Grady (2010: 96) points out: "Outside art provides resources to help sustain the creation of their sacred art. Both art forms simultaneously work to insulate the culture. By creating a separate art for sale, the Huichol people have elegantly mediated the risks associated with compromising their traditional and historical cultural experience. In this way, they are continuing to choose when and how to interact with the outside dominant society on their own terms. They remain firm in their commitment to maintain balance in the world, while adapting to change over time and space."

FIG. 10.25
OLLA MAIDEN DOLLS, C. 1960

Maker: Winifred Caweyoke?

Zuni Pueblo, New Mexico, USA

Cloth armature, glass beads

Tallest: 12 3/8 in. (31 cm)

Museum of International Folk Art, Gift of Girard Foundation Collection, A.1980.8.769–70, 802, 835, 838–9, 858x, 860

In the twentieth century, handmade dolls, intended as collectibles rather than playthings, became a popular item for sale to tourists. Usually costumed in their traditional dress, the dolls allowed the buyers to take home a miniature version of these Native peoples. Here the dolls are dressed as the Zuni

Olla Maidens, a group who parades and performs while carrying water jars on their heads.

At Zuni Pueblo, "older beadworkers say that during the 1920s traders suggested the beading of small dolls as curios. Early trader C. G. Wallace said that he initiated beadworking at the Pueblo because pottery, although in demand, was too difficult to ship (Batkin 1987:165)." (Ostler and Rodee 1989: 32).

In the Southwestern United States in the early twentieth century, non-Native traders with the Indians introduced a number of innovations, which they encouraged the Native artists to make in order to please the buying public, who visited by train or selected the wares from mail-order catalogs. One of these innovations was to make their arts smaller, so that the objects would fit into a traveler's suitcase. Many of these innovations have now become a mainstay in the arts of Native peoples.

FIG. 10.26B

PHOTO 10.7
ZULU RICKSHAW PULLERS ON THE DURBAN
BEACHFRONT, EARLY 1980S

The McGregor Museum, Kimberly, South Africa

Photograph by Jean Morris

FIGS. 10.26A (HEADDRESS),
Opposite, AND B (COSTUME)
RICKSHAW PULLER'S COSTUME
AND HEADDRESS, 1980S

Zulu peoples, KwaZulu-Natal,
South Africa

Glass beads, yarn, feathers, fur, ox
horns, mirrors, cotton, cardboard

Headdress: 59 x 28⁷/₈ in. (150 x
73 cm)

Costume: 81 ½ x 57 in. (207 x
145 cm)

Fowler Museum of UCLA

Photograph by Don Cole,
X97.4.1a&b

Rickshaws were first imported into Durban in 1892 as a new mode of transportation. Zulu men became the exclusive pullers, providing the main source of transport in the city center and harbor. By 1902 2,170 rickshaws were pulled by 24,000 Zulu registered pullers. The city mandated that the pullers wear a uniform to make them identifiable to the police. This law set into motion an era of competitive creativity between Zulu pullers to adorn themselves in the most wildly elaborate headdresses and costumes imaginable. The addition of oxen horns to the headdress equated the strength of the ox to that of the puller.

Not only did these outfits attract clientele; the South African tourism industry promoted their image in the international media. The headline in a 1935 U.S. Time magazine advertisement accompanied by a photo read: "A Zulu Warrior pulled my rickshaw!" (Time, June 1935: 25). Clearly the nineteenth-century colonial stereotype of the Zulu warrior—wild, dangerous, and exotic—had been transferred onto these pullers imaginatively dressed in feathers and beads. For all of its negatives, this image did allow the puller an opportunity to demonstrate his strength and regain some acclaim, while garnering economic benefit. By the 1980s rickshaw pulling, now confined to beachfront tourist rides, began to greatly decline, with only a handful of pullers still in business.

Fashion by definition is fickle and changeable as opposed to that which is deeply imbedded in tradition. Beads have been "in" fashion and "out" of fashion for the past two centuries. They were in fashion during the Victorian era (1837–1901) in England and again in the swinging 20s in Europe and the U.S. (Figs. 10.32 and 10.33). In the 1950s France made evening dresses (Fig. 10.35) and bags (Fig. 10.34) festooned with beads. Again in the 60s and 70s "love" beads signaled a young and restless American culture. Twenty-first century high fashion is once again incorporating glass beads into *haute couture* (Fig. 10.36).

The ushering in of the machine age in the nineteenth century, led to a revival of fancy sewing as an important signifier of the accomplished woman. Cloth weaving now produced by machines freed women from this mundane task, allowing them to turn to ornamentation, particularly embroidery and beadwork on commercial cloth, and knitting and crocheting with beads. Mass circulation of home craft magazines, such as *The Ladies' Companion* and *The Englishwoman's Domestic Magazine* proliferated in England, and *Godey's Lady's Book* in the U.S. and Canada, stimulated by the new printing technologies. In these home craft magazines, Victorian women found patterns and instructions to make purses (Figs. 10.27, 10.28, and 10.29) and all manner of household and sewing items (Figs. 10.30 and 10.31) in their pursuit of the cult of domesticity.

FIG. 10.27

FIG. 10.27
LADIES' PURSES, 1840-60

England?

Knitted silk, metal, glass beads

Left: 13 3/8 x 8 7/16 in. (34 x 21.4 cm); right: 12 1/2 in. (31.7 cm)

Museum of International Folk Art, Gift of Charmay Allred, A.1997.45.2–3

FIG. 10.28, *Opposite*
GENTLEMAN'S PURSES, MID-NINETEENTH CENTURY

England

Crocheted fiber, glass and cut steel beads

Left: 11 5/8 x 2 3/4 in. (29.5 x 7 cm); right: 15 3/8 x 2 9/16 in. (39 x 6.5 cm)

Museum of International Folk Art, Gift of the Girard Foundation Collection, A.1984.153.702–3

These purses earned the nickname "miser's" purse, because they made it so difficult for their owner to extract the coins.

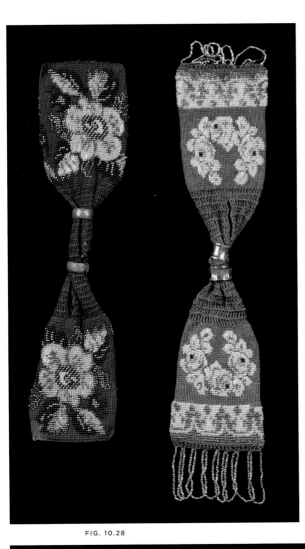

FIG. 10.28

FIG. 10.29
LADY'S PURSE, 1850-80

England?

Satin, metal, glass beads

8^{7}/$_{16}$ x 7^{1}/$_{2}$ in. (21.5 x 19 cm)

Museum of International Folk
Art, Gift of Kathryn O'Keeffe,
A.1997.17.1

FIG. 10.29

FIG. 10.30

FIG. 10.30 AND DETAIL
SAMPLER, 1840

México

Fiber, glass beads

Without frame: 17^{1}/$_{2}$ x 15^{7}/$_{16}$ in.
(44 x 38^{1}/$_{2}$ cm)

Los Poblanos Collection

This totally beaded sampler's
inscription reads: "Hécho por
Antonia Corina de Obregon.
El Año de 1840 y lo Dedica á
su Esposo é Hijos" (Made by
Antonia Corina de Obregon.
The year of 1840 and she
dedicates it to her husband
and children).

FIG. 10.30 DETAIL

237

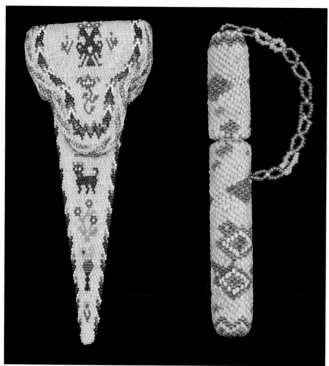

FIG. 10.31
SEWING SCISSORS
COVER AND
NEEDLE CASE,
1820–50

México

Silk, glass beads

Scissors cover:
$4^{11}/_{16}$ x $1^{1}/_{2}$ in. ($11^{1}/_{2}$
x $4^{1}/_{2}$ cm); needle
case: $4^{7}/_{16}$ x $4^{1}/_{2}$ in.
(11 cm x $1^{1}/_{2}$ cm)

Los Poblanos
Collection

FIG. 10.32 AND DETAIL
FLAPPER-STYLE DRESS, C. 1927

House of Paquin?, Paris, France

Silk, glass beads

New Mexico History Museum, owned by Eugenia Shonnard,
2006.40.1

The loose-fitting, dropped waist, and knee-length hemline are
characteristics of the 1920s era evening dresses in Europe and the
United States.

FIG. 10.32

FIG. 10.32 DETAIL

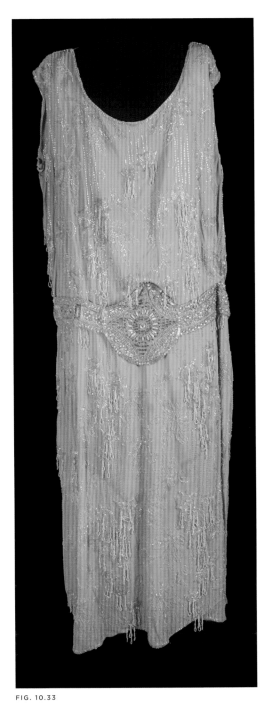

FIG. 10.33

FIG. 10.33 DETAIL

FIG. 10.33 AND DETAIL
FLAPPER-STYLE DRESS, 1920S

Origin unknown

Silk, glass beads

New Mexico History Museum, 2978.45a

FIG. 10.34
PURSE, 1950S

Jorelle by Llewellyn. Handmade in France

6 x 10 x 2 in. (15.24 x 25.4 x 5 cm)

Glass beads, metal

Felicia Katz-Harris Collection

Tee-Ca Modes dress manufacturer, Benjamin Katz, had this dress made for his wife, Matty Katz. The purse completed the evening dress ensemble.

FIG. 10.35
EVENING DRESS, 1950S

Tee-Ca Modes, New York, New York, USA

Silk satin, glass beads

Felicia Katz-Harris Collection

FIG. 10.34

FIG. 10.35

FIG. 10.36 AND DETAIL EVENING GOWN, 2014

Maker: Orlando Dugi (b. 1978, Navajo nation)

Silk, glass and sterling silver beads

Collection of the artist

Up-and-coming dress designer, Orlando Dugi, learned beadworking at a young age from his Navajo grandmother and father, and how to use a sewing machine in seventh grade home economics class. The evening gown is from Dugi's ten-piece Red Collection. He dyes the fabric, using the natural insect dye, cochineal; makes the dress; and does the beadwork. The beadwork is based on Pueblo Indian pottery patterns. In fall 2015, Dugi's Red Collection appeared on the runway at the Oklahoma Fashion Week in Oklahoma City.

FIG. 10.36

HIGH ART

In the twentieth and twenty-first centuries, beadwork artists have been stretching the boundaries of so-called "traditional" beadwork. Jacobs (2012: xxvi) makes this observation regarding the Naga people of India, but it has applications worldwide: "It is wrong to believe that so-called 'traditional' cultures never undergo change, even in the material world. Dress, ornament, arts and crafts are always transforming, among the Nagas as well as in all other world regions. Western observers are tempted to judge these changes as a 'decline' in culture, or as an unflattering adjustment to an assumed tourist taste. But seen from a local perspective, these changes are a necessary development between the past and the present, and a means of building a bridge between the two."

FIG. 10.37
"SUNBOYZ" HIGH TOPS, 2009

Maker: Teri Greeves (b. 1970, Kiowa nation)

All Star tennis shoes, glass beads

10 x 9 x 3 in. (25.4 x 22.9 x 7.6 cm)

New Mexico Arts, Art in Public Places Permanent Collection

Photograph by Dan Barsotti

FIG. 10.37

FIG. 10.38

Beadmaker Teri Greeves takes traditional Plains beaded moccasins and turns them into contemporary high tops and high-heeled shoes. She explains: "In the mid 1980s, a Lakota woman brought a pair of fully beaded Converse tennis shoes into my mom's trading post in Wyoming. My sister and I thought they were the coolest things we had ever seen; they were a mixture of traditional beadwork and design on a pair of modern-day shoes and spoke to us as Indian kids living in the modern world.

Later on, when I was going to college . . . my mother suggested I make a pair for her shop in Santa Fe. The very first pair I made, in 1994, had very traditional designs on them like something that would be on a pair of moccasins. The second pair I made had a pictorial design, and the third pair had a pictorial narrative. By the third pair, I stopped looking at them as shoes and started looking at them sculpturally: They didn't have to match; they could be viewed all the way around and they could tell a story." (Greeves 2015: 102).

FIG. 10.38
"NDN GIRLZ / REZ GIRLZ", 2009

Maker: Teri Greeves (b. 1970, Kiowa nation)

High-heeled canvas sneakers, glass beads

10 x 9 x 3.5 in. (25.4 x 22.9 x 8.9 cm)

New Mexico Arts, Art in Public Places Permanent Collection

Photograph by Dan Barsotti

FIG. 10.39

FIG. 10.39
"THE TRIUMPH OF INDIAN ART"
STEERING WHEEL AND GEAR
SHIFT KNOB COVERS, 2002

Steering wheel cover made by Teri Greeves (b. 1970, Kiowa nation)

Gear shift knob cover made by Marcus Amerman (b. 1957, Choctaw nation)

Brain-tanned hide, glass beads

Museum of Indian Arts and Culture / Laboratory of Anthropology, Gift of Elizabeth Sackler, 58510/12b

FIG. 10.40A

FIGS. 10.40A (FRONT VIEW) AND B (SIDE REAR VIEW)
"VOCHOL", 2010

Wíxaríka (Huichol) peoples, Jalisco, México

Volkswagen, resin, paint, yarn, 2,277,000 glass beads

59 x 161 x 68 in. (149.8 x 408.9 x 172.7 cm)

Museo de Arte Popular, México City, México

Photograph by: Alejandro Piedra Buena

Using their traditional beadworking designs and techniques and commissioned by the Museo de Arte Popular, eight Huichol artists covered an entire full-size VW bug with their paintings in glass beads. Even the hubcaps, the mirrors, and bumpers are covered in beads in this tour-de-force creation, which took 9,000 hours to complete.

FIG. 10.40B

ART FOR SOCIAL ISSUES

"Although it is true that many of the bead sculptures made in KwaZulu incorporate something of a broadly ethnic image because they are clearly of black people . . . , their makers have . . . moved beyond an ethnic image to make a clear statement about contemporary life." (Preston-Whyte and Thorpe 1989: 151).

BREAKING THE SILENCE

Beginning in 1980, Zulu beadworker Thembi Mchunu initiated a new form of beadwork, creating a 3-dimensional beaded doll constructed from fabric and adorned with beadwork. Her fellow beadworkers from the Thousand Hills followed her lead and began creating beaded sculptures, ushering in a new form that provided a platform for creating compositional tableaus of social life.

In 1996–1997, Kate Wells, from the Department of Design Studies at the now Durban Institute of Technology, offered a series of workshops to improve the technical skills and materials of these beadworkers. During these workshops, the Zulu women discussed problems in their daily lives, in particular the illness suffered by many in their community. It became clear to Wells that the women knew little or nothing about the transmission of HIV/AIDS, so she arranged a series of intervention workshops on this topic. At that time more than 10 percent of the South African population was infected with AIDS, where it is a heterosexual disease, and KwaZulu-Natal, the homeland of these women, had the highest infection rate of all of the South African provinces.

Long-standing cultural taboos prevent rural Zulu women from discussing matters of love, intimacy, and sexuality. Traditionally the mechanism to express these subjects has been mediated through beadwork, such as the love letter (*ibique*) (Figs. 2.52 and 2.53). "All traditional Zulu beadwork relates in some way to courtship and marriage." (Wells, et. al. 2004: 74). Thus began the Siyazama Project, housed at the Durban Institute, which developed into an effective HIV/AIDS campaign. "It happened because the communication mode in which the women were skilled also was the mode used traditionally and historically to circumvent the social female taboo on discussion of matters of emotional and sexual intimacy. The women used the medium of beadwork communication passed down to them by their mothers and grandmothers to express their new understanding of sexual and sex-AIDS interface insights, and their work became untraditionally sexually explicit" (Fig. 10.41). (Wells, et. al. 2004: 77–78). Through these beaded tableaus, Zulu beadworkers are combating silence in a culturally acceptable way, visually educating other KwaZulu-Natal women about the impact of HIV/AIDS and how to prevent its transmission (Figs. 10.42, 10.43, 10.44).

Near Capetown, South Africa, the nonprofit Art Aids Art runs a community art program, eKhaya eKasi Art & Education Centre. Using glass beads and

FIG. 10.41
"SEXUAL HARASSMENT,"
(*UKUHLUKUNYEZWA NGOCANSI*),
2010

Maker: Gabi Gabi Nzama (Zulu)

Ndwedwe, KwaZulu-Natal, South Africa

Wood, cloth, glass beads

6⅛ x 8⅝ x 5 in. (15.6 x 22 x 12.7 cm)

Museum of International Folk Art, Purchase funds from the Barbara Lidral Bequest, A.2014.15.3

Nzama's tableau depicts a rape scene, a common problem in South Africa that contributes to the spread of AIDS.

FIG. 10.41

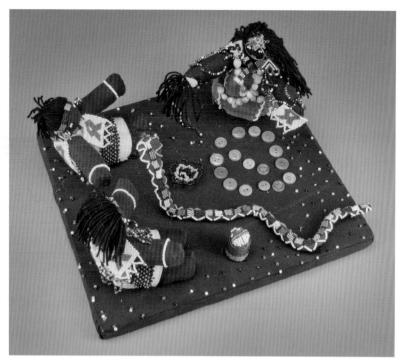

FIG. 10.42

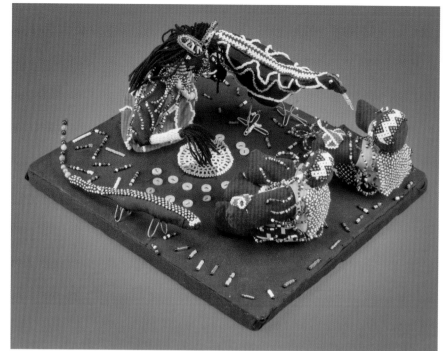

FIG. 10.43

galvanized wire, the members, most originally from rural provinces, make beaded figures incorporating daily life issues, such as the AIDS epidemic. Their skull and skeleton figures (Photo 10.8) remind us that death can result from the HIV/AIDS infection.

As folk artisans we recognize our responsibility to communicate to the world and, in particular, our immediate community, about contemporary issues by depicting subject matter that impacts us, even when they might be controversial. Folk art is about carrying on traditions, but it is also continuously evolving and must address our daily lives here and now, our culture and our values. We do so not at the whim of individual artistic impulse, but through careful observation of our neighbors and group deliberation among the members of our collective. Folk Art must speak to people—that is part of what puts the 'folk' in folk arts. The AIDS epidemic and the devastation it has wrought was the inspiration for the very difficult skeleton figures (Fig 10.45) that we have designed, showing that death can be the result of unsafe practices. We must educate each other about the myths surrounding HIV/AIDS and speak out against the stigmatization that pressures people into keeping their status secret. There is enough suffering in our lives without oppressing each other for no good reason. The spirit of Ubuntu means that we must support one another and gain strength through our interconnectedness. In this way, we use a respected traditional art form to reach the minds of our people, for there will be no folk art if there are no people left to make it. (Lulama Sihlabeni 2013).

FIG. 10.44

FIG. 10.45

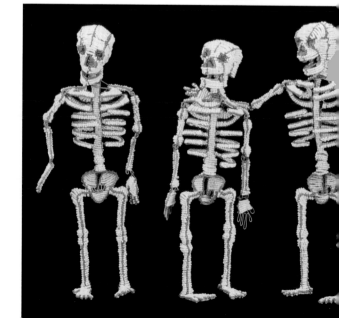

FIG. 10.42, *Opposite*
"SNAKE STORY," 2010

Maker: Celani Njoyeza (Zulu)

Ndwedwe, KwaZulu-Natal, South Africa

Wood, cloth, glass beads, metal wire

6 3/4 x 12 3/4 x 11 1/4 in. (17.1 x 32.4 x 28.6 cm)

Museum of International Folk Art, Purchase funds from the Barbara Lidral Bequest, A.2014.15.1

In Njoyeza's "Snake Story," a snake threatens a young girl with the sexually transmitted disease of AIDS, while a healer gives advice to her and her family member. The figures wear the beaded red AIDS ribbon, a visual metaphor for AIDS awareness.

FIG. 10.43, *Opposite*
"*UMPUNDULA* BIRD, 2010

Maker: Celani Njoyeza (Zulu)

Ndwedwe, KwaZulu-Natal, South Africa

Wood, cloth, glass beads, metal wire

6 1/8 x 12 3/4 x 11 3/16 in. (15.6 x 32.4 x 28.4 cm)

Museum of International Folk Art, Purchase funds from the Barbara Lidral Bequest, A.2014.15.2

In this tableau, an imaginary bird represents the dangers of HIV/AIDS. Two children arrive home to find their parents missing. They consult with a healer who has learned via a lizard that their parents have been killed by the bird. The scene reminds of the all too common circumstance whereby Zulu children are orphaned when their parents die of the HIV/AIDS virus.

FIG. 10.44, *Opposite*
"WOMEN CRUCIFIED TO AIDS", 2010

Maker: Lobolile Ximba (Zulu)

KwaZulu-Natal, South Africa

Wood, cotton, wool, glass beads, hair

20 5/16 x 16 7/8 x 3 in. (51.6 x 42.9 x 7.6 cm)

Museum of International Folk Art, Purchase funds from the Barbara Lidral Bequest, A.2014.15.4

Ximba illustrates the disproportionately high incidence of HIV/AIDS infection among the women of KwaZulu-Natal, and the suffering that results, using the highly charged image of the Christian crucifix.

FIG. 10.45, *Opposite*
SKELETONS, 2013

Designer: Abisha; made by members of eKhaya eKasi Art & Education Centre

Khayelitsha township, South Africa

Metal wire, glass beads

15 5/8 x 7 in. (39.7 x 17.8 cm)

Museum of International Folk Art, Purchase funds from the Barbara Lidral Bequest, A.2016.31.1–3

PHOTO 10.8
LULAMA SIHLABENI (EKHAYA EKASI ART & EDUCATION CENTRE COORDINATOR), 2013

Khayelitsha township, South Africa

Photograph by Bob Smith, courtesy of International Folk Art Alliance

PHOTO 10.8

FIG. 10.46
GAS MASK, 2010

Maker: Naomi Bebo (b. 1979, Menominee / Ho-Chunk)

Deer hide, ermine, silk, Iraqi gas mask, glass beads

9 1/2 x 7 1/2 x 6 1/2 in. (24.1 x 19 x 16.5 cm)

Tweed Museum of Art, University of Minnesota, Marguerite L. Gilmore Charitable Foundation Fund, D2014.8

ART FOR SOCIAL ISSUES ELSEWHERE

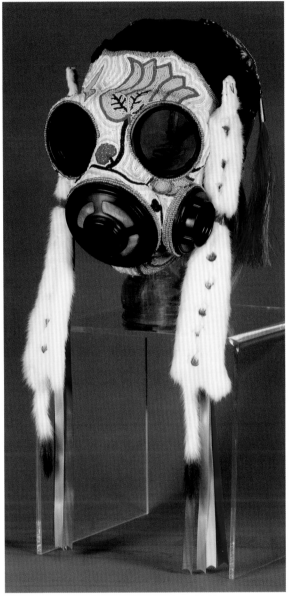

FIG. 10.46

Bebo explains her intent in creating this mask: "It has been a journey for me to reclaim an object that I initially perceived to be cold and repugnant and to take part in its metamorphosis; to watch it emerge with a life of its own into a thing of beauty. By intricately beading the mask in delicate floral designs, the Beaded Mask is a visual contradiction to its origins as a tool of war and a symbol of oil dependence and environmental destruction." (Bebo 2013).

LIZA LOU'S KITCHEN

Contemporary American beadwork artist, Liza Lou, spent five years completing her first full-scale installation—a kitchen, covered fully in millions of glass beads. Using a pair of tweezers, she placed each glass bead to adorn every surface and each object in the room totally with beads. As her second project in 1999 to accompany the kitchen, Lou created a "Backyard", using over 30 million beads, complete with a barbeque, picnic table, grass, flowers, pink flamingos, and a lawn mower.

Lou's artwork is about women's work. In 2005 she moved to South Africa, where she established a studio with Zulu beadworkers. She continues to maintain a studio in KwaZulu-Natal and another in Los Angeles. Lou says:

> For the past ten years, I've been living and work-ing in Durban, South Africa. I wanted to do a project working with Zulu bead workers, wanted to see what could happen, if process could have real-world reso-nance in terms of helping a community of women to create a stable economic entity on which to build their businesses and lives. . . .
>
> I never planned to be in South Africa for ten years. The plan was to come for two weeks, to do a one-time project and then to go home. But within minutes of meeting the women, I knew I was in trouble. For one thing the women sing while they bead. It is a cultural thing. . . .
>
> Year after year, the project stretched. Another work and another, and I found I could not leave. My work was growing and changing and the thirty women in my studio were building their lives upon the work we were doing. . . . (Lou 2015).

FIG. 10.47 AND DETAILS
"KITCHEN", 1991–96

Maker: Liza Lou (b. 1969, American)

Artist's used appliances, wood, wire, plaster, glass beads

168 sq. ft. (5,120 sq. cm)

Whitney Museum of American Art, New York, 2008.339a-x

Photos courtesy of the artist

Photographs by: Tom Powell (full kitchen, sink detail, Lays chips and beer detail, Tide detail); Aaron Chang (Oven/pie detail, cookbook detail)

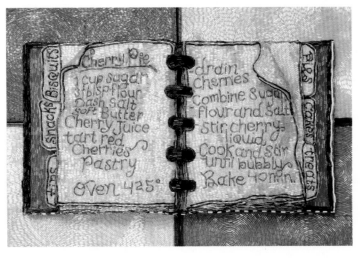

BIBLIOGRAPHY

GENERAL

Allen, Jamey D., and Valerie Hector, eds. *2007 International Bead and Beadwork Conference*. Istanbul, Turkey: Rezan Has Museum, November 22–25, 2007.

Anawalt, Patricia Rieff. *The Worldwide History of Dress*. New York: Thames and Hudson, 2007.

Barr, Ronald G., and Urs A. Hunziker. "Infants Who Are Carried More Cry Less." In *Generations: A Universal Family Album*. Eds. Anna R. Cohn and Lucinda A. Leach. Washington, D.C.: Smithsonian Institution and Pantheon Books, 1987: 196–99.

Biebuyck, Daniel P., and Nelly Van den Abbeele. *The Power of Headdresses: A Cross-Cultural Study of Forms and Functions*. Brussels: TENDI S.A. Published under the patronage of the Leopold III Foundation for Exploration and Nature Conservation, 1984.

Coles, Janet, and Robert Budwig. *Beads: An Exploration of Bead Traditions around the World*. New York: Simon & Schuster Editions, 1997.

Coomaraswamy, Ananda K. *Christian and Oriental Philosophy of Art*. New York: Dover Publications Inc., 1956.

Crabtree, Caroline, and Pam Stallebrass. *Beadwork: A World Guide*. London: Thames & Hudson, 2002, 2009.

Dubin, Lois Sherr. *The History of Beads from 30,000 B.C. to the Present*. New York: Harry N. Abrams, 1987.

Gennett, Adrienne V. *Glass Beads: Selections from the Corning Museum of Glass*. Corning, New York: The Corning Museum of Glass, 2013.

Ice, Joyce, ed. *On Collecting: From Private to Public, Featuring Folk and Tribal Art from the Diane and Sandy Besser Collection*. Santa Fe, New Mexico: Museum of International Folk Art, 2009.

Kahlenberg, Mary Hunt, ed. *The Extraordinary in the Ordinary*. New York: Harry N. Abrams, Inc., 1998. In association with the Museum of International Folk Art.

Linn, Priscilla Rachun. "No Object Too Small: A Thought on Babies, Things, and Culture." In *Generations: Generations: A Universal Family Album*. Eds. Anna R. Cohn and Lucinda A. Leach. Washington, D.C.: Smithsonian Institution and Pantheon Books, 1987: 180–85.

Murdoch, George P., and Catarina Provost. "Factors in the Divisions of Labor by Sex: A Cross-Cultural Analysis." *Ethnology* 12 (1973): 203–25.

Ortner, Sherry B., and Harriet Whitehead. *Sexual Meanings: The Cultural Construction of Gender and Sexuality*. Cambridge: Cambridge University Press, 1981.

Pokornowski, Ila. "Beads and Personal Adornment." In *The Fabrics of Culture: The Anthropology of Clothing and Adornment*. Eds. Justine M. Cordwell and Ronald A. Schwarz. The Hague: Mouton Publishers, 1979: 103–17.

Roach, Mary Ellen, and Joanne Bubolz Eicher. "The Language of Personal Adornment." In *The Fabrics of Culture: The Anthropology of Clothing and Adornment*. Eds. Justine M. Cordwell and Ronald A. Schwarz. The Hague: Mouton Publishers, 1979: 7–21.

Sciama, Lidia D., and Joanne B. Eicher, eds. *Beads and Beadmakers: Gender, Material Culture and Meaning*. Oxford: Berg, 1998.

Sumberg, Bobbie. *Textiles: Collection of the Museum of International Folk Art*. Layton, Utah: Gibbs Smith Publishers, 2010.

Turner, Victor, ed. *Celebration: Studies in Festivity and Ritual*. Washington, D.C.: Smithsonian Institution Press, 1982.

van Dongen, P. L. F., Th. J. J. Leyenaar, and K. Vos, eds. *The Seasons of Humankind*. Leiden: Rijksmuseum voor Volkenkunde, 1987.

Woodward, Kathryn, ed. *Identity and Difference*. London: Sage Publications, 1997.

AFRICA

Anderson, Jon Lee. "A History of Violence." *New Yorker* (23 July 2012): 49–59.

Angas, George French. *The Kafirs Illustrated: A facsimile reprint of the original 1849 edition of hand-coloured lithographs*. Cape Town: A.A. Balkemia, 1849.

Arnoldi, Mary Jo, and Christine Mullen Kreamer. *Crowning Achievements: African Art of Dressing the Head*. Los Angeles: UCLA Fowler Museum of Cultural History, 1995.

Asiw Aju, A. I. "Political Motivation and Oral Historical Traditions in Africa: The Case of Yoruba Crowns, 1900–1960." *Africa: Journal of the International African Institute* 46, no. 2 (1976): 113–27.

Becker, Rayda. "'Ku veleka vukosi . . .' To bear children is wealth . . ." In *Evocations of the Child: Fertility figures of the southern African region*. Eds. Elizabeth Dell, Nessa Leibhammer, and Karol Nel. Cape Town: Human & Rousseau and Johannesburg Art Gallery, 1998: 119–30.

Becker, Rayda, and Anitra Nettleton. "Tsonga-Shangana Beadwork and Figures." In *Catalogue: Ten Years of Collecting (1979–1989)*. Eds. David Hammond-Tooke and Anitra Nettleton. Johannesburg: University of the Witwatersrand Art Gallery, 1989: 9–15.

Bedford, Emma, ed. *Ezakwantu: Beadwork from the Eastern Cape*. Cape Town: South African National Gallery, 1993.

Beier, Ulli. *Yoruba Beaded Crowns: Sacred Regalia of the Olokuku of Okuku*. London: Ethnographica, 1982.

Best, Gunter. *Marakwet and Turkana: New Perspectives on the Material Culture of East African Societies*. Frankfurt am Main: Museum für Völkerkunde, 1993.

Blier, Suzanne Preston. "Kings, Crowns, and Rights of Succession: Obalufon Arts at Ife and Other Yoruba Centers." *Art Bulletin* 67 (1985): 383–401.

Boram-Hays, Carol. "Borders of Beads: Questions of Identity in the Beadwork of the Zulu-Speaking People." *African Arts* 38, no. 2 (2005): 38–49, 92–93.

Bouttiaux, Anne-Marie. "The Attributes of Power." *Persona, Masks of Africa: Identities Hidden and Revealed*. Tervuren, Belgium: Royal Museum for Central Africa, 2009: 75–87.

Brain, Robert, and Adam Pollock. *Bangwa Funerary Sculpture*. Toronto: The University of Toronto Press, 1971.

Brotem, Bronwyn V., and Ann Lang. "Zulu Beadwork." *African Arts* 6, no. 3 (1973): 8–13, 64, 83–84.

Bryant, A. T. *Olden Times in Zululand and Natal: Containing Earlier Political History of the Eastern-Nguni Clans*. London: Longmans, Green and Co., 1929.

Burgard, Timothy Anglin, Karin Breuer, and Jill D'Alessandro. *The Diane and Sandy Besser Collection: A Gift to the Fine Arts Museums of San Francisco*. San Francisco, CA: Fine Arts Museums of San Francisco, 2007.

Cameron, Elisabeth L. *Isn't S/He a Doll? Play and Ritual in African Sculpture*. Los Angeles: UCLA Fowler Museum of Cultural History, 1996.

Carey, Margret. *Beads and Beadwork of East and South Africa*. Aylesbury, UK: Shire Ethnography, 1986.

———*Beads and Beadwork of West and Central Africa*. Aylesbury, UK: Shire Ethnography, 1991.

———"Gender in African Beadwork: An Overview." In *Beads and Bead Makers: Gender, Material Culture and Meaning*. Eds. Lidia D. Sciama and Joanne B. Eicher. Oxford: Berg, 2001: 83–93.

Cole, Herbert M., "Vital Arts in Northern Kenya." *African Arts* 7, no. 2 (1974): 12–23, 82.

———"Artistic and Communicative Values of Beads in Kenya and Ghana." *The Bead Journal* 1, no. 3 (1975): 29–37.

———"Living Art among the Samburu." In *The Fabrics of Culture: The Anthropology of Clothing and Adornment*. Eds. Justine M. Cordwell and Ronald A. Schwarz. The Hague: Mouton Publishers, 1979: 87–102.

———*Icons: Ideals and Power in the Art of Africa*. Washington, D.C.: Smithsonian Institution Press for the National Museum of African Art, 1989.

Cole, Herbert M., and Doran H. Ross. *The Arts of Ghana*. Los Angeles: University of California Press, 1977.

Cornet, Joseph. *Art Royal Kuba*. Milan: Edizioni Sipiel Milano, 1982.

Courtney-Clarke, Margaret. *Ndebele: The Art of an African Tribe*. New York: Rizzoli, 1986.

Davison, Patricia. "Art Unframed: Aesthetic Expression among Black Women." In *Women Artists in South Africa*. Eds. Lynn McClelland and Lucy Alexander. Cape Town: South Africa National Gallery, 1985.

———"Ambiguity, Style and Meaning." In *Arts and Ambiguity: Perspectives on The Brenthurst Collection of Southern African Art*. Johannesburg: Johannesburg Art Gallery, 1991: 12–18.

D'Awol, Anyieth. Correspondence with author. 1 September 2013.

Dederen, Jean-Marie. *Toy or Treasure? Exploring N'wana, the Tsonga 'Doll'*. In *Dungamanzi: Stirring Waters*. Ed. Nessa Liebhammer. Johannesburg, South Africa: Johannesburg Art Gallery and Wits University Press, 2007: 104–19.

Delius, Peter. "The Ndzundza Ndebele: Indenture and the Making of Ethnic Identity." Unpublished paper, History Workshop, University of the Witwatersrand, 1987.

——— "The Ndzundza Ndebele: Indenture and the Making of Ethnic Identity, 1883–1914." In *Holding Their Ground: Class, Locality and Culture in 19th & 20th Century South Africa*. Eds. Philip Bonner, Isabel Hofmeyr, Deborah James, and Tom Lodge. Johannesburg: Ravan Press and Witwatersrand University Press, 1989: 227–58.

Dell, Elizabeth, Nessa Leibhammer, and Karel Nel, eds. *Evocations of the Child: Fertility Figures of the Southern African Region*. Cape Town: Human & Rousseau and Johannesburg Art Gallery, 1998.

Djaba, Nomoda Ebenezer, "Cedi's Beads Industry." Interview by Barbara Henderson. In *The Bead Is Constant*. Ed. Alexandra Wilson. Accra: Ghana Universities Press, 2003: 103–109.

Drewal, Henry John, and John Mason. *Beads, Body and Soul: Art and Light in the Yoruba Universe*. Los Angeles: ULCA Fowler Museum of Cultural History, 1998.

——— "Beads, Body, and Soul: Art and Light in the Yoruba Universe." *African Arts* 31, no. 1 (1998): 18–27, 94.

Drewal, Henry John, and John Pemberton III. *Yoruba: Nine Centuries of African Art and Thought*. New York: The Center for African Art, 1989. In association with Harry N. Abrams Inc.

Drewal, Margaret Thompson. "Projections From the Top in Yoruba Art." *African Arts* 11, no. 1 (1977): 43–49, 91–92.

Fagg, William. *Yoruba Beadwork: Art of Nigeria*. New York: Rizzoli International Publications, Inc., 1980. In cooperation with the Pace Gallery.

Fisher, Angela. *Africa Adorned*. New York: Harry N. Abrams, 1984: 26–29.

Fraser, Douglas, and Herbert M. Cole, eds. *African Art and Leadership*. Madison: University of Wisconsin Press, 1972.

Geary, Christraud M. "Bamum Thrones and Stools." *African Arts* 14, no. 4 (August 1981): 32–43, 87–88.

——— "Elephants, Ivory, and Chiefs: The Elephant and the Arts of the Cameroon Grassfields." In *Elephant: The Animal and Its Ivory in African Culture*. Ed. Doran H. Ross. Los Angeles: Fowler Museum of Cultural History, University of California, Los Angeles, 1992: 229–57.

Gianturco, Paola, and Toby Tuttle. "South Africa: Dinah and the Ndebele Bead Women." In *Her Hands: Craftswomen Changing the World*. 2nd ed. Brooklyn, New York: Powerhouse Books, 2004: 104–17.

Gilvin, Amanda. "Cedi and Krobo Hotworked Glass Beads." *Ornament* 26, no. 3 (2003): 62–63.

Godby, Michael. "Alfred Martin Duggan–Cronin's Photographs for 'The Bantu Tribes of South Africa' (1928–1954): The Construction of an Ambiguous Idyll." *Kronos*, 36 (November 2010): 54–83.

Gott, Suzanne. "The Power of Touch: Women's Waist Beads in Ghana." In *Dress Sense: Emotional and Sensory Experiences of the Body and Clothes*. Eds. Donald Clay Johnson and Helen Bradley Foster. Oxford: Berg, 2007.

——— "Ghana's Glass Beadmaking Arts in Transcultural Dialogues." *African Arts*, 47, no. 1 (2014): 10–29.

Hammond-Tooke, David, and Anitra Nettleton, eds. *Catalogue: Ten Years of Collecting (1979–1989)*. Johannesburg: University of the Witwatersrand Art Galleries, 1989.

Harries, Patrick. "Exclusion, Classification and Internal Colonialism: The Emergence of Ethnicity among the Tsonga-Speakers of South Africa." In *The Creation of Tribalism in Southern Africa*. Ed. Leroy Vail. Berkeley and Los Angeles: University of California Press, 1989: 82–117.

Hart, Robert. "The McGregor Museum's Photographic Collections with a Special Emphasis on the Historic Negatives." World Library and Information Congress: 73rd IFLA General Conference and Council, August 19–23, 2007, Durban, South Africa.

Houlberg, Marilyn Hammersley. "Ibeji Images of the Yoruba." *African Arts* 7, no. 1 (1973): 20–27, 91.

Huber, Hugo. *The Krobo: Traditional, Social and Religious Life of a West African People*. Studia Instituti Anthropos 16 (1963): 165–92.

Jick, Millicent. "Bead-Net Dress from Giza Tomb G7740Z, Old Kingdom, Dynasty IV, Reign of Khufu." *Ornament* 14, no. 11 (1990): 50–53.

Jolles, Frank. "Traditional Zulu Beadwork of the Msinga Area." *African Arts* 26, no. 1 (1993): 42–53, 101–102.

——— "Zulu Trade Dolls from Natal: Toward an Aesthetic of Tourist Art." *Museum Anthropology* 17, no. 1 (February 1993): 37–49.

——— "Contemporary Zulu Dolls from kwaLatha: The Work of Mrs. Hluphekile Zuma and Her Friends." *African Arts* 27, no. 2 (1994): 54–69, 95.

Kennedy, Carolee. *The Art and Material Culture of the Zulu-Speaking Peoples*. UCLA Museum of Cultural History Pamphlet Series, 1, no. 3. Los Angeles: Regents of the University of California, 1978.

Klopper, Sandra. "Women's Work, or Engendering the Art of Beadwork in Southern Africa." In *Ezakwantu: Beadwork from the Eastern Cape*. Ed. Bedford, Emma. Cape Town: South African National Gallery, 1993: 28–33.

Klump, D., and Corinne Kratz. "Aesthetics, Expertise and Ethnicity: Okiek and Masai Perspectives on Personal Ornament." In *Being Masai: Ethnicity and Identity in East Africa*. Eds. T. Spear and Richard Waller. London: Currey, 1993: 195–221.

Knight, Natalie, and Suzanne Priebatsch. *Ndebele Images*. Johannesburg: Natalie Knight Productions, 1983.

Kotz, Suzanne, ed. *Selected Works from the Collection of the National Museum of African Art*. Washington, D.C.: National Museum of African Art, 1999.

Kreamer, Christine Mullen. *African Vision: The Walt Disney–Tishman African Art Collection*. Washington, D.C.: National Museum of African Art, Smithsonian Institution, 2007.

Labelle, Marie-Louise, ed. *Beads of Life: Eastern and Southern African Beadwork from Canadian Collections*. Gatineau, Quebec: Museum of Civilization Corporation, 2005.

Lainé, Daniel. *African Kings*. English translation. Berkeley: Ten Speed Press, 2000.

Lamb, Alastair. "Krobo Powder-Glass Beads." *African Arts* 9, no. 3 (1976): 32–39.

——— "Some 17th Century Glass Beads from Ghana, West Africa." *The Bead Journal* 3, nos. 3 and 4 (1978): 23–27.

Lambrecht, Frank L., and Dora J. Lambrecht. "Leather and Beads in N'gamiland." *African Arts* 10, no. 2 (1977): 34–36.

Larson, Thomas J. *The Hambukushu Rainmakers of the Okavango*. San Jose, CA: Writers Club Press, 2001.

Levinsohn, Rhoda. "Ndebele Beadwork." *Ornament* 4, no. 2 (1979): 61–63.

——— "Symbolic Significance of Traditional Zulu Beadwork." *Black Art* 3, no. 4 (1979): 29–35.

——— *Art and Craft of Southern Africa: Treasures in Transition*. Johannesburg: Delta Books, 1984.

Levy, Diane. "Ndebele Beadwork." In *Catalogue: Ten Years of Collecting (1979–1989)*. Eds. David Hammond-Tooke and Anitra Nettleton. Johannesburg: University of the Witwatersrand Art Galleries, 1989: 24–31.

——— *Continuities and Changes in Ndebele Beadwork: c.1883 to the Present*. Unpublished M.A. Dissertation. University of the Witwatersrand, 1990.

——— "Southern African Beadwork: Issues of Classification and Collection." In *Art and Ambiguity: Perspectives on the Brenthurst Collection of Southern African Art*. Johannesburg: Johannesburg Art Gallery, 1991: 99–122.

Liebhammer, Nessa, ed. *Dungamanzi: Stirring Waters*. Johannesburg, South Africa: Johannesburg Art Gallery and Wits University Press, 2007.

Liu, Robert K. "African Mold-Made Glass Beads." *The Bead Journal* 1, no. 2 (1974): 8–14.

Mahlangu, Esther Nikwambi. Interview with author. Santa Fe, New Mexico. 15 July 2012.

Mphahlele, Es'kia. "Introduction." *Art and Ambiguity: Perspectives on the Brenthurst Collection of Southern African Art*. Johannesburg: Johannesburg Art Gallery, 1991: 6–9.

Monkeybiz. *Bead by Bead: Reviving an Ancient African Tradition: The Monkeybiz Bead Story*. South Africa: Jacana Media Ltd, 2007.

Morris, Jean, and Eleanor Preston-Whyte. *Speaking with Beads: Zulu Arts from Southern Africa*. New York: Thames and Hudson, 1994.

Nettleton, Anitra. "Breaking Symmetries: Aesthetics and Bodies in Tsonga-Shangaan Beadwork." In *Dungamanzi: Stirring Waters*. Ed. Nessa Liebhammer. Johannesburg, South Africa: Johannesburg Art Gallery and Wits University Press, 2007: 78–101.

——— "Jubilee Dandies: Collecting Beadwork in Tsolo, Eastern Cape 1897–1932." *African Arts* 46, no. 1 (2013): 36–49.

——— "Of Severed Heads and Snuff Boxes: 'Survivance' and Beaded Bodies in the Eastern Cape, 1897–1934." *African Arts* 48, no. 4 (2015): 22–33.

Northern, Tamara. *The Sign of the Leopard: Beaded Art of Cameroon*. Storrs, Connecticut: The William Benton Museum of Art/The University of Connecticut, 1975.

——— *The Art of Cameroon*. Washington, D.C.: National Museum of Natural History, Smithsonian Institution, 1984.

Pemberton III, John. "The Oyo Empire." In *Yoruba: Nine Centuries of African Art and Thought*. New York: The Center for African Art, 1989: 170–75. In association with Harry N. Abrams Inc.

——— *African Beaded Art: Power and Adornment*. Northampton, Massachusetts: Smith College Museum of Art, 2008.

Pokornowski, Ila. "Beads and Personal Adornment." In *The Fabrics of Culture: The Anthropology of Clothing and Adornment*. Eds. Justine M. Cordwell and Ronald A. Schwarz. The Hague: Mouton Publishers, 1979: 103–17.

Preston-Whyte, Eleanor. "Ways of Seeing, Ways of Buying; Images of Tourist Art and Culture Expression in Contemporary Beadwork." In *African Art in Southern Africa: From Tradition to Township*. Johannesburg: AD. Donker/Publisher, 1989: 123–151, 244–246.

———"Zulu Bead Sculptors." *African Arts* 24, no. 1 (1991): 64–76, 104.

Priebatsch, Suzanne, and Natalie Knight. "Traditional Ndebele Beadwork." *African Arts* 11, no. 2 (January1978): 24–27.

Proctor, Andre, and Sandra Klopper. "Through the Barrel of a Bead: The Personal and the Political in the Beadwork of the Eastern Cape." In *Ezakwantu: Beadwork from the Eastern Cape*. Ed. Emma Bedford. Cape Town: South African National Gallery, 1993: 57–65.

"Rebecca Lolosoli, Kenya: She Decided It Takes a Village to Be Safe." In "150 Women 2011 Who Shake the World." *Newsweek* (14 March 2011): 63.

Rubin, Arnold. "Accumulation: Power and Display in African Sculpture." *Art Forum*, May 1975: 35–47.

Scherz, A., E.R. Scherz, G. Taapopi, and A. Otto. *Hairstyles, Head-dresses & Ornaments in Namibia and Southern Angola*,1992.

Schildkrout, Enid. "Africa—Sub-Sahara." In *The Extraordinary in the Ordinary*. Ed. Mary Hunt Kahlenberg. New York: Harry N. Abrams, Inc, Publishers, 1998: 189. In association with the Museum of International Folk Art.

Schneider, Elizabeth Ann. "Art and Communication: Ndzundza Ndebele Wall Decorations in the Transvaal." In Nettleton, Anitra & Hammond-Tooke, David (eds.). *African Art in Southern Africa: From Tradition to Township*. Johannesburg: Ad. Donker, 1989: 103–122, 242–244.

———"Ndebele umndwana: Ndebele dolls and walls." In *Evocations of the Child: Fertility Figures of the Southern African Region*. Eds. Elizabeth Dell, Nessa Leibhammer, and Karol Nel. Cape Town: Human & Rousseau and Johannesburg Art Gallery, 1998: 139–150.

Schoeman, H.S. "A Preliminary Report on Traditional Beadwork in the Mkhwanazi Art of the Mtunzini District, Zululand." (Part one) *African Studies* 27, no. 2 (1968): 57–81. (Part two) *African Studies* 27, no. 3 (1968): 107–133.

Sihlabeni, Lulama. Taped interview for radio broadcast "Let's Talk about This." Youth Media Project, Santa Fe, New Mexico. 20 December 2013.

Steiner, Christopher B. "Body Personal and Body Politic: Adornment and Leadership in Cross-Cultural Perspective." *Anthropos* 85 nos. 4–6 (1990): 431–45.

———"West African Trade Beads: Symbols of Tradition." *Ornament* 14, no. 1 (1990): 58–61.

———*African Art in Transit*. London: Cambridge University Press, 1994.

Stevenson, Michael, and Michael Graham-Stewart, eds. *South East African Beadwork, 1850–1910: From Adornment to Artefact to Art*. Vlaeberg, South Africa: Fernwood Press, 2000.

Stewart, Kearsley (producer) and Harlan Wallach (director). *Controlling the Fire. The Value of the Beads: Beauty and Personhood in Contemporary Ghana*. Durham, North Carolina: Duke University, 2011.

Stokes, Deborah. "Rediscovered Treasures: African Beadwork at the Field Museum, Chicago." *African Arts* 32, no. 3 (1999): 18–31, 91.

Straight, Bilinda. "Umoja: No Men Allowed." *American Anthropologist* 15, no. 1 (2013): 135–37.

Thompson, Robert Farris. "The Sign of the Divine King: An Essay on Yoruba Bead-Embroidered Crowns with Veil and Bird Decorations." *African Arts* 3, no. 3 (Spring 1970): 8–17, 75–80.

———"Bead-Embroidered Crowns, Scepters, Panels." *Black Gods and Kings: Yoruba Art at UCLA*. Occasional Papers of the Museum and Laboratories of Ethnic Arts and Technology, Number 11. Los Angeles: University of California, 1971: 8/1–3.

———"Sons of Thunder: Twin Images among the Oyo and other Yoruba groups." *African Arts* 4, no. 3 (1971): 8–13, 77–80.

———"The Sign of the Divine King: Yoruba Bead-Embroidered Crowns with Veil and Bird Decorations." In *African Art and Leadership*. Eds. Douglas Fraser and Herbert M. Cole. Madison: The University of Wisconsin Press, 1972: 227–60.

Twala, Regina G. "Beads as Regulating the Social Life of the Zulu and Swazi." In *Every Man his Way: Readings in Cultural Anthropology*. Ed. Alan Dundes. Englewood Cliffs, N. J.: Prentice-Hall, 1968: 364–79.

Vail, Leroy, ed. *The Creation of Tribalism in Southern Africa*. London: James Currey Ltd., 1989.

Van Wyk, Gary N. "Convulsions of the Canon: 'Convention, Context, Change' at the University of the Witwatersrand Art Galleries." *African Arts* 27, no. 4 (1994): 54–67, 95.

———"Illuminated Signs: Style and Meaning in the Beadwork of the Xhosa- and Zulu-speaking Peoples." *African Arts* 36, no. 3 (2003): 12–33, 93–94.

von Lintig, Bettina."A Grasslands Beaded Leopard Skin." *Tribal Art* 72 (Summer 2014): 108–117.

Wada, Shohei. "Female Initiation Rites of the Iraqw and the Gorowa," *Senri Ethnological Studies* 15, no. 3 (1984): 187–96.

Wells, Kate, Edgard Sienaert, Joan Conolly, Fokosile Ngema, Nzama, Celani Njoyeza, Bonangani Ximba, and Beauty Ndlovu. "The 'Siyazama' Project: A Traditional Beadwork and AIDS Intervention Program." *Design Issues*, 20, no. 2 (Spring 2004): 73–89.

Wilson, Alexandra. *The Bead Is Constant*. Accra: Ghana Universities Press, 2003.

ASIA

Adhyatman, Sumarah and Arifin Redjeki. *Manik-Manik di Indonesia/Beads in Indonesia*. Jakarta: Penerbit Djambatan, 1993.

Ao, Ayinla Shilu, and Robert K. Liu. *Naga Tribal Adornment: Signatures of Status and Self*. Washington, D.C.: The Bead Society of Greater Washington, 2003.

Beck, Horace C. "The Magical Properties of Beads." *The Bead Journal* 2, no. 4 (1976): 32–39.

Campbell, Margaret. *From the Hands of the Hills*. Hong Kong: Media Transasia, 1978.

Cheah, Hwei-Fe'n. "Between East and West: Peranakan Chinese Beadwork from Malaysia, Singapore and Indonesia." In *2007 International Bead and Beadwork Conference*. Istanbul: Rezan Has Museum, November 22–25, 2007: 13.55– 14.45.

Crowfoot, Grace M. and P. Sutton. "Ramallah Embroidery." *Embroidery*, March 1935: 37.

Deo, Shantaram Bhalchandra. *Indian Beads: A Cultural and Technological Study*. Pune, India: Deccan College Post-Graduate and Research Institute, 2000.

Diba, Layla S. "Turkoman Silver Ornaments From Central Asia." In *Faith and Transformation: Votive Offerings and Amulets from the Alexander Girard Collection*. Ed. Doris Francis. Santa Fe: Museum of New Mexico Press, 2007: 16–17. In association with the Museum of International Folk Art.

———*Turkman Jewelry: Silver Ornaments from the Marshall and Marilyn R. Wolf Collection*. New York: The Metropolitan Museum of Art, 2011.

Diran, Richard K. *The Vanishing Tribes of Burma*. New York: Amphoto Art, an imprint of Watson-Guptill Publications, 1997.

Elson, Vickie C. *Dowries from Kutch: A Women's Folk Art Tradition in India*. Los Angeles: Museum of Cultural History, University of California, 1979.

Fisher, Nora. *Mud, Mirror and Thread: Folk Traditions of Rural India*. Ahmedabad, India: Mapin Publishing Pvt. Ltd, 1993. In association with Museum of New Mexico Press.

Fitz Gibbon, Kate, and Andrew Hale. *Uzbek Embroidery in the Nomadic Tradition*. Minneapolis: Minneapolis Institute of Arts, 2007.

Fraser, Douglas. "The Heraldic Woman: A Study in Diffusion." In *The Many Faces of Primitive Art*. Ed. Douglas Fraser. Englewood Cliffs, New Jersey: Prentice Hall, 1966: 36–99.

Frater, Judy. *Threads of Identity: Embroidery and Adornment of the Nomadic Rabaris*. Ahmedabad, India: Mapin Publishing Pvt. Ltd., 1995.

Gabriel, Hannelore. "Shell Jewelry of the Nagas." *Ornament* 9, no. 1 (1985): 37–41.

Harvey, Janet. *Traditional Textiles from Central Asia*. London and New York: Thames and Hudson, 1997.

Hector, Valerie. "Prosperity, Reverence and Protection: An Introduction to Asian Beadwork." *BEADS: Journal of the Society of Bead Researchers* 7 (1995): 3–36.

Heppell, Michael, Limbang Anak Melak, and Enyan Anak Usen. *Iban Art. Sexual Selection and Severed Heads: Weaving, Sculpture, Tattooing and Other Arts of the Iban of Borneo*. Amsterdam and Leiden: KIT Publishers and C. Zwartenkot – Art Books, 2005.

Howard, Michael C. "SIREU: Beaded Skirts from Papua." *Hali* 125 (Nov/Dec 2002): 94–98.

Irwin, John, and Margaret Hall. *Indian Embroideries*. Vol. 2. Ahmedabad, India: Calico Museum of Textiles, 1973: 124–131, plates 69–70.

Jacobs, Julian. *The Nagas, Hill Peoples of Northeast India: Society, Culture and the Colonial Encounter*. Revised edition. London: Edition Hansjorg Mayer, 2012.

Janowski, Monica. "Beads, Prestige and Life among the Kelabit of Sarawak, East Malaysia." In *Beads and Bead Makers: Gender, Material Culture and Meaning*. Eds. Lidia D. Sciama and Joanne B. Eicher. Oxford: Berg, 1998: 213–247.

Kalter, Johannes. *The Arts and Crafts of Turkestan*. London: Thames and Hudson, 1984.

Kalter, Johannes, and Margareta Pavaloi. *Uzbekistan: Heirs to the Silk Road*. New York: Thames & Hudson, 1997: 286–87, 293.

Kanungo, Alok Kumar. "Impact of Social and Political Change on the Use of Beads among the Konyaks." In *2007 International Bead and Beadwork Conference*. Istanbul: Rezan Has Museum, November 22–25, 2007: 14.15–14.50.

Kawar, Widad. "Ethnographic Beads and Necklaces in the Middle East." In *2007 International Bead and Beadwork Conference*. Istanbul: Rezan Has Museum, November 22–25, 2007: 13.50–14.10.

Langgu, Dato Sri Edmund. Borneo Post online, November 18, 2010.

Lewis, Paul and Elaine. *Peoples of the Golden Triangle: Six Tribes in Thailand*. London and New York: Thames and Hudson, 1984.

Liu, Robert K. "Chinese Glass Beads and Ornaments." *The Bead Journal* 1, no. 3 (1975): 13–27.

Liu, Robert K., and Gail Rossi. "Chinese Tiger Hats." *Ornament* 14, no. 3 (1991): 22–25, 70, 73, 75–76.

Maramba, Roberto. *Form and Splendor: Personal Adornment of Northern Luzon Ethnic Groups, Philippines*. Makati City, Philippines: Bookmark, Inc., 1998.

McCulloch, Sarah. "Silversmithing in China's Guizhou Province." *Ornament* 16, no. 3 (1993): 56–9, 92, 95.

Morris, Desmond. *Body Guards: Protective Amulets and Charms*. Boston: Element Books Inc., 1999.

Munan, Heidi. "Social Status Gradations Expressed in the Beadwork Patterns of Sarawak's Orang Ulu." *BEADS: Journal of the Society of Bead Researchers*, 7 (1995): 55–64.

———*Beads of Borneo*. Singapore: Editions Didier Millet, 2005.

Ong, Edric. Email conversation with author. 15 August 2016.

Rossi, Gail. "Enduring Dress of the Miao: Guizhou Province, People's Republic of China." *Ornament* 11, no. 3 (1988): 26–31.

Schletzer, Dieter, and Reingold Schletzer. *Old Silver Jewellry of the Turkoman: An Essay on Symbols in the Culture of Inner Asian Nomads*. Trans. Paul Knight. Berlin: Dietrich Reimer Verlag, 1983.

Sellato, Bernard. *Hornbill and Dragon: Arts and Culture of Borneo*. 2nd edition. Singapore: Sun Tree Publishing, 1992.

Sethi, Cristin McKnight. Communication with author, 2016.

Smithsonian Institution Press. *Aditi: The Living Arts of India*. Washington, D.C.: Smithsonian Institution Press, 1985.

Stanislaw, Mary Anne. *Kalagas: The Wall Hangings of Southeast Asia*. Menlo Park, California: Ainslie's, 1987.

Stillman, Yedida Kalfon. *Palestinian Costume and Jewelry*. Albuquerque: University of New Mexico Press for the Museum of New Mexico and the International Folk Art Foundation, 1979.

Thannaree C. "The Art of Looking Akha." Ezistock.com/blog. Posted October 6, 2011.

Topham, John, with Anthony Landreau and William E. Mulligan. *Traditional Crafts of Saudi Arabia*. London: Stacy International, 1981.

Untracht, Oppi. *Traditional Jewelry of India*. New York: Harry N. Abrams, Inc., 1997: 53–68.

Weir, Shelagh. *Palestinian Costume*. Austin: University of Texas Press, in co-operation with British Museum Publications, 1989.

Whiting, Mrs. J. D. "Charms and Amulets." Unpublished paper. Accession file FA.1981.48.1/190. Museum of International Folk Art, 1981.

Whittier, Herbert L., and Patricia R. Whittier. "Baby Carriers: A Link Between Social and Spiritual Values Among the Kenyah Dayak of Borneo." *Expedition* 30, no. 1 (1988): 51–58.

Worcester, Dean C. "Head-hunters of Northern Luzon." *National Geographic* 23, no. 9 (1912): 833–930.

EUROPE

Birkalan-Gedik, Hande. "The Evil Eye in Turkey." In *Faith and Transformation: Votive Offerings and Amulets From the Alexander Girard Collection*. Ed. Doris Francis. Santa Fe: Museum of New Mexico Press, 2007: 106–7. In association with the Museum of International Folk Art.

Celik, Ethem. "Products of Patience." In *2007 International Bead and Beadwork Conference*. Istanbul: Rezan Has Museum, November 22–25, 2007: 09.10–10.00.

Clabburn, Pamela. *Beadwork*. Shire Album 57. UK: Shire Publications, Ltd., 1980.

Jargstorf, Sibylle. *Glass Beads from Europe*. Atglen, PA.: Schiffer Publishing, 1995.

Kimball, Jane A. "Turkish Prisoner of War Inscribed Beadwork of the Great War." In *2007 International Bead and Beadwork Conference*. Istanbul: Rezan Has Museum, November 22–25, 2007: 10.35–11.25.

———"World War I Turkish Prisoner-of-War Beadwork." *BEADS: Journal of the Society of Bead Researchers* 19 (2007): 5–16.

Milgram, Miriam. "Ethnographic Perspectives on the Use of Seed Beads in the Textile Folk Art in the Balkans: 3 Case Studies." In *2007 International Bead and Beadwork Conference*. Istanbul: Rezan Has Museum, November 22–25, 2007: 13.00–13.50.

Parker, Rozsika. *The Subversive Stitch: Embroidery and the Making of the Feminine*. New York: Routledge, 1989.

Recklies, Adele Rogers. "Turkish Prisoner-of-war and Balkan Beadwork." In *2007 International Bead and Beadwork Conference*. Istanbul: Rezan Has Museum, November 22–25, 2007: 10.35–11.25.

Sumberg, Bobbie, ed. *Young Brides, Old Treasures: Macedonian Embroidered Dress*. Santa Fe: Museum of International Folk Art and the Macedonian Arts Council, 2012.

Yurova, Elena. *The Glorious Epoch of Beads in Russia*. Moscow: Interbook Business, 2003.

LATIN AMERICA (INCLUDING MEXICO)

Belote, Linda. "Ecuadorian bead weaving: Unusual Netting by the Saraguro Indians." *Bead and Button*, June 2002: 88–89.

——— Email correspondence with author. Hancock, Minnesota, 3 September 2013.

Cordry, Donald. "Pendant Glass Beads from San Pedro Quiatoni, Oaxaca, Mexico." *The Bead Journal* 1, no. 4 (1975): 10–11.

Cordry, Donald, and Dorothy Cordry. *Mexican Indian Costumes*. Austin: University of Texas, 1968.

Delismé, Mireille. 2012 Santa Fe International Folk Art Market Application Form. 2011: 1–8.

Dransart, Penny. "A Short History of Rosaries in the Andes." In *Beads and Bead Makers: Gender, Material Culture and Meaning*. Eds. Lidia D. Sciama and Joanne B. Eicher. Oxford: Berg, 1998: 129–146.

Grady, C. Jill. "Huichol Art Inside and Out." In *Huichol Art and Culture: Balancing the World*. Eds. Melissa S. Powell and C. Jill Grady. Santa Fe: Museum of New Mexico Press, 2010: 88–96.

———"Huichol Votive Art." In *Huichol Art and Culture: Balancing the World*. Eds. Melissa S. Powell and C. Jill Grady. Santa Fe: Museum of New Mexico Press, 2010: 33–47.

Mauldin, Barbara. *Folk Art of the Andes*. Santa Fe: Museum of International Folk Art and Museum of New Mexico Press, 2011.

Polk, Patrick Arthur. *Haitian Vodou Flags*. Jackson: University Press of Mississippi, 1997.

Shelton, Anthony. "Predicates of Aesthetic Judgement: Ontology and Value in Huichol Material Representations." In *Anthropology, Art and Aesthetics*. Eds. Jeremy Coote and Anthony Shelton. Oxford, Great Britain: Clarendon Press, 1992: 209–44.

Schindler, Helmut. "Silver Jewelry of the Mapuche." *Ornament* 8, no. 3 (1985): 32–37.

Yturbide, Teresa Castelló, and Carlotta Mapelli Mozzi. *La Chaquira en México*. Museo Franz Mayer y Artes de México, 1998.

NORTH AMERICA (EXCLUDING MEXICO)

Anderson, Jeffrey D. *Arapaho Women's Quillwork: Motion, Life, and Creativity*. Norman: University of Oklahoma Press, 2013.

Barten, W. H. *Barten's Activities as Wild West Show Contractor for the Sioux Indians at Pine Ridge Agency, 1904–24 Papers*. Manuscript 406. Lincoln: Nebraska State Historical Society Archives, 1904–24.

Bebo, Naomi/Tweed. "Naomi Bebo Biography." Naomi Bebo website, 29 August 2013.

Bol, Marsha Clift. "Lakota Beaded Costume of the Early Reservation Era." *Phoebus: A Journal of Art History*: 70–77. Reprinted 1993 in *Arts of Africa, Oceania, and the Americas: Selected Readings* Eds. Janet Catherine Berlo and Lee Anne Wilson. New Jersey: Prentice-Hall, Inc., 1985: 363–70.

———"Lakota Women's Artistic Strategies in Support of the Social System." *American Indian Culture and Research Journal* 9, no. 1 (1985): 33–51.

———"Defining Lakota Tourist Art, 1880–1915." *Unpacking Culture: Art and Commodity in Colonial and Postcolonial Worlds*. Eds. Ruth Phillips and Christopher Steiner. Berkeley: University of California Press, 1999: 214–228.

Bol, Marsha C., and Nellie Z. Star Boy Menard. "I Saw All That: A Lakota Girl's Puberty Ceremony." *American Indian Culture and Research Journal* 24, no. 1 (2000): 25–42.

Brackett, Albert G. "The Sioux or Dakota Indians." *Smithsonian Institution Annual Report*, 1976: 446–472.

Coleman, Winfield W. "The Cheyenne Women's Sewing Society." In *Plains Indian Design Symbology and Decoration*. Eds. Gene Ball and George P. Horse Capture. Cody, Wyoming: Buffalo Bill Historical Center, 1980: 50–69.

Conn, Richard. *Native American Art in the Denver Art Museum*. Denver: Denver Art Museum, 1979.

Deloria, Ella C. *Dakota Commentary on Walker's Texts*. No. 834. Philadelphia: American Philosophical Society, 1937.

———*Teton Myths*. Manuscript texts collected by George Bushotter, 1887–1888. No. 852. Philadelphia: American Philosophical Society, 1937?.

———*Speaking of Indians*. Reprint. Vermillion: University of South Dakota, 1983.

———*The Dakota Way of Life*. Manuscript on file. Vermillion: Institute of Indian Studies, University of South Dakota, n.d.

DeMallie, Raymond J. "Male and Female in Traditional Lakota Culture." In *The Hidden Half: Studies of Plains Indian Women*. Eds. Patricia Albers and Beatrice Medicine. Lanham, Maryland: University Press of America, 1983: 237–61.

Dewey, Marcus. Interview with author. Sioux Falls, South Dakota. 23 September 1995.

Driscoll, Bernadette. "*Sapangat*: Inuit Beadwork in the Canadian Arctic." *Expedition* 26, no. 2 (1984): 40–47.

Dubin, Lois S. *Floral Journey: Native North American Beadwork*. Los Angeles: Autry National Center of the American West, 2014. In association with the University of Washington Press.

Elliott, Dolores N. "Two Centuries of Iroquois Beadwork." *BEADS: Journal of the Society of Bead Researchers* 15 (2003): 3–22.

Ewers, John C. *The Blackfeet: Raiders on the Northwestern Plains*. Norman, Oklahoma: University of Oklahoma Press, 1958.

Ewers, John C., Marsha V. Gallagher, David C. Hunt, and Joseph C. Porter. *Views of a Vanishing Frontier*. Omaha: Center for Western Studies/Joslyn Art Museum, 1984.

Gerdes, Scott. "In a small circle: Eah Ha Wa (Eva Mirabal): the best unknown Taos artist." *Taos News/Taos Woman*, 2016: 26–27.

Greene, Candace. "Soft Cradles of the Central Plains." *Plains Anthropologist: Journal of the Plains Anthropological Society* 37, no. 139 (1992): 95–113.

Greeves, Teri. "The Tale of the First Beaded Sneakers." Indian Market insert. The Santa Fe New Mexican. August 2015.

Grimes, John R., Christian F. Feest, Mary Lou Curran. *Uncommon Legacies: Native American Art from the Peabody Essex Museum*. Seattle: American Federation of Arts, 2002. In association with University of Washington Press.

Hassrick, Royal B. *The Sioux: Life and Customs of a Warrior Society*. Norman: University of Oklahoma Press, 1964.

Haukaas, Tom. "2 Be(ad) or Not 2 Be(ad), That is the Question." In *Changing Hands: Art Without Reservation 2*. Eds. David Revere McFadden and Ellen Napiura Taubman. New York: Museum of Arts and Design, 2005: 139–143.

———Email conversation with author, 24 January 2010.

———Email conversation with author, 6 January 2014.

———Email conversation with author, 17 August 2015 and 15 May 2015.

———Email conversation with author, 12 January 2017.

Hirschfield, Alan J., with Terry Winchell. *Living with American Indian Art: the Hirschfield Collection*. Layton, Utah: Gibbs Smith Publisher, 2012.

Hungry Wolf, Adolf and Star. *Children of the Circle*. Summertown, Tennessee: Book Publishing Company, 1992.

Lang, Sabine. *Men as Women, Women as Men: Changing Gender in Native American Cultures*. Austin: University of Texas Press, 1998.

Little Thunder, Rosalie. Interview with author. Rapid City, South Dakota, 2 August 1993.

Logan, Leslie. "A Life in Beads: The Stories a Plains Dress Can Tell." Education packet. National Museum of the American Indian Education Office, Smithsonian Institution, Washington, D.C., n.d.: 9–10.

Logan, Michael H., and Douglas A. Schmittou. "Tribal Styles in Plains Indian Art." *With Pride They Made These: Tribal Styles in Plains Indian Art*. Occasional Paper No. 12. Knoxville: Frank H. McClung Museum, University of Tennessee, 1995: 38–52.

Lou, Liza. "2015 Passionate Artist Award Acceptance Speech, Neuberger Museum of Art." Liza Lou website. 7 November 2015.

Lyford, Carrie. *Quill and Beadwork of the Western Sioux*. Reprint. Boulder, Colorado: Johnson Publishing Co., 1979.

McFadden, David Revere, and Ellen Napiura Taubman. *Changing Hands: Art without Reservation 2: Contemporary Native North American Art from the West, Northwest & Pacific*. New York: Museum of Arts and Design, 2005.

McNenly, Linda Scarangella. *Native Performers in Wild West Shows: From Buffalo Bill to Euro Disney*. Norman: University of Oklahoma Press, 2012.

Medicine Crow, Joseph. *From the Heart of the Crow Country: The Crow Indians' Own Stories*. New York: Orion Books, 1992.

Michelson, Truman. "Narrative of an Arapaho Woman." *American Anthropologist* 35 (1933): 595–610.

Moore, Ellen K. "Designing with Light: Navajo Beadwork Today." *American Indian Art Magazine* 20, no. 4 (Autumn 1995): 70–79.

———*Navajo Beadwork: Architectures of Light*. Tucson: University of Arizona Press, 2003.

Moses, L.G. *Wild West Shows and the Images of American Indians, 1883–1933*. Albuquerque: University of New Mexico Press, 1996.

New Holy, Alice. Interview with author. Pine Ridge Reservation, South Dakota. 17 September 1992.

Ostler, James, and Marian Rodee. "Zuni Beaded Dolls: From Curio to Folk Art." *American Indian Art Magazine* 14, no. 2 (1989): 32–37.

Penney, David, Ruth Phillips, and David Wooley. *On the Border: Native American Weaving Traditions of the Great Lakes and Prairie*. Moorhead, Minnesota: Plains Art Museum, 1990.

Phillips, Ruth B. *Trading Identities: The Souvenir in Native North American Art from the Northeast, 1700–1900*. Seattle: University of Washington Press, 1998.

Pohrt, Richard A. "Plains Indian Moccasins with Decorated Soles." *American Indian Art Magazine* 2, no. 3 (1977): 32–39, 84.

Pohrt, Richard, Jr., ed. *Bags of Friendship: Bandolier Bags of the Great Lakes Indians*. Santa Fe: Morningstar Gallery, 1996.

Powers, Marla. "Menstruation and Reproduction: An Oglala Case." *Signs* 6, no. 1 (1982): 54–65.

———*Oglala Women: Myth, Ritual, and Reality*. Chicago: University of Chicago Press, 1986.

Roscoe, Will. *Changing Ones: Third and Fourth Genders in Native North America*. New York: St. Martin's Griffin, 1998.

Snow, Dean R. *The Iroquois*. Oxford, UK, and Cambridge, USA: Blackwell Publishers, Ltd., 1994.

Torrence, Gaylord. *The Plains Indians: Artists of Earth and Sky*. Paris: Musée du quai Branly/Skira Rizzoli, 2014.

Walker, James R. *Lakota Society*. Ed. R. J. DeMallie. Lincoln: University of Nebraska Press, 1982.

———*Lakota Myth*. Ed. Elaine A. Jahner. Lincoln: University of Nebraska Press, 1983.

Williams, Walter L. "Persistence and Change in the Berdache Tradition Among Contemporary Lakota Indians." In *The Many Faces of Homosexuality: Anthropological Approaches to Homosexual Behavior*. Ed. Evelyn Blackwood. New York: The Haworth Press, Inc., 1986: 191–200.

Winnepeg Art Gallery, The. *The Inuit Amautik: I Like My Hood Full*. Winnepeg, Canada: The Winnepeg Art Gallery, 1980.

Wissler, Clark. Letter to Boas. 3 August 1902. Department of Anthropology. New York: American Museum of Natural History.

INDEX

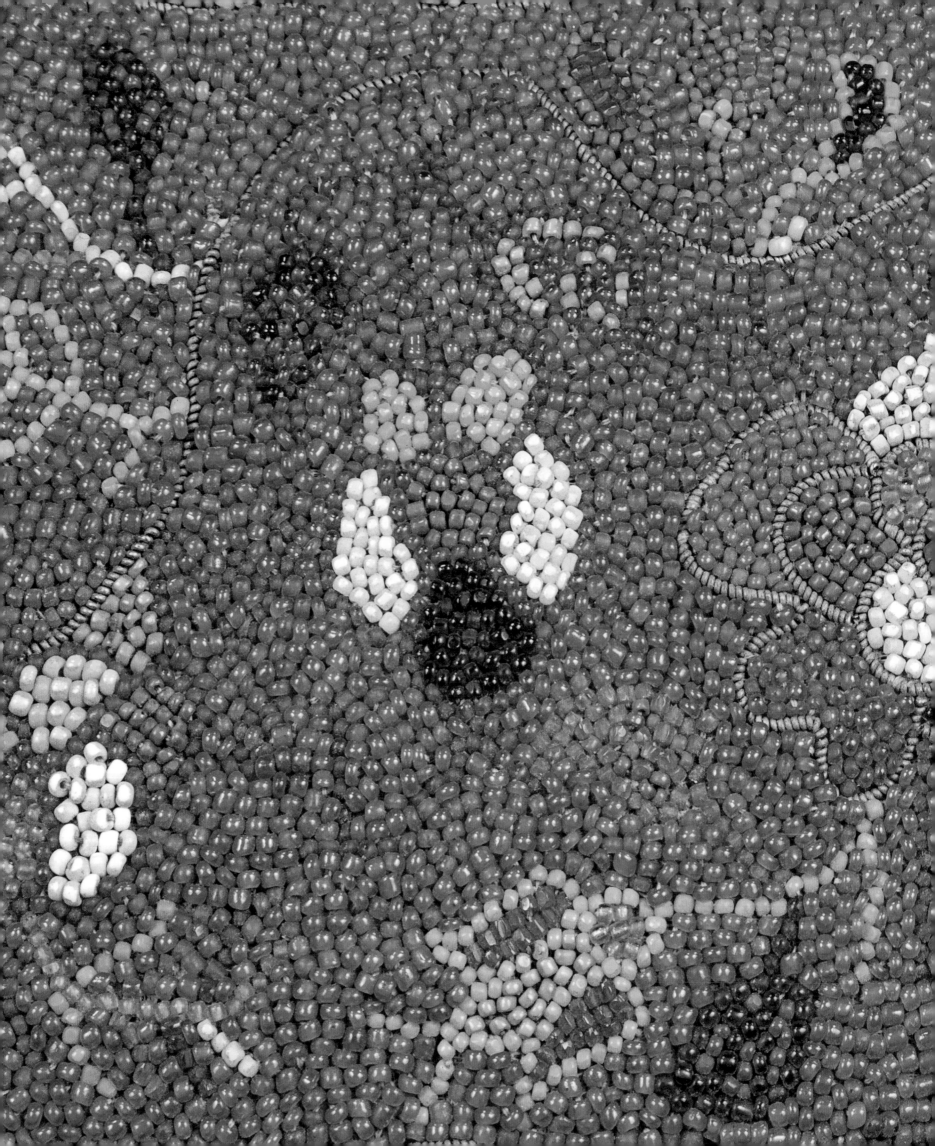